Brazil in Transition

THE PRINCETON ECONOMIC HISTORY OF THE WESTERN WORLD

Joel Mokyr, Series Editor

A list of titles in this series appears at the back of the book

BRAZIL IN TRANSITION

Beliefs, Leadership, and Institutional Change

Lee J. Alston, Marcus André Melo,
Bernardo Mueller, and Carlos Pereira

PRINCETON UNIVERSITY PRESS

Princeton and Oxford

Published by Princeton University Press, 41 William Street, Princeton, New Jersey 08540

In the United Kingdom: Princeton University Press, 6 Oxford Street, Woodstock, Oxfordshire OX20 1TR

press.princeton.edu

Jacket art: Tarsila do Amaral, *São Paolo*, 1924. Oil on canvas, 57" × 90". Courtesy of Pinacoteca do Estado de São Paulo.

Library of Congress Cataloging-in-Publication Data

Names: Alston, Lee J., 1951– author.
Title: Brazil in transition : beliefs, leadership, and institutional change / Lee J. Alston,
    Marcus André Melo, Bernardo Mueller, and Carlos Pereira.
Description: Princeton : Princeton University Press, [2016] | Series: The Princeton
    economic history of the Western world | Includes bibliographical references and index.
Identifiers: LCCN 2016005035 | ISBN 9780691162911 (hardcover : alk. paper)
Subjects: LCSH: Brazil—Economic policy. | Brazil—Social policy. | Brazil—Politics and
    government.
Classification: LCC HC187 .A55875 2016 | DDC 330.981—dc23
LC record available at http://lccn.loc.gov/2016005035

British Library Cataloging-in-Publication Data is available

This book has been composed in Sabon and Helvetica Neue

Printed on acid-free paper. ∞

Printed in the United States of America

10 9 8 7 6 5 4 3 2 1

To Mary, and our grandchildren, Anya and Luke,
  who were born while this work was in progress
To Bella, Binha, and Dani with love
To Suely, Beatriz, and Henrique and to my parents,
  Charles and Suzana
To the memory of my father, Carlos,
  and to my mother, Annete

CONTENTS

ILLUSTRATIONS

TABLES

PREFACE

WHY ISN'T THE WHOLE WORLD DEVELOPED? WHY DO SOME COUNTRIES break from their past and enter the rank of sustainable economic, legal, and political development? These questions are the Holy Grail for the social sciences and motivate our book. We chip away at the fundamental question of development by building a framework to understand the dynamics of development of Brazil, from 1964 to 2014. Brazil is currently on the trajectory of a critical transition to sustainable development. To complete a transition requires an iterative process of institutional deepening. Our analytical framework is inductive from the case of Brazil, but it can yield insights for development in other countries. Our hope is that other scholars will take the framework, and with modifications, apply it to understand development in other countries, and ultimately better understand the general process of development.

In our intellectual journey, we acquired many debts to many scholars and organizations. The project got off the ground thanks to the Rockefeller Foundation hosting us as residents in Bellagio. It was an intellectual experience we will never forget. We benefitted enormously from detailed comments provided by the anonymous reviewers for Princeton University Press and from a book conference at Northwestern University, funded by President Schapiro at Northwestern University and Princeton University Press. Joel Mokyr and Marlous van Waijenburg organized the conference, and the participants deserve to be named: Hoyt Bleakley, Alan Dye, Joseph Ferrie, Brodwyn Fischer, Regina Grafe, Stephen Haber, David D. Haddock, Anne Hanley, Daniel Immerwahr, John Londregan, Noel Maurer, Joel Mokyr, Aldo Musacchio, Nicola Persico, Frank Safford, William Summerhill, Marlous van Waijenburg, John Wallis, and Sam Williamson. Sonja Opper kindly organized an earlier book conference at Lund University in November 2013. We thank the discussants—Thomas Brambor, Christer Gunnarsson, and Carl Hampus-Lytkens—and the participants.

We benefitted greatly from lengthy discussions and correspondence at critical times of our journey with Alan Dye, Thráinn Eggertsson, Avner Greif, Murat Iyigun, Douglass North, James Robinson, John Wallis, and Barry Weingast. We thank William Summerhill for a discussion about the substance of our afterword. From a variety of people we received helpful comments on drafts: Eric Alston, Martin Andersson, Andy Baker, Robert Bates, Michael Bordo, Eric Brousseau, David Brown, Charles Calomiris, Victor Fleischer, Patrick François, Steven Haber, Joseph Jupille,

John Londregan, Thomas Mayer, Tomas Nonnenmacher, Sonja Opper, Samuel Pessoa, Laura Randall, Hugh Rockoff, Jerome Sgard, Kenneth Shepsle, Richard Sicotte, Stefan Voigt, Steven Webb, and Eugene White. Throughout the project and for suggestions for a title we thank Robert Higgs. Presenting seminars and receiving comments at the following conferences and universities clarified where we were going astray: Getulio Vargas Foundation; a conference at Washington University honoring Douglass North's ninetieth birthday; the Economic History Association Annual Meetings (Boston and Washington, DC); the workshop on Legal Order, the State, and Economic Development in Florence, Italy; the International Society for the New Institutional Economics Annual Meeting; and seminars at Columbia University, Indiana University, Rutgers University, University of British Columbia, University of Chicago, University of Colorado (Institutions Program and School of Law), and the University of Hamburg (Institute of Law and Economics).

We thank our series editor, Joel Mokyr, and our editor at Princeton University Press, Seth Ditchik, for believing in the project, for their comments, and for their patience. We thank Patty Lezotte at the Ostrom Workshop at Indiana University for copyediting and cheerfully pulling it all together during crunch times. Lee Alston thanks the faculty and staff at the Institute for Behavioral Science at the University of Colorado for their support from 2002 to 2014 and the staff at the Ostrom Workshop at Indiana University for helping to finish the project. The material is based on work by Alston supported by the National Science Foundation under Grant No. OISE-1157725. Any opinions, findings, and conclusions or recommendations expressed in this material are those of the author(s) and do not necessarily reflect the views of the National Science Foundation. Carlos Pereira is grateful to the National Council for Scientific and Technological Development (CNPq) for a research fellowship and Frederico Bertholini for research assistance.

Our personal debts know no bounds. Lee Alston thanks his wife, Mary, who believed in the project and who patiently listened to endless laments and lectures at dinners. Marcus André Melo thanks his family for supporting him throughout the entire journey of discussing, writing, and rewriting the book materials. Bernardo Mueller thanks Suely, Beatriz, and Henrique. For encouragement, support, and endless interactions in what sometimes seemed an interminable process, Carlos Pereira would like to thank his wife, Ana Paula.

ABBREVIATIONS

ARENA   Aliança Renovadora Nacional
BNDES   Brazilian Development Bank
BNH   National Housing Bank
BRIC   Brazil, Russia, India, China
CIESP   Center of the Industries of the State of São Paulo
CIP   Inter-ministerial Price Council
CNI   National Confederation of Industry
CPI   Corruption Perceptions Index
FHC   Fernando Henrique Cardoso
FIESP   Federation of the Industries of the State of São Paulo
FSE   Fundo Social de Emergência
GDI   gross domestic income
GDP   gross domestic product
IA   Institutional Act
IDB   Inter-American Development Bank
IEDI   Instituto para o Estudo do Desenvolvimento Industrial
IMF   International Monetary Fund
IPEA   Institute for Applied Economic Research
IPF   institutional possibility frontiers
ISI   Import Substitution Industrialization
MDB   Movimento Democrático Brasileiro
MP   Ministério Público
MST   Landless Peasant Movement
NBER   National Bureau of Economic Research
OECD   Organization for Economic Cooperation and Development
PACTI   Program of Support to the Improvement of the Technological Capability of Industry
PAEG   Economic Action Program
PBQP   Brazilian Program of Quality and Productivity
PCI   Program of Industrial Competitiveness

PDC	Christian Democratic Party
PDS	Partido Democrático Social
PFL	Liberal Front Party (Partido da Frente Liberal)
PICE	Industrial and Foreign Trade Policy
PISA	Programme for International Student Assessment
PL	Liberal Party
PMDB	Brazilian Democratic Movement Party (Partido do Movimento Democrático Brasileiro)
PND	National Development Plan
PR	proportional representation
PROES	Program of Reduction of the State Participation in Banking Activity
PSD	Social Democratic Party
PSDB	Brazilian Social Democracy Party
PSOL	Partido Socialismo e Liberdade
PT	Workers' Party
PTB	Brazilian Labor Party
SOE	state-owned enterprise
SUS	Unified Health System
TCU	National Audit Tribunal
UDN	União Democrática Nacional
URV	Unidade Real de Valor
WVS	World Values Survey

PART I

An Overview of Brazil in Transition:
Beliefs, Leadership, and Institutional Change

CHAPTER 1

Introduction

SINCE 1994, BRAZIL HAS BEEN ON A RELATIVELY VIRTUOUS PATH OF economic and political development, though there have been bumps in the road. Is twenty years long enough to conclude that Brazil is still on the road to a sustainable developmental path whose hallmarks are social inclusion with steady economic and political development? Or, were the past twenty years simply a flash in the pan similar to the short-lived Brazilian miracle of the late 1960s and early 1970s? This time, the miracle is for real because of a change in beliefs in Brazilian society and consequent changes in economic and political institutions. Today, the dominant belief held among those in power as well as the majority of the population is in "fiscally sound social inclusion." How did this belief emerge? And, moreover, what are the forces that will sustain it? To understand the changes in Brazil over the past fifty years, we wed the concepts of windows of opportunity, beliefs, dominant network, leadership, institutions, and economic and political outcomes into a framework to understand the dynamics of institutional change and the beliefs within which they are nested.[1] Development is contextual; that is, each country must find its own way. Brazil is no exception, though the concepts developed in this book have purchase in understanding institutional development or persistence elsewhere.

Economic Development and Critical Transitions

Our main theme is the process of development in the modern world. The purpose is to better understand the forces leading some contemporary societies to achieve economic and political development while most societies remain in autopilot. "Development" may seem fairly intuitive; yet, all countries manage to grow during some periods and almost all develop to

---

[1] We build on an expanding literature on institutions, beliefs, and leadership. For books for the primarily academic audience, see Acemoglu and Robinson (2006); Eggertsson (2005); Greif (2006); North (2005); North, Wallis, and Weingast (2009); North et al. (2012); and Schofield (2006). A recent contribution reaching the general audience is Acemoglu and Robinson (2012). The list of articles dealing with the topic is voluminous and we will reference them when specifically relevant.

some extent over time. However, few countries manage to complete what we call the "critical transition," which is a more fundamental change in a country's circumstance than simply increases in GDP.

To see that the process of development entails a transition from one state to another, rather than simply an incremental change along a continuum, note that it is common for analysts—whether growth theorists, development economists, political scientists, journalists, or others—to classify countries into two broad groups. There are rich and poor countries; developed and developing; center and periphery; First World and Third World (the Second World disappeared with the fall of communism); industrialized and nonindustrialized; and open-access and limited-access orders. Although the labels and the associated theoretical approaches differ, the basic notion is that there are two categories. It is natural then for the interest to center on trying to understand the determinants of the transition from one group to the other. It turns out that recent cases of countries making the transition are quite rare. It is not simply a matter of time until most countries grow themselves from the bottom to the top category. In table 1.1, we used the Maddison Project data set to classify each of the countries for which there was GDP per capita data, as being in the high income, low income, and middle/transition categories.[2] We did this for three different years spanning the data set—1900, 1950, and 2008. In order to classify the countries, the choice of cutoff for the high group was chosen somewhat arbitrarily to include countries that are normally accepted as being "developed" at that time, and the cutoff for the low group was set at two-thirds (66.7 percent) of that level. Given the propensity to classify all countries into just two groups, the countries between the low and the high groups are considered as being in transition from one to the other. As expected, there are fewer countries in the high GDP per capita group than the low group (note that in 1900, the limited data availability biases upward the proportion of those in the high group). Strikingly, the number of countries in the transition group is always relatively small—less than 10 percent. The last row in the table names the countries in the transition group, which allows one to see that this group would be even smaller if we reassigned the special cases (Puerto Rico, Kuwait, UAE in 2008, and war-torn Europe in 1950). Furthermore, some of the transition countries are transitioning downward (such as Argentina and Uruguay in 1950), corroborating the notion that countries making the transition from the bottom to the top group is a relatively rare occurrence. Although the numbers in table 1.1 depend on the criteria used to classify the countries (see note to table), the general conclusion that there is a small high-income group and a

2 The Maddison Project data is described in Bolt and van Zanden (2013).

TABLE 1.1. Number and Percentage of Countries: High, Low, and Transition

Stage of development	2008			1950			1900		
	GDP/P	N	%	GDP/P	N	%	GDP/P	N	%
High	>$18K	27	17	>$5.5K	13	9	>$2.8K	13	30
Low	<$12K	121	74	<$3.7K	116	84	<$1.9K	26	60
Transition	>$12K and <$18K	13	9	>$3.7K and <$5.5K	10	7	>$2.8K and <$1.9K	4	9
Countries in transition	Greece, Portugal, Spain, Czech, Slovakia, Belarus, Latvia, Lithuania, Chile, Puerto Rico, Kuwait, UAE, Mauritius			Austria, Belgium, Finland, France, Germany, Norway, Argentina, Chile, Uruguay, Trinidad, Tobago			Norway, Sweden, Chile, Uruguay		

Source: Calculated using data from the Maddison Project (Bolt and van Zanden 2013).

Note: Data: GDP per capita in 1990 Int. GK$. Countries classified by the following criteria: 2008—High (GDP/P > $18,000), Low (GDP/P < $12,000), Transition ($12,000<GDP/P<$18,000); 1950—High (GDP/P > $5,500), Low (GDP/P < $3,666), Transition ($3,666<GDP/P<$5,500); 1900—High (GDP/P > $2,800), Low (GDP/P < $1,866), Transition ($1,866<GDP/P<$2,800). Upper bound is 1.5 times the lower bound.

large low-income group, with few transitioning countries in between, is quite robust. This flies in the face of the notion that poor countries will inexorably grow over time and catch up with richer countries, known as the convergence hypothesis, which has been a major debate in economics in the past decades.[3]

The evidence in table 1.1 refers solely to GDP per capita. Although higher levels of income and wealth are necessary for a critical transition, this concept requires important changes in several other dimensions as well. Many times, an increase in GDP per capita can take place in circumstances that are not sustainable or that compromise future growth, creating a middle-income trap. A critical transition, in contrast, requires not only economic improvements but also accompanying changes in social relations (e.g., greater equality) and political institutions (e.g., alterations of power and checks and balances). Therefore, a country that has achieved a critical transition has done something significantly harder and more fundamental than simply raising its GDP. Note that according to

---

3 See Barro and Sala-i-Martin (2004: 16–21) for a history of the literature.

the classification in table 1.1, Argentina was a high-income country in 1900 (GDP per capita $2,875), in transition in 1950 ($4,987), and in the low-income group in 2008 ($9,715), suggesting that although incomes were high at the outset, other conditions were lacking. In the opposite direction, although Austria, Belgium, France, and Germany are classified as in the transition group in 1950, this was a temporary setback due to the two world wars, suggesting that the other fundamental conditions besides GDP that had promoted the development of these countries in the nineteenth century were still in place.

The conditions besides GDP growth that are necessary for a critical transition vary from country to country. By examining those countries that have achieved sustainable development, we can see that there are many common features, such as rule of law for all, political openness and universal participation, free entry and exit for all sorts of organizations (business, political, religious, and associational), checks and balances, electoral uncertainty *ex ante*, and certainty *ex post*. No country has all these features, and each has its own set of quirks and dysfunctionalities, but by and large their institutions share a related set of such characteristics and generally lack other conflicting elements, such as authoritarianism, inequality, segregation, favoritism, and systemic violence.

Brazil is currently poised to make the critical transition. Given that only a handful of countries have managed to do this in the past decades, it is incumbent on us to back up this claim with evidence and argumentation. Furthermore, given that Brazil's performance in terms of GDP growth has been merely mediocre in past decades, we need to make a strong case that other fundamental changes are taking place that are setting the stage for economic growth to follow. In chapter 2, we present a basic framework for understanding how countries develop or fail to do so. In chapters 3–6, we provide a detailed analysis of the changes in Brazil since the 1960s. We show that the country has become economically orthodox, politically open, and socially inclusive, with all these three areas marked by a general respect for the rules. The characteristics, which are now firmly rooted and less likely to be reverted by eventual shocks, have never been aligned in such a way in Brazilian history and contrast markedly with the state of the country just a few decades ago. Previously, chronic fiscal and monetary indiscipline kept the country in a perpetual inflationary state with high internal and external indebtedness. Misguided and excessive state intervention fostered inefficiencies, distorted markets, reduced productivity, and left market failures unaddressed. Politics was at different times mired in different combinations of authoritarianism, corruption, clientelism, populism, nepotism, electoral fraud, gridlock, and exclusion. Socially, the country was highly unequal— among classes, races, regions, and sectors—with lack of opportunity for the disadvantaged and few effective policies seeking to address these imbalances through redistribution. Though some of these problems persist, there have been huge strides.

BRAZIL: THIS TIME FOR REAL?

Brazil currently boasts the world's sixth largest economy, and it has been undergoing a profound transformation toward its critical transition. At first blush, this is a bold claim because the rates of GDP growth during the past twenty years, especially at the start of its transition, have been generally unremarkable and often disappointing. But, as noted earlier, a critical transition is about more than GDP growth; it also includes economic opportunity and distribution as well as genuine political competition and democratic stability. On these scores, we demonstrate in the empirical section that Brazil is a different country now than it was twenty years ago.

We are bullish about the changes in Brazil, but the perception by much of the media inside and outside of Brazil is that the slowdown in economic growth is an indication that once again the glory years are lost. This replacement of hope and confidence with skepticism and despondency is not hard to understand. From 1975 to 1994, the country underwent two decades of unrelenting economic decline during which a crippling process of hyperinflation wreaked havoc with individuals', organizations', and governments' attempts to structure their lives and to plan for the future. To many, the repeated frustrations and failures of this period destroyed the country's self-esteem and instilled a sense that perhaps this dysfunctional state of affairs was not a phase to be overcome, but rather a natural Brazilian characteristic.

Since 1994, things have changed for the better. Inflation has been kept under control, and several economic indicators have clearly improved, some of them remarkably so. Poverty and inequality have been falling for more than ten years; the country's debt ranks as investment grade; agriculture and other exports are booming; international reserves are above US$350 billion; extensive oil reserves have been discovered; and powerful politicians involved in corruption scandals have faced tremendous reputational costs, and some have been tried and punished by the Supreme Court. Over this period, Brazil has consolidated a vibrant, competitive, and liberal democracy in a global context in which generalized elections have often not resulted in guarantees and safeguards to citizens' civil and individual rights.

And yet, there remains a nagging feeling among analysts and the Brazilian public that these achievements may merely be a temporary good spell of the sort the country has often had in the past, but which inevitably ends in tears. Perhaps the most salient argument along these lines is that all these achievements are a direct consequence of the world's commodity boom since 2003 and now that this has ended, everything will come crashing down.

Skepticism about Brazil's achievements as well as its future prospects is not gratuitous. An examination of several indicators of performance and prosperity provides sufficient ground to be suspicious of claims that the country has deeply changed. Figure 1.1 shows Brazilian GDP per capita growth rates from 1950 to 2010. For the purpose of comparison, the figure also shows the average GDP per capita among all countries as well as the boundary for the top 20 percent and bottom 20 percent countries in each year. The figure differentiates when GDP per capita in Brazil grew above and below the average. The data show that prior to 1980, Brazil performed overwhelmingly above the world average and often above the top 20 percent mark. Since then, however, its performance has been, more often than not, below average. This is not an obvious candidate for a study of a country on a successful transition to sustainable development.

Other indicators are equally ominous. In the United Nations' Human Development Index, Brazil was only 85th out of 187 countries in 2011. In the *World Bank's 2011 Doing Business* ranking, which compares the ease of doing business across countries, Brazil was ranked 126th out of 183. The Legatum Prosperity Index puts Brazil at 42nd out of 110 in 2011. In the Heritage Foundation's 2012 Index of Economic Freedom, Brazil was in the "mostly unfree" category, ranking 99th out of 179 countries. In terms of corruption, Transparency International's Corruption Perceptions Index (CPI) places Brazil at 69 out of 174 countries in 2012. In 2012, Reporters without Borders ranked Brazil at 99 out of 179 countries in terms of the freedom of press. In the 2009 OECD PISA test for educational attainment for fifteen-year-olds, Brazil came in 50th, 55th, and 51st out of 62 countries in reading, math, and science, respectively.[4] These are clearly not the kind of rankings that would make a country stand out as an example of successful development. In most categories cited above, Brazil seems woefully distant from the leading group. How

4 The sources of the indexes cited in this paragraph are as follows: Human Development Index (http://hdr.undp.org/en/humandev/); Doing Business Index (http://www.doing business.org/rankings/); Legatum Prosperity Index (http://www.prosperity.com/default .aspx); Heritage Foundation Index of Economic Freedom (http://www.heritage.org/index /default); Corruption Perceptions Index (http://cpi.transparency.org/cpi2011/); Reporters without Borders Press Freedom Index (http://en.rsf.org/press-freedom-index-2011-2012 ,1043.html); and OECD Programme for Student Assessment (http://www.oecd.org/pisa /46643496.pdf).

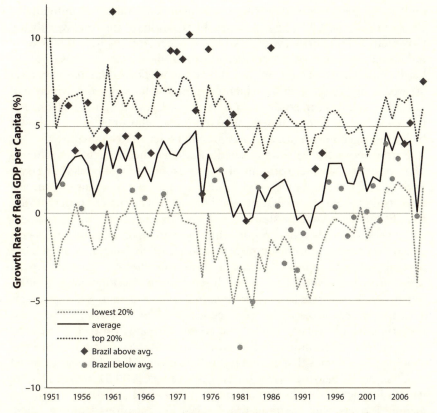

Figure 1.1. Brazilian GDP per capita growth relative to the rest of the world. Sources: Heston, Summers, and Aten (2009) data for 1950–2007 in constant 2005 prices; IMF for 2008–2010 data, http://www.imf.org/external/pubs/ft/weo/2010/02/weodata/download.aspx.

is it then that we justify our choice of Brazil as a country on the road to prosperity?

Rather than trying to discredit these indexes and the comparisons they purport to allow, we find that such attempts at measuring different dimensions of a country's performance can often be quite useful. It is naive, however, to expect a successfully developing country to simultaneously and monotonically improve all or even most of these dimensions throughout that process. The process of development is inherently messy and contextual, and no combination of indicators ever provides a sure telltale sign of whether a definitive transition is really underway. Many of the indicators measure performance variables that vary widely over time, reflecting cyclical rather than deeper determinants. Other indicators are built using perceptions by experts, businessmen, and other individuals, for example, the CPI (Transparency International) and the Worldwide Governance Indicators (World Bank). Yet, perceptions are often overly influenced by more salient current information and are often subject to herd behavior. Tetlock (2006) has shown the weakness of expert opinion at predicting issues such as which countries will thrive and which will fall. His twenty-year study with a large and varied sample of experts from various fields concluded that even those who by definition should be knowledgeable predict only marginally better than chance.

Furthermore, there are several indicators in which Brazil fares remarkably well, for example, 10th out of 133 in "soundness of banks" in 2009; 15th out of 236 in number of documents published in scientific journals from 1996 to 2010; and first in a ranking of developing countries' efforts to fight hunger.[5] Another shortcoming of using any arbitrary assortment of indexes and indicators to infer the true nature of a country's process of development is that they typically measure levels when it is often more revealing to analyze how a particular society evolves over time. Indeed, a serious methodological flaw in much research in development is to infer longitudinal processes from cross-sectional data. Brazil, for example, typically scores very low in indexes of educational level or attainment. Analysts rightly hold this as one of the country's major obstacles if it is to develop. However, simply looking at the level of the country's latest PISA score masks the fact that "average PISA scores for Brazil have improved in all subjects measured over the last ten years" (OECD 2010). Despite its still low level, the quality of education has had a distinctive upward evolution over recent years in Brazil. Even in education—an area where Brazil's performance is admittedly dismal—it ranks third in a sample of 49 countries for the annual growth rates in students' achievements between 1995 and 2009 (Hanushek, Peterson, and Woessmann 2012). What has caused this change? Investigation into this issue, as done by the OECD (2010) and the World Bank (Bruns, Evans, and Luque 2012), reveals that Brazil has implemented coherent and innovative reforms that have started addressing the underlying causes of poor education in ways that promise significant long-term changes. The reforms have targeted several different dimensions of the educational system and at several different levels— federal, state, and municipal. Funding, which is constitutionally hardwired, is high by world standards, but, more importantly, the productivity of the

5 The sources of the indexes mentioned in this paragraph are: "Soundness of Banks" (World Economic Forum, Executive Opinion Survey 2008, 2009); SCImago Journal and Country Rank (http://www.scimagojr.com/countryrank.php); ActionAid (2010); and "Who's Really Fighting Hunger?" (The Hague: ActionAid International, http://www .actionaid.org.uk/doc_lib/hungerfree_scorecard.pdf).

expenditures has improved and become more equitable. The government created several new funds to assure resources for different educational purposes: they increased teacher salaries, especially in the poorer regions, and emphasized better training for teachers; government-mandated local education councils increased community participation; conditional cash transfers have been extremely successful and have been expanded to cover more than 11 million families, contributing to reduced absenteeism, repetition, and child labor; and completion rates also improved. With school attendance now nearly universal, Brazil has directed efforts to increase the length of the school day and the school year. Brazil also extended the number of years in the curriculum to twelve. This additional temporal information not only provides a much more complete and informative picture than a lone indicator but may temper or even invert an analyst's assessment of the state of education in Brazil.

The areas where improvement has been the clearest and most impressive are poverty and inequality reduction. From 1990 to 2009, approximately 60 percent of Brazilians moved to a higher economic group, and extreme poverty was practically eliminated. Only 4 percent remain in poverty in 2013 (Báez et al. 2015). The World Bank report *Shared Prosperity and Poverty Eradication in Latin America and the Caribbean* places Brazil as the country with the greatest improvement in poverty reduction in the region, home to "one in every two people who escaped poverty in the Latin America and Caribbean region during the period" (Báez et al. 2015: 65). Since the mid-1990s, the Gini coefficient of income inequality has been steadily declining, leading that index to uncharted territory in a country that has always been one of the most unequal in the world. This has taken place during a period in which, worldwide, inequality within countries has been on the rise. As a result of these improvements, the structure of society has changed with a perceptibly larger middle class and upper class, which has meant greater access to markets for goods and services, including public services such as education and health, and greater participation in national affairs, all of which should work to reinforce these trends. While the World Bank report attributes the improvements to stable growth since 2001, stronger policy focus on poverty, and the dynamics of the labor market (Báez et al. 2015: 65–66), these are merely proximate causes. The deeper determinants are the beliefs that produced the institutions that underlie those proximate causes. As with the case of education, the level of poverty and inequality in Brazil is still unsatisfactory, and much improvement is necessary in the future; nevertheless, the magnitude of change and the concerted way in which it has been achieved are highly relevant.

Still, identifying development is more difficult than simply looking at different indicators over time. A profound process of reform may have been initiated with no discernible effect yet apparent. The impact of reform may materialize with a hard-to-quantify lag during which policies, programs, and new ways of doing things have been implemented and yet no results have emerged. In some cases, things might even get worse before they get better. In other cases, some indicators might never improve or even get permanently worse, and this might still be accommodated within a successful process of development. To see this, note that even highly advanced nations fare badly along some dimensions or others: Italy was 69th out of 182 in the 2010 CPI (Transparency International); the United States had the highest prisoner population per 100,000 people in 2007 and was 29th out of 223 countries in prevalence of diabetes in 2010; the United Kingdom fared fourth lowest in a Privacy Index ranking of 48 countries in 2007; and Belgium was 57th out of 149 in the Environmental Performance Index.[6] The upshot of this discussion is that although indexes and rankings may be useful to categorize highly dysfunctional or highly successful countries, they may be less precise to distinguish between countries that are transitioning to development from those that are going through a cyclical good or a bad period.

If not indexes, what evidence can we provide to support the choice of Brazil to illustrate our approach to development? A large literature consolidated in the past two decades argues that institutions, rather than geography, culture, policies, or luck, are the fundamental cause of long-term growth (North 1990, 2005; Acemoglu and Robinson 2006, 2012; Engerman and Sokoloff 2000; Eggertsson 2005; Greif 2006; North, Wallis, and Weingast 2009; and Rodrik, Subramanian, and Trebbi 2004, among many others). If we are correct that Brazil is on the path to a more prosperous level of economic and political development, then we should be able to provide an argument where changing institutions must play a central role. It is necessary that we show that a dramatic transformation has taken place in the country's institutions between the previous history of boom and busts to the current period that we identify as a transition to a new order.

Further, we go beyond simply chronicling the change in institutions, and propose (chapter 2) a framework to understand the changes that transpired. We give a general interpretation of the changes in Brazil (chapter 2) and a detailed analysis of recent Brazilian history, also based

6 The sources of the indexes mentioned in this paragraph are: Corruption Perceptions Index (http://cpi.transparency.org/cpi2011/); Prison Population (International Center for Policy Studies, cited in http://www.allcountries.org/ranks/prison_incarceration_rates_of _countries_2007.html); Diabetes Atlas (International Diabetes Federation, http://www.idf .org/diabetesatlas/); Privacy Index (Privacy International, https://www.privacyinternational .org/); and Environmental Performance Index (Yale University, cited in http://www.photius .com/rankings/environmental_performance_index_2008.html).

on the framework (chapters 3–6). Here, our goal is to convince the reader that something truly remarkable is taking place in Brazil.

While it might seem obvious that things have improved since the 1980s in Brazil, our claim is much bolder. Not only have outcomes changed—for example, inflation is under control, and the external debt is lower than international reserves, inter alia—but more importantly, institutions, beliefs, and those in power have also changed because the process of development has changed. This is a much more controversial position. Despite occasional glowing endorsements, like pieces on Brazil in the *Economist* (2009), the *New Yorker* (Lemann 2011), and *Spiegel* (Follath and Gluesing 2012), the more typical position is of sharp skepticism about the Brazilian economy's prospects. An emblematic example of this point of view is the book *Breakout Nations: In Pursuit of the Next Economic Miracles* by Ruchir Sharma of Morgan Stanley:

> While in recent years Brazil has been widely touted as a rising regional superpower, on the relevant fundamentals Brazil is the anti-China, a nation that invested in the premature construction of a welfare state rather than the roads and wireless networks of a modern industrial economy. Nations that have grown dependent on booming prices for raw materials such as oil and precious metals—namely, Russia and Brazil—face a hard decade ahead. (Sharma 2012: 10)

Sharma (2012: 64) predicts that countries like India, South Korea, and Thailand "are the real or potential breakout nations, while Brazil is not."

Like Sharma, the *Economist* (2013) now casts a gloomier forecast consistent with our view that much of the content of the media is noise based on assessments of recent policies and outcomes rather than the deeper and more stable fundamental determinants, the changes in beliefs and institutions. Sharma (2012), for example, puts much weight on the overvalued exchange rate in Brazil and on the poor state of infrastructure as part of his argument for why Brazil will not be a "breakout nation." Admittedly, these are important variables that seriously impact Brazilian development. Yet they are outcomes that, to a large extent, are deliberate consequences of policies. Analysts frequently act as if countries did not face budget or political constraints. For example, there has been considerable criticism that Brazil neglected to sufficiently invest in infrastructure. But, what is the opportunity cost? Which will yield a higher rate of return: infrastructure or education? Brazil chose education as noted above.

Without a clear understanding of why Brazil took decisions and actions that led to outcomes, one does not have the full picture of the trade-offs. To have this understanding, it is necessary to posit the constraints and incentives faced by all the relevant players. The major determinants of the incentives and constraints are beliefs and institutions, which is why these concepts are central to our framework in chapters 2 and 7.

This means that to show that Brazil is in the midst of a dramatic transformation, we cannot rely on a list of outcomes or policies. Instead, we need to show evidence that both institutions and beliefs have changed in such a way that the content and timing of their change coincides with the switch from dysfunctional policies and poor outcomes of the past to improved, albeit still imperfect, policies and outcomes of the present. The advantage of analyzing a single country in great detail, as opposed to a sample of countries with more generality, is that we can be very explicit about the specific institutions and beliefs and how they change. Moreover, Brazil is an important world economic and political player.

We focus on the beliefs—the mental constructs mapping institutions onto outcomes—that motivated the choice of institutions. There are two sets of beliefs that have been the driving force of the process of change in Brazil since 1985. The first is a belief in social inclusion that arose as a reaction to the oppressive experience under military dictatorship and the inequalities and injustice inherited from the country's history. The second is an aversion to inflation born from the traumatic experience under hyperinflationary years of 1985 to 1994. Together, these two separate strands form a belief in fiscally sound social inclusion that constrains and influences the choice of institutions by the dominant coalition, thereby crucially affecting the selection of policies and the incentives influencing outcomes. It might seem that the beliefs we identified for Brazil are arbitrary and unfounded. After all, many countries had traumatic experiences with authoritarianism and monetary instability, and there is no indication that such experience inevitably leads to the sort of beliefs we attribute to Brazil. These beliefs are mental models about how the world works and are not reducible to preferences or values. In chapter 2, we elaborate on the beliefs and provide evidence that there has been a sharp change in beliefs in Brazil in the past three decades.

A SKETCH OF THE CONCEPTUAL FRAMEWORK

Institutions matter for economic development. This statement has now become part of mainstream economics. Alone, understanding the importance of institutions is insufficient for understanding economic and political development because there is no recipe for institutional change. Institutional change is highly contextual to time and place. All countries have to find their own way to develop. Most countries are more or less in an autopilot mode where institutions change on the margin, but there are generally not fundamental changes in institutions followed by institutional deepening. Why? Typically, those in power structure the formal rules of the game in a manner to produce outcomes that are in their economic and political interests. For those in power, there are rents from a stable status quo where not much changes. Citizens, as well, become accustomed to the status quo, and there are few gains and, at times, high costs to rocking the boat.

Yet, there are some countries that break away from their autopilot mode and move toward a more virtuous trajectory, implementing institutional changes that lead to sustained economic and political development. We seek to better understand what undergirds institutional change. To do so, we need to better understand the role of beliefs and tie them to institutional change (Eggertsson 2005; North 2005; Greif 2006). If beliefs are the key to understanding institutional change, we need to understand what leads to changes in beliefs, especially among those in the dominant network of power that structures institutions. Beliefs are generally quite stable because most economic and political outcomes are at the margin. But, at times, economic and political outcomes diverge considerably from what those in the dominant network expected. When this happens, we call it a window of opportunity for institutional change because the powerful actors may have changed, bringing with them different beliefs, or the beliefs of those in power change. During windows of opportunity, the beliefs of those in power as well as among the citizens become malleable. "Outcomes are not normal, what is going on?"

During windows of opportunity, beliefs are up for grabs to some extent, but often not much happens because no one seizes the opportunity. During these times, we see leadership playing a role to circumvent the free-rider problem. We are not proposing a "great men make history" view of beliefs and institutional change but, rather, that leaders are shaped by the context of the situation. A leader senses and acts on the major anxiety facing a society. Leaders take the pulse of citizens and act on it. Leadership entails cognition (understanding the problem facing society), coordination (getting others in power to "give it a go"), and moral authority (citizens trusting in leaders' motives to try to do the right thing).[7] In Brazil, President Fernando Henrique Cardoso came to power with some moral authority because of his political exile during the military regime in Brazil. In addition, Cardoso, both as an academic professor as well as a political figure (he was a former senator and played a key role during the Constituent Assembly), developed a reputation for knowledge and leadership. Naturally, leaders can and do act selfishly, but we are interested in leaders who act for the betterment of society and how they will be viewed historically.

7 See Riker (1996) on leadership and coordination, and Greif (2012) on moral authority.

Windows of opportunity are seemingly quite frequent, but the combination of windows of opportunity with the right leaders with beliefs that foster institutions that increase economic and political development is rare. This is why most countries remain in a cycle of more or less the status quo, where people see only marginal changes during their lifetimes. Our framework—only sketched out here in general terms, but developed more thoroughly in chapters 2 and 7—helps us to better understand both institutional persistence and institutional change. It allows us to better understand transitions from one relatively stable process of institutional change on the margin to a new set of beliefs with a similar dynamic, but with a significantly different set of institutions and outcomes. Understanding the concepts behind transitions is the key to understanding why some countries make the "critical transition." In our analysis, we stress the *process* of economic and political development more so than the short-run variations in economic growth or seemingly political competition. Achieving a truly open society takes decades (North, Wallis, and Weingast 2009).

ANALYTICAL NARRATIVES AND ECONOMIC DEVELOPMENT

This book is about understanding the developmental path of Brazil, which we hold up as a country that has embarked toward a critical transition. This claim derives not from a mechanical extrapolation of the past but rather is based on a framework that stresses windows of opportunity, beliefs, and leadership. This section discusses some epistemological issues related to the kind of evidence that we present. Because there will always be ambiguities whether a given country is making a transition or is merely experiencing a transient period of growth, no use of the data can make a definitive case one way or the other. Any judgment will necessarily be inductive rather than deductive.

This difficulty of judging the evidence is not exclusive to the setting being considered here; rather, it is common to a broad set of scientific inquiries. Whenever direct evidence is not available to test a given hypothesis, it is still possible to rely on circumstantial evidence. This involves showing that certain events or circumstances that are often associated with that hypothesis have taken place so that one can then infer, with a given probability, that the hypothesis should not be rejected. The quality of that inference will depend of course on the strength of the link between the circumstantial evidence and the hypothesis. The greater the amount of circumstantial evidence and the stronger the link between each strand of that evidence and the hypothesis, the stronger will be the case that is being made. Fogel (1982) argues that areas like economic history, like many court cases, often have no choice but to rely on circumstantial evidence.

Brazil has been going through a remarkable transformation in which the fundamental roles of windows of opportunity, beliefs, institutions, and leadership can be clearly identified. The transformation will eventually lead to a critical transition for Brazil across the gap to join the select group of developed nations. It is important to make it as clear as possible what we are and what we are not saying. In particular, it is important to distinguish what we claim from what we predict. The claims involve things that have already happened, can be expressed in greater detail, and can be confronted with evidence. The predictions, on the other hand, are of a very different nature. Inevitably, they are a guess of what we think will happen in the future. All predictions have an element of hubris, yet the level of epistemological arrogance depends on various elements of the prediction (Taleb 2010). The first is the time span and the level of detail of the prediction. The further into the future and the more specific the prediction, the less reliable it will be. The second is the underlying *process* on which the prediction was based.

So, what exactly are our claims and predictions about Brazilian development, and how can they be assessed? Consider first the claims. In the last three decades, new beliefs have taken hold that wed social inclusion to fiscal and monetary orthodoxy. The beliefs affected formal and informal institutions that in turn have led to many positive outcomes. We are not saying that the transformation is all encompassing, that it is complete, or that it has not in the process also produced distortions and waste. It is not enough to produce evidence of inefficiencies and dysfunctional behavior to refute our claims. The access to economic and political markets has made Brazil a fundamentally more inclusive society than it has ever been. The unprecedented recent fall in inequality and poverty and the growth of the middle class are evidence for our claims. The changes are also extending to more inclusion in education, less tolerance for corruption, and greater respect for the rule of law.

Simply put, we predict that Brazil will establish institutions that lead to stable economic rates of growth and increasingly less dysfunctional politics and corruption. Sustaining this path will enable Brazil to transition from the lower-growth to the higher-growth groups of countries in the world. This prediction is based on the framework we present in chapters 2 and 7. The framework emphasizes the role of beliefs and institutions in determining economic and political outcomes (as well as the role of windows of opportunity and leadership in determining which beliefs and institutions emerge). The beliefs foster institutions pushing Brazil in the direction of outcomes such as lower inequality, lower poverty, a bigger middle class, more competitive economic and political markets, impersonality, and rule of law. Myriad distortions, inequalities, and inefficiencies accompany the process of what we term "dissipative inclusion." But, dissipation does not cancel out the transformative nature of the changes.

Much of the recent literature on redistribution and growth has come to accept that redistribution, and thus inclusion, often have a positive effect on growth (P. Lindert 2003; Perotti 1995; Bénabou 2002; Easterly and Rebelo 1993; Sala-i-Martin 1997; Saint Paul and Verdier 1996; Aghion and Bolton 1997; Galor, Moav, and Vollrath 2009; Engerman and Sokoloff 2000; Galor 2011; Acemoglu and Robinson 2006, 2012; North, Wallis, and Weingast 2009). If the predictions fail to materialize, we can then assess whether they failed because the inclusion did not really take place in Brazil or because the notion that inclusion translates into growth is wrong.

Our prediction has relatively large confidence intervals (low epistemological arrogance), as we are vague on timing and details. We are not venturing to predict exactly how the transition will happen, except that it will be driven by the *beliefs in fiscally sound social inclusion*. We are not predicting which sectors/areas/domains will improve and which will remain mired in inefficiencies, nor how fast or smoothly the transition proceeds. We do not predict these details because neither the framework nor the literature provides a basis for making such inferences. The lack of detail does not make the prediction less striking or controversial.

Finally, our analysis is in no way an endorsement of whatever party or president was, is, or may come to be in power. Similarly, we do not endorse or criticize any specific current policy or program, as our justification for expecting Brazil to thrive is not based on the analysis at this level. Instead, in our framework the main determinant of outcomes are institutions, which in turn are determined by beliefs. Although we are very explicit about which beliefs and institutions are responsible for the fundamental changes in Brazil, we understand that there is an infinite number of specific policies, programs, and other manifestations through which these beliefs and institutions can lead to change. We have no way of telling whether the specific set of government efforts that have materialized are the best path to economic growth. In fact, given the messy nature of politics and the complexity of the task, it is quite likely that the observed policies are probably not the best that could be done and may often be counterproductive. What we do expect, however, is that the beliefs and institutions are such that there will be forces that push for those policies and programs to be eventually revised as they prove to be mistaken. Whereas in many countries institutions are such that inefficiencies may be there by design, as they suit the ruling elite, we see Brazilian institutions as providing the incentives and the means for the inefficiencies to be continually, though imperfectly, transacted away in political markets. Like cointegrated variables that may stray apart but are always eventually pulled back together, our view does not require that government policy be always efficient and in line with the beliefs in fiscally sound inclusion. We do expect, however, that there will be forces to pull them back toward those beliefs.

A careful reading of our application of the framework makes it clear that our analysis is not a stamp of approval (or disapproval) of current governments or policies. We identify the period during and closely after the *Real Plan* in 1994 as a window of opportunity in which a crucial role was played by leadership, which initiated institutional changes and sustained institutional deepening, moving Brazil toward a critical transition. This was an occasion where individuals mattered. But since then—including the second term of Cardoso, the two terms of Luiz Iná-cio "Lula" da Silva, and the first term of Dilma Rousseff—we see less of a role for leadership. The framework is such that except during windows of opportunity, there is little scope for leadership, and the country is on autopilot. Of course, each specific dominant network is able to affect the details and imprint its own style, but the essence and general direction are ultimately determined by beliefs and institutions.

Road Map for the Book

A large part of the evidence consists of analytical narratives in which we use both quantitative and qualitative evidence to provide support for the application of our concepts to historical periods in the last fifty years of Brazilian history. Analytical narratives are much more nuanced than running a regression from which the scholar interprets causation because of a "significant" coefficient.[8] With analytical narratives, there are not significant coefficients, but there is considerable evidence, much of which is independent and as a result can be very convincing. As in courts of law or in medical diagnoses, the plethora of circumstantial evidence can make a compelling case for guilt or innocence, or for the course of medical treatments. In chapter 2, we lay out a brief conceptual dynamic to interpret the past fifty years in Brazil. We developed the framework to understand Brazilian development, though we believe it can also aid the understanding of development elsewhere, particularly in Latin America. Our framework rests on tying together the key concepts of windows of opportunity,

---

8 We recognize that not all scholars use regression analysis so naively, and indeed, regression results are useful evidence when viewed along with qualitative evidence, making the results more convincing.

beliefs, dominant network, leadership, institutions, and outcomes. It is the dynamics of the concepts that led to institutional change in Brazil and in turn a new trajectory. We then discuss the important dominant networks in power, along with their beliefs, in four periods: 1964–1984 (the military years); 1985–1993 (the early years back to democracy); 1993–2002 (Cardoso years); and 2002–2014 (the Lula and Dilma years). Here we give an overview of the fifty years.

We delve into the details of the development of Brazil over fifty years starting, in chapter 3, with the military government. The belief in "developmentalism" motivated the institutions put in place by the military regime. Developmentalism rested on top-down technocratic planning and was a coalition between the military and the business community, both domestic and foreign. Import substitution policies along with state-led industrialization brought economic growth in the late 1960s and into the mid-1970s. Economic growth resulted essentially because the military regime solved a coordination problem for business. Given the low level of GDP in Brazil at the time, there was low-hanging fruit to be reaped with planning. But, the Brazilian miracle of the late 1960s and early 1970s began to sputter out, and, moreover, political rights became more constrained. The threat of torture was present; censorship was dominant; and a considerable number of people left the country. The years of censorship and a closed political system sowed the seeds for a more open political order. Above all, the failure of the expansionist strategy of growth through import substitution accompanied by inflation and external debt became self-evident. Citizens also began to blame the government for not reducing economic and social inequality. The dominant belief that economic growth should precede social inclusion started losing political support.

In chapter 4, we discuss the factors, especially changing beliefs, that led to redemocratization and the subsequent institutional changes during the years 1985–1993. After the military government, the middle class demanded more inclusion in the political arena. To a certain extent, this happened with multiple parties, and only one claiming to be a right-wing party. Unexpectedly, the franchise was given to illiterates seemingly because the belief in social inclusion warranted it; the illiterates were not in the streets clamoring for the vote. The granting of the franchise to illiterates had few short-term, but many long-run, consequences. The business sector was less open than the political sector, with the initial maintenance of import substitution programs. Business was still in the hands of elites with lots of regulations as well as ways to avoid regulations—for a price.

We explore the role of the Constitution of 1988 in the critical transition process. We make four points about what we call a decade-long "constitutional moment." The first is that the constitution embraced the set of beliefs in Brazilian democracy, which evolved out of the fight against military rule. We view the constitution as both a crystallization of beliefs and a focal point for policy. By playing these roles, it legitimized procedure over substance, which is an essential part of democratic life. The "constitutional moment" created a consensus by Brazilian "elites" on the importance of social inclusion with fiscal sustainability, on the one hand, and powerful presidents operating in a constrained institutional environment, on the other.

Second, the Constitution of 1988 redesigned in fundamental ways the country's social contract. Reflecting the change in beliefs, the constitution stipulated new foundations for public policies to incorporate inclusion and redistribution. Third, the constitution vested the presidency with great powers while also strengthening the judicial and the legislative branches. Fortifying the presidency reflected a deep-rooted concern of the elites; these enhanced executive powers, in turn, were to operate in a constrained institutional space. The constitutional process was markedly erratic, underscoring the uncertainties surrounding a transition period. The consensus around the rights constitution—the provisions pertaining to social rights, individual liberties, and rule of law—persisted throughout the constitutional process. Nonetheless, the economic and fiscal constitution was subsequently extensively amended. A core set of beliefs, however, has not changed, and they relate to rights, checks and balances, and a powerful presidency. It took years of experimentation for the recognition that changes to the constitution and policy had to be made, but ultimately it became apparent that unbounded inclusion was not fiscally sustainable.

The period 1985–1993 witnessed several hyperinflations akin to those in Germany during the 1920s. It presented the right leader with a window of opportunity to put Brazil on a new trajectory, at least fiscally. Cardoso seized the window of opportunity (chapter 5), first as the finance minister and later as president. His leadership was not solely top-down; rather, the Cardoso team coordinated other organizations and citizens to buy into the *Plano Real*. In chapter 5, we make three fundamental points. First, Brazil entered into a virtuous path toward a critical transition, which was not inevitable. The outcome was a contingent process shaped by an array of factors. Many alternative coalitions could have emerged with very different outcomes. Actors faced high uncertainty and looked backward in a problem-solving fashion, but also looked forward toward the necessary institutional deepening.

Second, to quell inflation entailed up-front costs and coordination problems that required leadership. Later, at the end of the second term of President Cardoso, Brazilian society had adopted a belief in strong inflation aversion, maintaining the belief in inclusion. That is, social inclusion would still be given priority as long as it was fiscally sound. Once society internalized the new beliefs, leadership was no longer critical, and the institutional dynamics and deepening entered an autopilot mode. Third, new economic and political actors developed a stake in the reform process and formed a constituency that did not exist before: firms redeployed their assets in new profitable ways (as opposed to rent seeking) and politicians increasingly voted for public goods. In addition, citizens as consumers updated their beliefs in the benefits of liberalization and price stability.

In chapter 6, we discuss institutional deepening and the subsequent economic and political outcomes in the two terms of Lula and first term of Dilma. We also advance three main arguments. First, markets, as evidenced by exchange rate movements, did not anticipate the smooth political transition process from Cardoso to Lula. High uncertainty about a Lula presidency was the norm. After the initial shock resulting from the electoral results, Lula drastically reduced uncertainty by providing credible evidence that his administration would not abandon fiscal and monetary orthodoxy. Second, the new beliefs and institutions (e.g., constitutional constraints that emerged in the 1980s and 1990s) effectively constrained political and economic elites in their interaction, thereby enabling competitive processes in the political and economic arenas. The established political institutions locked-in and reinforced the direction of change by affecting the incentives facing individuals, organizations, and politicians.

The functioning of these economic and political institutions largely explains policy continuity in key areas such as macroeconomic management. But they ultimately reflected the new beliefs emerging out of the transition process and the Cardoso era. Unlike the Cardoso years, however, developments in the economic and social realms entered an autopilot mode. Indeed, there was no necessity for the exercise of leadership: institutional change took place essentially at the margin and within the prevailing bands of the new status quo of beliefs. In other words, outcomes matched expectations, and rents started to move toward a "normal" form—that is, away from the prevailing mechanisms based on control of political property-rights mechanisms.

Lula was a highly charismatic figure who exercised strong personal leadership in the conventional meaning of the expression, but not a leader as defined in chapter 2. Not only did he come from the largest opposition party—the Workers' Party (PT)—he was also the first nonelite politician to hold the chief executive post in the country, and one of the few ever to do so in Latin America. At the most general level, this was highly significant for the new era of inclusive politics.

Third, social redistribution was intensified in the wake of the new social contract that emerged from the change in beliefs in the 1980s and

1990s. However, there was no discontinuity in social policy: old programs were scaled up rather than dismantled or created ex nihilo. Unlike the 1985–1993 period of populist inclusion, the new redistribution was to occur within the constraints of macroeconomic policy.

The continuity of beliefs, institutions, and even policies does not mean that the process was smooth nor that the new government did not seek to imprint its own vision of where the country should go. Rather, the extant beliefs and institutions contain forces that pull policies and behaviors back to a set of bounds compatible with beliefs. Although Lula and Dilma continually tested the bounds and even crossed them on occasions, the country stayed on track. It makes development markedly messy and often disordered. We call the process "dissipative inclusion." Because inclusionary policies naturally redistribute, there will almost always be losers who will resist and oppose those policies. This resistance may or may not be sufficient to stop the redistribution, but in either case, it means that many of the rents dissipate and obvious inefficiencies emerge. The upshot is that the push for greater social inclusion is full of distortions.

In chapter 7, we flesh out an inductive framework for understanding stasis and critical transitions. We developed the framework with a lens on Brazil, but it has more general applicability that we illustrate with a brief application to Argentina. In the final concluding chapter, we offer some conjectures about the future of Brazil, especially in light of recent declarations that the Brazilian miracle has vanished once again.

CHAPTER 2

A Conceptual Dynamic for Understanding Development

BELIEFS, LEADERSHIP, DOMINANT NETWORK,
AND WINDOWS OF OPPORTUNITY

Brazil is well on the way to transitioning to a society whose hallmarks consist of four pillars: (1) powerful organizations in society agree to play by the rules (e.g., the constitution and other formal laws), (2) politics are competitive and transparent, (3) those in power and citizens have a strong preference for macroeconomic stability, and (4) economic outcomes should be "fair"; that is, a critical role of the state is to assist inclusion through redistribution and quotas. In the subsequent chapters, we chronicle the transition with evidence. But, evidence needs interpretation. The tools of interpretation for analytical narratives are a set of concepts that yield a dynamic framework. We developed our framework inductively by studying the Brazilian historical experience. In this section, we sketch the concepts of the framework along with the dynamic that we use to interpret the narrative in chapters 3–6.

No society starts a transition in a historical vacuum. At any time, there are a group of organizations that, collectively, have political power and influence over changing the formal laws in a society.[1] We call the organizations in power the *dominant network*, which stresses the multitude of relationships among those in power.[2] Those in the network have a stake in sustaining it in order to maintain their rents, which can be economic, political, or reputational. The dominant network in Brazil always includes the executive branch and certain business organizations. Other organizations have exited and entered at various times.

Actors in organizations in the dominant network have a subjective view of the way institutions will affect outcomes (North 2005). *Institutions* include rules and norms along with their enforcement mechanisms and, as such, provide an incentive for behavior (Alston, Mueller, and

---

1 By organization, we mean a collection of individuals who share a goal or set of goals. These include business corporations, whether state-owned, private, or a mix; trade unions; the Catholic Church; the judiciary; the legislature; and numerous other groups.
2 We borrow the term "dominant network" from Wallis (2014).

Nonnenmacher forthcoming). We label the set of perceived impacts of formal laws (a subset of institutions) on outcomes as core *beliefs* (Greif 2006; Schofield 2006).[3] The beliefs about how the world works guide the choices of the dominant network over which institutions to put in place to most likely get their desired outcomes. In equilibrium, institutions must be consistent with the beliefs of those in the dominant network and in representative democracies with the majority of citizens. Different organizations have differing interests and preferences, but most of the time their beliefs about the impact of laws on outcomes are relatively consistent. Which laws will be chosen depends on the relative bargaining power of the organizations and side payments that they make among the network. But, when shocks hit a society, beliefs of some of the actors become malleable.

To understand the transition of Brazil, we need to understand which shocks called into question the core beliefs of some in the dominant network. Shocks can also cause exit or entry from the dominant network. Shocks shake core beliefs when outcomes differ dramatically from expectations. We call such moments *windows of opportunity*. Beliefs become malleable, and there is a coordination problem among those in the dominant network about which new laws to pass/impose. Windows of opportunity present a role for *leadership*.[4] By leadership, we mean that certain individuals at certain moments in a country's history make a difference because of their actions. The fact that history is replete with the mention of individuals lends considerable anecdotal weight and circumstantial evidence to the argument that certain individuals *did* make a difference. Leadership comprises several concepts that are not mutually exclusive: (1) cognition; (2) *heresthetics* or coordination (strategic manipulation); and (3) moral authority.[5] First, leaders must be aware that a window of opportunity exists. In addition, they must know how to take advantage of the window of opportunity. Cognition entails being able to address two questions: What is the problem or opportunity that we face? How can we solve the problem or take advantage of the situation? Leaders never act alone; it is the orchestration or coordination of other powerful

3 Greif (2006) has analyzed the role of beliefs and institutions in detail in a deductive game-theoretic fashion. Similarly, Schofield (2006) argues that most of the time, societies operate on a "core" set of beliefs, but during "constitutional quandaries" core beliefs become fragile. It is the fragile moments that enable societies to change their trajectories.
4 We thank Avner Greif, Patrick François, and Barry Weingast for discussions on the roles of leadership and beliefs. For an excellent analytical survey of recent contributions to literature on leadership, see Ahlquist and Levi (2011). In chapter 7, we elaborate on the role of leadership, and contributions of others on influencing our framework.
5 We elaborate in chapter 7. See Greif (2012, esp. chap. 3) for the leadership roles of cognition, moral authority, and coordination. See Riker (1986) on heresthetics.

organizations in the network that allows initial change to take place. Some leaders have moral authority either because of their past or because they earned it. Moral authority gives leaders more influence, which in turn induces others in the dominant network (as well as the public) to trust their motives, which may lead more readily to accepting new beliefs during windows of opportunity. Belief changes lead to institutional changes, but it is equally important for the initial institutional changes to be followed by institutional deepening. Through iterative changes in outcomes, institutional deepening solidifies core beliefs. It also solidifies the dominant network because when institutional changes produce outcomes that benefit extant organizations or create new organizations that win, the beneficiary organizations now have a stake in sustaining and deepening the new institutions and play by the rules established by the institutions.

When outcomes match expectations, we will see only marginal changes in laws. Societies are more or less on autopilot, as depicted at the bottom of figure 2.1 (and in greater detail in chapter 7).[6] This does not mean that laws do not change, but rather that they change on the margin, which reflects marginal changes in the dominant network. An exogenous or endogenous shock to the economic and political autopilot can open a _window of opportunity_ for significant changes in underlying beliefs and institutions. A shock, indicated by the box at the bottom left of figure 2.1, occurs when observed outcomes diverge dramatically from expected outcomes. The shock emanates from a host of factors (e.g., the threat of invasion by another country, or an economic or natural disaster).[7] During such moments, there is a role for leaders, who take advantage of the shock to shape underlying beliefs and constitutional-level institutions. By constitutional-level institutions, we mean both constitutions but also certain laws that fundamentally change incentives. In the United States, we consider the Civil Rights Act (1964) and the Voting Rights Act (1965) as constitutional-level institutions in that they were not marginal changes in legislation. However, in the event that leaders do not step forward to take advantage of the windows of opportunity, the moment can pass without any change in beliefs or fundamental institutions. Members of the dominant network regroup and make marginal placating changes.

---

6 We acknowledge the input of Tomas Nonnenmacher in composing figure 2.1, a variant of which is contained in Alston, Mueller, and Nonnenmacher (forthcoming).
7 In chapter 7, we consider "tipping points" that result from long endogenous changes. Tipping points still require leadership to coordinate beliefs among the dominant network. Street protests in the twenty-first century have not led to dramatic changes in the dominant network in part because no leader embraced them, for example, both the "Arab Spring" and the "Occupy Wall Street" movements lacked leadership to coordinate actions.

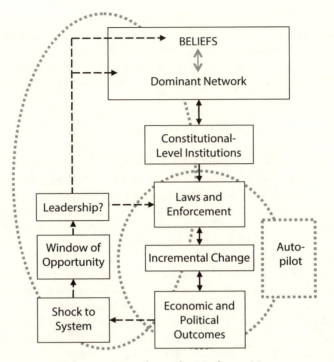

Figure 2.1. Autopilot and critical transitions

In chapter 5, we analyze Brazil's "constitutional moment" as a specific example of a window of opportunity and the interplay among leadership, belief structures, and the changing organizations in the dominant network. At constitutional moments, the organizations revamp the rules under which political and economic organizations interact and contract. This process begins with the autopilot at the bottom of figure 2.1, which is instigated by a shock to the system that creates a window of opportunity, which prompts a leader (at times) to shape beliefs of the dominant network in such a way as to generate constitutional change. As such, the process can be thought of as a single loop beginning with the "business as usual" and ending with a constitutional-level institutional change.

One loop is not sufficient to change societies. Deep changes in economic and political trajectories entail more than a single "constitutional moment." They require reinforcing institutional changes to alter and solidify core beliefs. The institutional deepening requires multiple loops around the circuit to shape and solidify beliefs among the dominant network. Institutional deepening is an endogenous interactive process entailing legislation that supports and deepens the belief change set in motion by the constitutional moment. The process ends in a "new autopilot," in which core beliefs are again in alignment with the outcomes of the economic and political systems. During the process, citizens also update their beliefs as the new institutions produce new outcomes that change the beliefs of citizens about the actions of the dominant network.

Difference in Difference in Changing Beliefs

The key force pushing Brazil toward making the critical transition are the beliefs that led it to adopt the enabling institutions and policies. We first show evidence that beliefs have changed over the period considered. A problem with basing a theory on beliefs is that they cannot be measured or quantified in any perfectly rigorous way. Nevertheless, we provide here some quantitative evidence that beliefs have changed considerably over the relevant period of time.

A Brazilian who entered into a coma in the early 1980s and awoke today would be massively surprised at the changes the country has been through. Some of the most surprising changes would involve problems that had previously seemed insurmountable and out of hand, but were now under control, such as inflation and the dreaded external debt. Even if the end of the dictatorship could have been surmised in the early 1980s, the extent to which democracy, openness, and participation have taken root would certainly cause an impression. Perhaps the most surprising development would be the unprecedented fall in inequality that has incorporated previously excluded masses into markets for all sorts of goods and services, such as durable goods and air travel. Events that no longer stir surprise in the citizenry today would be hard to believe at first, such as a common worker becoming president, and politicians serving time in jail. Many more subtle changes would be comprehended in time, such as the larger involvement in world trade and the smaller direct participation of the state in the economy. But all these changes would soon be assimilated as they are easy to perceive. Some other changes, however, would not be that salient, as they are behavioral, including perceptions, attitudes, and ultimately beliefs. Eventually, the former coma patient would realize the greater adherence to rules. Even today, Brazil sees itself as a place where many laws stay only on paper, but we suspect that a serious attempt to quantify this would find renewed levels of deference and conformity. Similarly, the notion of the *jeitinho brasiliero*—the Brazilian way of doing things by circumventing rules and conventions—would probably be found to crop up less and less in daily life and discourse. As would the need for *despachantes*—hired intermediaries and bureaucratic fixers—to obtain official documents. Certainly, it has become very rare to see the old habit of authorities and their relatives gaining access by stating "Do you know who you are talking to?" (DaMatta 1991). If you asked a Brazilian if any of these changes had taken place, we suspect that the answer would be no, but the former coma patient through his or her unique before-and-after perspective would perceive the differences.

Confronted with such a remarkable transformative process, the question that naturally arises is: what put Brazil on the critical transition? The choice of appropriate institutions is clearly the direct cause that led to the policies and actions that produced the changes. But that still leaves unanswered why the country got those institutions right this time. A central contribution of our book is our emphasis on the role of beliefs in modulating the choice of institutions and the interactive process involving beliefs, institutions, and outcomes. Beliefs emanate from the dominant network and represent the networks' expectation of the impact of institutions on outcomes.

Many of the changes described for Brazil could be argued to be merely following global trends that have affected many other countries simultaneously, such as a greater emphasis on redistribution. Alternatively, they could be conceived as the expected consequence from the universalization of the franchise that took place in Brazil in the mid-1980s. As the median voter's income is below average, it would be natural to expect politicians to redistribute and promote inclusion for purely electoral reasons. So why appeal to something as ethereal and hard to measure as beliefs when the more standard arguments seem to explain the facts sufficiently well? We make the case that beliefs are the key factor underpinning change rather than other more proximate transformative processes, such as universal franchise.

We present evidence that a change in beliefs has occurred and that the change is a crucial factor in the broader institutional change that the country has undergone. The evidence shows that the changes in beliefs are exceptional to Brazil and not general to many other countries simultaneously. And, in particular, it differs from other Latin American countries. Because the entire region tends to move in synch in many aspects, as seen by the proximate synchronicity of independence, import substitution, dictatorship, redemocratization, and privatization, it is natural to expect the same general forces to operate across these countries. In terms of beliefs, this synchrony can be seen in the greater focus on redistributive policies in the past decade as the countries embraced more inclusive policies, stances, and rhetoric. Changes in Brazil due to the "treatment" of its own specific history, experiences, and other factors that formed beliefs led to beliefs that are significantly different from those in other (control) countries that underwent their own distinct formative processes, even if the resulting beliefs might have superficial similarities.

Beliefs are admittedly hard to pin down and even harder to quantify. Whereas institutions, which are also often elusive concepts, have been proxied and instrumented in a variety of creative ways, there has been less progress measuring beliefs. Yet, there has been much recent research on beliefs using data from surveys such as the World Values Survey (WVS), which surveys individuals across a group of countries in different waves over time.[8] In particular, scholars use two specific responses in the WVS for comparative analysis of beliefs on the appropriate level of inequality and redistribution. In the first response, respondents place their views on a scale of 1 to 10, where 1 is the position that "People should take more responsibility to provide for themselves," and 10 is the position that "The government should take more responsibility to ensure that everyone is provided for." In the second response, the choices are (1) "In the long run, hard work usually brings a better life," and (10) "Hard work doesn't generally bring success—it's more a matter of luck and connections." The understanding behind the use of the results is that they bring out beliefs related to the social contract, that is, inequality, redistribution, and fairness. Averaging across the sample of respondents in each country gives us a proxy for each country's prevailing belief. We interpret the view that luck and connections are mostly responsible for success in life, and that government should actively redress the resulting inequality through redistributive policies as indicating beliefs that social inclusion is a necessary condition for a country to develop. We do not compare the different levels of measured beliefs across countries at any point in time, but rather we compare how much they changed over time.

In figures 2.2 and 2.3, we plot the averaged proxied belief for all the countries that were included in both the 1989–1993 and the 2010–2014 waves of the WVS for each of the respective questions about attitudes toward work and redistribution. The 45-degree line shows where the belief would be in the second wave if there had been no change over time. In figure 2.2, Chile, South Africa, Nigeria, Peru, and Turkey have practically not budged their position, as measured by the question on government vs. individual responsibility, in more than two decades. On the other extreme, Russia, South Korea, India, and Brazil had a major change of beliefs, with all four dramatically moving toward the view that government rather than individuals should be responsible for providing for its citizens'

---

8 The extensive literature on beliefs, social contracts, and the use of survey data to measure beliefs includes Alesina, Glaeser, and Sacerdote (2001); Alesina and Glaeser (2004); Alesina and Giuliano (2009); Alesina and La Ferrara (2005); Alesina, Cozzi, and Mantovan (2012); Alesina and Angeletos (2005); Bénabou and Tirole (2006); Bénabou (2000, 2005); Fong (2001); Giuliano and Spilimbergo (2009); Jusko (2011); and Handler (2003). For the WVS, see http://www.worldvaluessurvey.org/wvs.jsp.

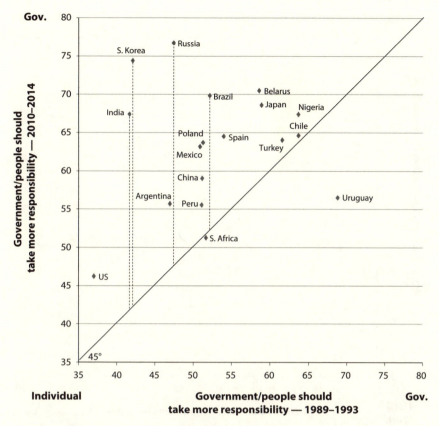

Figure 2.2. Comparative change in beliefs: government vs. individual responsibility, 1989–1993 and 2010–2014. Sources: World Values Survey, fifth wave WVS 2005–2008 for 2005 data and Four Wave Aggregate for 1991 data. The data refer to the mean percent in each country positioning themselves in relation to the following issue: "V118.–Right—People should take more responsibility to provide for themselves; Left—The government should take more responsibility to ensure that everyone is provided for." http://www.wvsevsdb.com/wvs/WVSAnalize Question.jsp.

welfare. In figure 2.3, most countries exhibit little change in terms of their view whether success in life is due to luck or hard work. Yet Brazil, South Africa, and China deviate significantly from their positions two decades earlier. The exceptional shift in Brazil from luck toward hard work as a determinant of success is a consequence of the demise in the later period of the hyperinflation that scourged the country at the time of the first survey. It is natural to despair at the value of hard work when the relentless

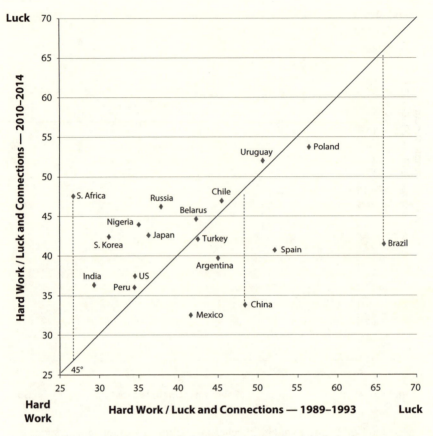

Figure 2.3. Comparative change in beliefs: hard work vs. luck and connections, 1989–1993 and 2010–2014. Sources: World Values Survey, fifth wave WVS 2005–2008 for 2005 data and Four Wave Aggregate for 1991 data. The data refer to the mean percent in each country positioning themselves in relation to the following issue: "V120.–Left—In the long run, hard work usually brings a better life; Right—Hard work doesn't generally bring success—it's more a matter of luck and connections." http://www.wvsevsdb.com/wvs/WVSAnalizeQuestion.jsp.

hyperinflationary process crushes even the most diligent projects and efforts. Other countries that underwent similar simultaneous hyperinflationary processes do not appear in the data to have been similarly scarred, which underscores that belief formation is specific and idiosyncratic.

Taken together, both of the graphs show that the countries with the largest shifts in beliefs are, in order, South Korea, Brazil, Russia, India, and China, that is, the original BRICs plus South Korea. These are all countries that have undergone dramatic changes and upheavals in the past decades, which gives credence to the use of the data for proxying beliefs. We provide much additional evidence that corroborates the central role played by the interaction among beliefs, institutions, and outcomes in the Brazilian transformation. There is not any silver bullet to prove our contention, but we rely on a plethora of circumstantial evidence in our empirical chapters.

OVERVIEW OF DOMINANT NETWORK, BELIEFS, AND INSTITUTIONS IN BRAZIL FROM 1964 TO 2014

Here we provide a brief overview of the interpretation describing the dominant network and the beliefs in each of the three periods, as well as the associated basic institutions and outcomes that emerged. Table 2.1 summarizes each of these elements for each period. This synopsis will provide a picture of the whole, which will facilitate the understanding of the detailed analysis in the subsequent chapters. "All regimes . . . rest on some explicit or implicit bargain between political leaders and key support groups" (Haggard and Kaufman 1995: 7). The kinds of bargains or interactions function as networks, which include diverse sectors of society, such as business groups, politicians, unions, banks, government agencies, and public bureaucracies. In this section, we identify the dominant network formed by the main political leaders and groups in Brazilian society responsible for the dominant beliefs in each of the three periods.

1964–1984

The dominant belief in Brazil preceding the military regime was nationalist development, driven primarily by state-led industrialization associated with foreign indebtedness. It is clear that the dominant network's belief was in developmentalism—the combination of industrialism, nationalism, and state intervention. Industrial entrepreneurs demanded and received protection against the competition of imported products through the Import Substitution Industrialization (ISI) model.

In the late 1950s and early 1960s, the industrialist-led dominant network collapsed, replaced by a new alliance of a military and civilian techno-bureaucracy. Central actors in the new dominant network included high-level civil and military technocrats, and industrial and banking sectors, working in close association with foreign capital. During the military regime, the bureaucratic-authoritarian dominant network had a faction within the army that was fully committed to a nationalist agenda of development of Brazilian industry. They believed that, after restoring the country's fiscal health, the state should play a key role with large-scale

TABLE 2.1. Brazilian Development, 1964–2014

Period	1964–1984	1985–1993	1994–2014
Dominant network	Bureaucratic-authoritarian: military and civil high-level techno-bureaucracy, national industrial and banking sectors, in close association with foreign capital	Populist developmentalist: national industrial and banking sectors, soft-liners (authoritarian side), and moderates (democratic side)	Open and stable economy: national and foreign banking sectors, national industrialists. Trade unions. Agribusiness.
Beliefs	Developmentalism	Social inclusion	Fiscally sound social inclusion
Institutions	Economic: technocratic social planning, import substitution Political: curtailment of civil liberties	Economic: subsidies to business elites and import substitution Political: "Christmas tree" constitution, franchise for illiterate. Strengthened accountability institutions. Strong executive.	Economic: fiscal and monetary orthodoxy Political: restraints on state governments with power shifting to the federal government. Strengthened accountability institutions. Strong executive.
Economic and political outcomes	Economic: initially high growth, "Brazilian Miracle" followed by slower growth Political: authoritarian rule with exclusion, censorship, and oppression	Economic: hyperinflation and uncertainty Political: democracy without checks and balances, e.g., populist land reform, judiciary siding for labor	Economic: price stability with mediocre growth Political: increasing social inclusion if fiscally sound. Checks and balances and rule of law.

intervention and participation in the economy. The dominant network shared the belief that economic growth controlled by the state should precede social inclusion.

The bureaucratic-authoritarian regime emerged in a complex economic environment, in which ISI deepened. Although the initial phase of industrialization reduced dependence on imported consumer goods, the costs of importing the intermediate goods and capital equipment needed for the production of consumer goods were high, producing or increasing deficits in the balance of payments, foreign indebtedness, and inflation. These problems led to a "zero-sum" economic situation that undermined the character of earlier coalitions prior to the military regime. The new long-term solution was the "vertical integration" or the "deepening" of industrialization through domestic manufacture of intermediate and capital goods.

The combination of economic growth with a strong repressive authoritarian regime resulting from the close alliance between hard-liners in the military, developmentalists, and technocrats produced institutional stability and generated some legitimacy for the military regime during the Miracle Years (1968–1973). The dominant network adopted an economic policy of state intervention and protection of all sectors of the national economy in the process of the national development. "The hardline military needed the technocrats to make the economy work. The technocrats needed the military to stay in power. The high growth rates in turn gave legitimacy to the authoritarian system" (Skidmore 1988: 110).

Circa 1974, it became clear that the exclusionary profile of the military regime was no longer capable of maintaining its original bureaucratic-authoritarian network united. Important weaknesses in the "tripod" pact between the military techno-bureaucracy, the national industry, and foreign investors emerged.

> Though the military techno-bureaucracy understood that it would have to make alliances with the dominant industrial and banking capitalists, and make them the great beneficiaries of the system, it maintained its political control as the ruling group, also determining economic policy. The military's political tutelage over the bourgeoisie created a fundamental contradiction that, together with the lack of popular support due to its exclusivity, set off in 1974 a process of institutional crises and also a process of partial re-democratization of the nation. (Bresser-Pereira 1984: 190)

The collapse of the alliance between the national industrial and financial sectors and the military techno-bureaucracy increased the understanding that redemocratization was inevitable not merely as a consequence of the military's strategy to regain some degree of legitimacy and avoid potential future retaliations, but also as a consequence of the breakdown of the bureaucratic-authoritarian dominant network itself. This process did not take place only in Brazil; rather, the

> democratization in Latin America in the last decades of the twentieth century broke up many cozy backroom relations between business

groups and authoritarian governments. However, business groups in democratizing polities learned quickly to avail themselves of new venues such as parties, elections, courts, and the media. These democratic means were more costly, complex, and indirect, but when they worked to further business preferences, they could be more reliable and enduring than ad hoc relations with authoritarian leaders. (Schneider 2013: 140)

The lifting of press censorship in late 1977 was the first concrete sign that liberalization—a process of making effective certain rights that protect both individuals and social groups from arbitrary or illegal acts by the state—was on the horizon. The liberalization process started with a crack within the dominant network. The Brazilian military regime was not a personalistic dictatorship but rather relied on periodic changes in the presidency. Although only the military elite participated in the choice of presidents, there were often intense internal disputes. The change toward liberalization started in 1974 with the tight choice of General Geisel, a moderate reformer, to replace General Medici, a hard-liner who presided over an era of harsh repression. In June 1978, President Geisel announced a preview for opening: suspending IA #5 (Institutional Act #5, which suspended various constitutional guarantees). In the protracted and gradual process of democratic liberalization, many social movements, such as the Catholic Church, left-wing intellectuals, urban workers, the middle class, and the emerging professional bureaucracy, played an important role demanding the restoration of civil and political rights. However, national industrial and banking sectors played the pivotal role in forcing the opening by their retraction of support for the military.

1985–1993

At the political level, the PDS (Partido Democrático Social) party—which used to represent the interest of the dominant network coalition during the dictatorship—split, and its soft-liners formed a new political party, the PFL (Partido da Frente Liberal). The PFL, in coalition with the PMDB (Partido do Movimento Democrático Brasileiro), the political party of the moderates, formed the Democratic Alliance, which successfully indirectly elected Tancredo Neves in 1984 as the first civilian president after twenty-one years of authoritarian regime. Tragically, on the eve of his inauguration as the new president, Tancredo fell ill and died five weeks later. José Sarney, a conservative politician representing the soft-liners, replaced Tancredo.

Sarney took office under great pressures and growing demands for social and political inclusion. The emergence of the belief in social inclusion as a precondition for effective development was a natural reaction to the extreme social-economic inequality of the authoritarian period.

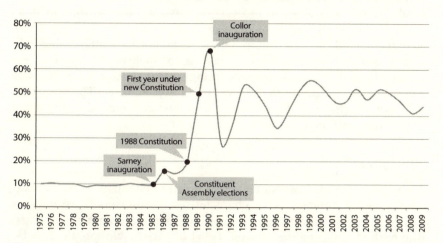

Total Expenditures — % of GDP

Figure 2.4. Total governmental expenditures (percent of GDP). Source: Ipeadata (2012), www.ipeadata.gov.br.

The belief produced a feedback loop with growing political awareness among political and social groups of the need for radical changes through massive political and social inclusion. The lack of political legitimacy of President Sarney made the transition to the first civilian government vulnerable to pressures for immediate structural changes not only in the economic and political spheres but also in social policies. The new government owed an immense social debt to those excluded from the "economic miracle." The impressive rate of economic growth achieved during the years of the miracle had accentuated rather than diminished income inequality. Sarney tried to respond to pressures from the new dominant coalition network by imprinting the label "*Tudo Pelo Social*" (everything for the social policy) as the top priority of his administration. Earlier, the political manifesto ("Commitment to the Nation") of Tancredo/Sarney presaged the ambitious agenda. With regard to social policies, the manifesto pointed to resolving income inequalities, implementing emergency measures against hunger and unemployment, and eliminating wage controls. The new constitution promulgated in 1988 codified these emerging beliefs but also allowed a varied array of groups to include and thus insulate their own private interests.[9]

With all these inclusive measures, overall government expenditure in the span between 1980 and 1990 grew dramatically (see figure 2.4). The massive increase in government expenditure was not sustainable and

9 Because of this characteristic it is sometimes referred to as a "Christmas tree" constitution.

had severe inflationary consequences. The expansion of government expenditure was a strategy to recover (or balance) political support in an environment of regulated competitive elections. Sarney, lacking political legitimacy, made the New Republic government extremely vulnerable. Sarney was unable to deny the demands for inclusion from organized groups in society. State governors facing similar pressures for inclusion contributed significantly to the increase in expenditures. The unsustainable social inclusion led to hyperinflation and economic disarray in the Brazilian transition to democracy.

1994–2014

After successive macroeconomic plans failed to eliminate hyperinflation, another belief, fundamentally characterized by an aversion to inflation and in favor of macroeconomic stability, became dominant in Brazil. Rather than replacing the previous belief of social inclusion, the new belief merged into a belief in fiscally sound social inclusion. The success of the *Real Plan* under the leadership of Fernando Henrique Cardoso (FHC) launched Brazil's critical transition in 1994 and placed Cardoso in the presidency. Transparency and a lack of coercion typified the *Real Plan*. Annual inflation fell from the four-digit level in 1994 to less than 5 percent in 1998. For the first time in decades, Brazil experienced sustainable price stability, and economic growth was encouraging.

Ironically, the national industrial sector supported the liberal and market-oriented reform agenda proposed by Cardoso. Ostensibly, these groups had a lot to lose if Brazil opened to foreign competition. The undeniable advantages of macroeconomic stability generated a positive net benefit to the national industrial sector even in the face of economic liberalization. The pro-reform network was much stronger than initially expected because both interest groups and politicians managed to coalesce under aligned preferences. "Instead of blocking reforms, these businesses, . . . pushed governments to adopt reforms, . . . and then become their coalition partners in supporting the new 'liberal' development model" (Schneider 2004: 463). Despite the financial costs involved, businesses remained surprisingly open to negotiation, something President Cardoso evidently learned during his repeated tactical maneuvers. In the end, Cardoso achieved a more open economy with the support of businesses that had previously sought protection from international trade.[10]

---

10 Contextual factors, like economic crisis, also played a role in altering the stakes facing business elites and other interest groups in supporting the reform agenda proposed by the Cardoso administration. For Kingstone (1999: 17), economic crises leave business more open to policy innovation because they perceive the status quo as untenable. Haggard

Surprisingly, great continuity in macroeconomic management and fiscal policy marked the ascendancy of Lula to the presidency in 2002. The strengthened institutions of checks and balances—including district attorneys, audit institutions, the judiciary, the bureaucracy, and regulatory agencies—constrained fiscal policy and restrained presidential abuse. Continued beliefs in fiscally sound social inclusion undergirded institutional change under Lula.

The international financial crisis of 2008 hit Brazil toward the end of Lula's second term of office. It represented an external shock to the country, as did the discovery and exploration of pre-salt oil reserves. Both prompted the government to increase state intervention in the economy, extend protectionist measures, introduce price controls, and provide massive quantities of subsidized credit to private and public sector companies. Under Dilma Rousseff, the measures continued, even as the crisis waned. The ever-expanding dominant network, which included public sector contractors, national industrialists, civil society organizations, and public sector unions, backed the Dilma interventionist agenda. Criticism accompanied Dilma's agenda: street demonstrations against price hikes, deficient public service delivery, and overall government underperformance. Fiscal sustainability constrained the overall change toward Dilma's social developmentalist program. Recent developments suggest a mixed record. The succession of primary fiscal surpluses has given way to a host of negative primary fiscal results. The system is in a partial autopilot: beliefs constrain government. The newly elected Dilma government has signaled to the dominant network its commitment to correct its recent economic choices following the negative economic outcomes of falling investment, rising inflation, and falling output.

SUMMARY

This brief overview of the three distinct periods of Brazilian history since 1964 will be expanded in chapters 3 to 6 using the concepts detailed at the beginning of the chapter: dominant network, institutions, beliefs, windows of opportunity, leadership, and critical transitions. By identifying how each of these concepts arose and interacted in the different historic circumstances, we have inductively developed a framework for

-----

(2000) also claims that crises reduce the value of rents gained under the old order, as well as incentives to defend the status quo, and usually weaken interest groups. Weyland (2002) argues that dire economic times make both voters and politicians less risk averse and hence more likely to accept radical reforms that promise large payoffs, even at the risk of potentially large losses. In our framework, the hyperinflation crisis created a window of opportunity for change.

understanding the dynamics of critical transitions in development, which we present in chapter 7. It is our expectation that this framework will be useful not only for understanding Brazilian development but also that of other countries. As an illustration of this greater generality, chapter 7 also contains an interpretation of Argentine history through the lens of the framework.

PART II

Introduction to the Case Study
of Brazil, 1964–2014

IN THIS PART OF THE BOOK, WE PUT IN ACTION THE FRAMEWORK SKETCHED in the previous chapters to analyze the evolution of Brazilian society since 1964. Brazil is one of the few countries currently making a transition to sustainable development. This is a bold claim because at this point there is not overwhelming evidence that Brazil is doing much better than many other middle-income countries. In terms of GDP per capita growth, the case is particularly weak. From 2003 to 2013, the average GDP per capita growth in all middle-income countries (according to the World Bank definition in its World Development Indicators[1]) was 6.3 percent; in Latin America, the average was 3.6 percent. During this period, the corresponding figure for Brazil was 3.5 percent. If GDP per capita is an indication of development, then Argentina—Brazil's southerly neighbor who averaged 6.2 percent growth in the same period—is a more likely candidate for a country that is making the transition.

But, we do not equate GDP growth with development. Development requires sustained economic growth and low volatility over very long periods that can only be achieved under open and inclusive institutions. Our case for Brazil hangs not on its recent growth performance but instead on a perception that it has been undergoing a fundamental transformation at the level of beliefs and institutions. In this regard, the comparison with Argentina is an almost perfect counterpoint, as the high levels of economic growth there in recent years have been accompanied by governmental behavior that subverts almost every tenet of what is usually considered a proper development-inducing institutional environment: subverting freedom of the press, infringement of judicial independence, masking and lying about inflation statistics, debt repudiation, intrusive controls over foreign currencies, forced nationalization of foreign companies, and rampant populism. In the meantime, Brazil has taken the opposite path, with moderate levels of GDP growth accompanied by greater rule of law, strengthened checks and balances, and unprecedented political, economic, and social inclusion. Clearly, what happens with these two countries in the coming decades will be a good test of the claim that open and inclusive institutions are the crucial determinant of long-run development.

1 The World Bank World Development data can be found at: http://data.worldbank.org /indicator/NY.GDP.MKTP.KD.ZG.

Whereas the previous chapters gave a preview of the basic argument explaining why we believe Brazil is going through a critical transition, in the second part of the book we spell out our detailed evidence. It is divided into four chapters that cover three periods that we see as crucial in giving rise to the beliefs and institutions that currently bolster the country's development process. A final chapter presents in greater detail the framework sketched out in chapter 2 and concludes with a brief application of our framework to Argentina and the conjecture that our framework has applicability in our countries and particularly in Latin America.

The first period covers the rise and fall of the military regime (1964–1984); the second period starts with redemocratization in 1985 and includes the hyperinflationary years up to 1993, when the *Real Plan* reinstated reasonable price stability; and the third period includes the years since the *Real Plan* to 2014.

In each of these periods, a full cycle of the dynamics that the framework portrays transpired. In describing and analyzing each of these periods, we identify each of the elements of the framework and show how they follow a pattern consistent with the dynamics. For example, each period starts with a shock that knocks outcomes off their expected path, generating a crisis where there is discontentment and desire for change among significant subsets of society. For each period, we describe the shock and its impact on outcomes. The upheaval that ensues forms a window of opportunity in which both the dominant network changes and the old beliefs no longer dominate. In the shifting period where the composition of the dominant network reformulates and no consensus over new beliefs emerges, a leader may arise to persuade and coordinate the dominant network toward new beliefs. For each period, we discuss the changes in the dominant network and the role (or absence) of leadership. The most important part of our interpretation is the identification of the new beliefs that emerged and how they map into the formal institutions enacted. Finally, for each period, we assess whether the outcomes that emerged at the end of this process match expectations, leading to stability subject to just incremental change, or whether the system heads toward unfulfilled expectations (and/or an external shock) that will knock it into another iteration of the dynamics.

The contribution of this part of the book is not to provide a detailed history of Brazil's recent past; there is already a large literature describing these events. The focus of the extant literature is usually on policies and outcomes, and in some cases even on institutions. Other treatments focus on leadership, stressing the supposedly game-changing role of an individual or political party (a very different and less nuanced approach to leadership than that which we adopt). Our approach is new because of its interpretation of events and outcomes through the lens of our framework.

It involves not simply a focus on beliefs, windows of opportunity, leadership, and institutions, but more importantly a unified treatment where these concepts are tied together in a coherent dynamic that can be applied more broadly to other countries and situations.

IDENTIFYING BELIEFS

Because of the central importance of beliefs in our framework, we describe not only the nature of the belief in each period but why that specific belief emerged instead of something else. The narrative has to provide a logically consistent account that is not refuted by the facts, events, and context. The better the description of the available quantitative and qualitative evidence, the easier for the reader to assess whether our narrative of which belief prevailed is consistent and believable. The following chapters provide thick description of the three periods Brazil has been through since 1964.

Each belief we identify is given a label. Although this runs the risk of making our interpretation seem somewhat reductionist, it helps the reader follow the narrative. In the remainder of this introduction, we summarize the beliefs that are the driving force behind each of the three periods we examine in the remaining chapters.

Developmentalism is the belief system that predominated during the authoritarian period from 1964 to 1984. This is not a new term; it has been widely used in many different contexts to describe this period in Brazil (see, e.g., Bresser-Pereira 2004). There is even a Wikipedia entry defining developmentalism as "a set of ideas which converge to place economic development at the center of political endeavors and institutions and also as a means through which to establish legitimacy in the political sphere."[2] The key aspect of this belief is the unambiguous prioritization of economic goals over others such as inclusion, voice, equality, and poverty reduction. Developmentalism also emphasized state-led technocratic, top-down means of achieving goals, all shrouded in nationalism and a military emphasis on discipline and order, achieved through force and violence if necessary. Part of the belief was already in place in the period before 1964. The central role of the state in planning and

2 See http://en.wikipedia.org/wiki/Developmentalism. The definition in the Portuguese version of Wikipedia does not treat developmentalism as an "idea" or belief; yet, in other ways, it is even closer to our use of the term: "any economic policy where the central objective is the growth of industrial production and infrastructure, with the active involvement of the state as the base of the economy and the consequent increase of consumption" (our translation) (see http://pt.wikipedia.org/wiki/Desenvolvimentismo).

implementing economic policy geared toward industrializing Brazil prevailed in the 1950s. Early developmentalism had been highly successful in transforming Brazil from a commodity exporter to an industrialized nation in a process that resulted in very high, if volatile, rates of growth. It is thus natural that the military maintained this aspect of the belief in developmentalism. The military changed developmentalism toward a more technocratic, authoritarian, and top-down style instead of the messier pattern of the previous period in which there was rampant clientelism, corruption, electoral fraud, political personalism, and ever more rambunctious dissent.

The belief in developmentalism was strong and stable while outcomes matched expectations. The high growth during the Brazilian Miracle Years (1968–1973) overshadowed the repressive and exclusive nature of the regime. But once economic outcomes faltered after 1974, adding to the discontent from the lack of voice and inclusion, not to mention the state-led violence and oppression, the belief in developmentalism weakened. The transition to a new window of opportunity and a new belief was in this case postponed, as the end of the military regime did not come about by revolution or sudden events but rather through a purposefully "slow, secure, and gradual" restitution of power by the military back to civilian rule labeled the "opening up" (abertura).[3]

The opening-up period was initiated in 1985 with a change in the dominant network and a corresponding change in beliefs (1985–1993). The period is often seen as a "lost decade" in Brazil's economic history, given the dismal economic outcomes marked by hyperinflations and low growth. The dissatisfaction with these outcomes would eventually induce a new window of opportunity for change in 1993, which we discuss in chapter 5. The notion that the 1985–1993 period was wasted time is reinforced by what followed: starting in 1993, outcomes systematically matched expectations, leading to sustained simultaneous satisfaction with economic, political, and social outcomes, inducing a deepening of beliefs and a virtuous perpetuation of the system.

And yet, despite the marked contrast between the foregone window of opportunity in 1985 and subsequent attempts at quelling hyperinflation, there is an important yet often unappreciated element of continuity that suggests that the early period was not completely wasted, but rather that it initiated changes that would be crucial for the subsequent success. The element is the belief in social inclusion that substituted the defunct belief in developmentalism that had prevailed over the previous period (1964–1984). The new belief was a reaction to the exclusion and oppression of

---

3 The military dictatorship often used this term to characterize the changes they planned to implement.

the authoritarian period.[4] Social inclusion crucially determined the underlying nature of the institutions and policies of the 1985–1993 period and as such can be held in large measure responsible for the disastrous outcomes experienced during that time. Counterintuitively, we also argue that social inclusion is partially responsible for the successful outcomes reached in the post-1993 period. Social inclusion means that government and its policies must always strive for inclusion, openness, participation, citizenship, transparency, equality, freedom, protection for the weak and helpless, and other related concepts.

The belief in social inclusion is highly consequential in Brazil. Many other countries have the trappings of social inclusion underlying the rhetoric of government and the policy-making process. In Latin America this is certainly the case, with manifestations of this belief written into law, present in the speech patterns of politicians, and apparent in the daily lives of citizens. But despite the remarkable similarity and historical synchronicity with which these manifestations came into being, the impact of social inclusion varies dramatically across countries. In some, it is just lip service to an ideal with no influence on policy or behavior, while in others it may be a key determinant of institutions and policies that emerged. Even when profession of the belief is meaningful, the actual impact in different countries varies significantly as the role of beliefs in development has the nature of a complex system, where small changes in parameters can lead to large differences in outcomes. It appears as if several Latin American countries almost simultaneously went through very similar experiences of independence, industrialization, dictatorship, democratization, hyperinflation, privatization, and commodity booms. The experiences seemingly led to the emergence of beliefs in social inclusion that look and sound very similar to one another, but the true nature and impact of social inclusion varied dramatically because of small differences in the details of the historical experience of each country. The details are events, such as the experience with slavery or lack thereof, the personal styles of a charismatic leader of the past (Perón [Argentina], Vargas [Brazil], or Chávez [Venezuela]), resentments from colonization, victories or defeats in wars of the past (Malvinas, Falklands), and probably more importantly even more abstract elements of national character that evolved through history in each country. In sum, beliefs are contextual.

So, how do we explain the paradox that the same belief in social inclusion could simultaneously be the basis of the negative outcomes of

---

4 Its roots probably go even further back in time as evidenced by occasional bursts of policies that sought to counterbalance the historical legacy of injustice and inequalities (dating as far back as slavery), such as the establishment of highly pro-worker legislation in the 1930s and land reform in the 1946 Constitution.

1985–1993 and of the virtuous transformation since 1993? It would be easier if during the first period social inclusion wasn't truly active and that only much later (possibly in 2003 when the Workers' Party [PT] came to power), did it really start to exert its influence over institutions and policy, leading to the unprecedented fall in poverty. But a careful examination of the historical record since 1985 makes it very clear that early on, social inclusion as an imperative was already present in very significant ways in many areas of Brazilian society, economy, and polity. Some noteworthy examples follow: The current Brazilian Constitution, which is considered one of the most inclusionary in the world (Ginsburg, Elkins, and Blount 2009: 208), was passed in 1988, with input from thousands of constitutional committees all over the country. Land reform was one of the flagship programs of the new civilian government in 1985. The motto of the Sarney government (1985–1989) was *Tudo Pelo Social* (everything for the social good). The constitutional requirement calling for the creation of participatory municipal sectoral councils in health, social assistance, education, and environment, which led to the creation of about 30,000 municipal councils all over the country, was first put in practice under Presidents José Sarney (1985–1989) and Fernando Collor de Mello (1990–1992). The origins of the new role of the Ministério Público (district attorney's office) as a major check on the abuse of power by the executive, legislative, and judiciary was the Civil Public Action Law (Law 7.347/85) passed in 1985 (Mueller 2010).[5] The continuous fall in equality that continues to the present day started in 1995. The massive expansion of the franchise, which included the illiterate and sixteen- and seventeen-year-olds, dates from the mid-1980s. The extension of social security to noncontributing rural workers, which had tremendous redistributive impacts in rural communities, started in the early 1990s. The universal health scheme, which extended medical treatment to the entire population rather than only those who had an official workbook (a much smaller subset of the population), was created in 1985. The decentralization of social provision, including the way it was financed through automatic disbursement from the federal government to the municipalities, tantamount to a revolution in intergovernmental relations, occurred under Sarney (1985–1989) and Collor (1990–1992). Not all the inclusive changes were positive or without problems. Many resulted in great distortions and unintended consequences. The nature of policies in the 1980s is consistent with a strong belief in social inclusion.

5 District attorney is not a completely accurate translation of *Ministério Público*. The role of Ministério Públicos is to act in the public or social interest. Ministério Públicos can (and do) sue private individuals, and corporations as well as government agencies and actors. For example, the Ministério Público has been active in pursuing corruption.

The belief in social inclusion was not abandoned in the early 1990s, despite the awful outcomes it induced, which is evidence of its deep roots.

How do we reconcile the claim that the belief in social inclusion has been present over both the dreadful 1985–1993 period and the virtuous period since 1993? The answer to this paradox is the rise of a second belief in the post-1993 period, which once grafted to the belief in social inclusion provided an overarching belief that induced very different institutions and policies. We call this second belief a "fear of inflation." It involves a perception by citizens and politicians of the costs and dangers of inflation and an understanding and acceptance that it is often necessary to bear up-front costs or refrain from some otherwise desirable behavior in order to avoid a relapse to the hyperinflationary past and all the suffering that would ensue. Fear of inflation arose from the traumatic experience with yearly inflation rates of more than 1,270 percent on average from 1985 to 1994 (2,851 percent in 1993). The belief induced and allowed presidents in Brazil to pursue very high primary surplus targets since 1999. Meeting ambitious primary surplus targets required that the executive make systematic cuts in budgeted expenditures across the board. Congressional budget expenditures are legitimate promised transfers to recipients across society, who naturally feel entitled to them and who complained when presidents discretionarily cut budgeted expenditures in the name of fiscal stability. The inflation aversion belief provides an environment where monetary stability and fiscal discipline trump other policies.

Once fear of inflation grafted to the belief in social inclusion, the result was an overarching belief in fiscally sound social inclusion. This, which we claim to be the prevailing belief still today in Brazil, tempers but does not eliminate the propensity of institutions and policies toward inclusion, openness, and participation. Rather, it provides a check that social inclusion will be pursued only in ways that are fiscally sustainable in the long term. Fiscally sound social inclusion sets a policy-making dynamic where programs and policies get created that have inclusion as a means or an end, but get suspended or postponed when inflationary pressures threaten stability. The fiscal imperative takes precedence over the inclusionary objectives. Politicians again pursue social inclusion objectives once assured of monetary stability. This makes for a slower pace of inclusionary policy with more volatility and less continuity, but at the same time more sustainable outcomes over time. In addition, not all growth-enhancing policies can be pursued simultaneously. For example, we argue that the Lula government pursued investments in education (socially inclusive) over investments in infrastructure.

During the period of the Dilma presidency that is under consideration (2010–2014), the belief in fiscally sound social inclusion remained in place, though it was increasingly put under strain as the government opted to counter the effects of the global crises through increased state intervention and expansionary fiscal policy, sometimes slipping into foolhardy habits of the past, such as trying to control energy prices. The mediocre levels of economic growth during the Dilma administration and the rising (though still controlled) level of inflation are moves toward outcomes no longer matching expectations, which started putting pressure on the prevailing beliefs in fiscally sound social inclusion. The government imposed several institutional changes that have pushed the boundary of this belief. A case could even be made that rather than simply being changes at the margin within the extant beliefs, the government's attempt at greater dirigisme represents a move to a new set of beliefs, possibly in social developmentalism. Yet the mounting criticism that this behavior attracted and the near defeat in the presidential election in 2014, despite the huge advantages in Brazil for the incumbent, are an indication that Brazilian society was still invested in the extant beliefs based on social inclusion and monetary stability and unwilling to risk adventures in the direction proposed by the Dilma government. Because the global crisis and Brazil's fragile situation persist, the belief in fiscally sound social inclusion will remain under pressure and will certainly suffer further changes at the margin. But, at least for now, the same twenty-year-old belief in fiscally sound social inclusion remains intact.

APPENDIX: A PRIMER ON THE BRAZILIAN POLITICAL SYSTEM

This section describes some basic characteristics of political institutions in Brazil.[6] The political process during the twenty-one years of the military regime was highly centralized. Over this period, five military presidents were indirectly elected via an electoral college in Congress, and the executive dominated the policy-making process. Although politically weak, the military kept Congress open, and it functioned during most of the authoritarian period. The first military government intended to stay in power for only a short period and consequently preserved many of the democratic features established in the 1946 Constitution, such as PR (proportional representation), the open-list electoral system for the legislature, the electoral calendar for congressional and subnational elections (governors, state assemblies, and mayors), and the multiparty system.

After being unexpectedly defeated in five states in the gubernatorial elections of 1965, the government decided to extinguish the multiparty

6 For a more detailed and analytical treatment of current political institutions in Brazil, see Alston et al. (2008).

system and impose a two-party system, composed of one party aggregating the political interests of the government (ARENA, Aliança Renovadora Nacional) and a second party representing the acceptable opposing interests (MDB, Movimento Democrático Brasileiro). The two-party system lasted until 1979, when the military once more allowed multiple parties as a strategy to weaken the growing opposition forces.

In 1968, the military closed Congress during the most repressive period of the dictatorship. During this period, the military increasingly resorted to torture and censorship. The opening process started in 1974 when the soft-liners in the military regained power. The pace of the democratic liberalization, however, was slow and tentative so as to avoid political risks for the dominant ruling network. In 1978, the military abolished Institutional Act #5, which ten years earlier suspended many constitutional guarantees, and it restored the amnesty law.

In 1982, the military allowed direct elections for governors, and there were great expectations for the same to happen at the presidential level in 1985. Despite the largest ever mass movement in Brazil, in favor of direct election for president, the opposition was unable to muster the two-thirds majority to approve a constitutional reform. A few years later, a new political alliance in favor of the democratization finally managed to elect the first civilian president after twenty-one years of dictatorship, though indirectly through the electoral college in Congress. Brazil approved a new constitution in 1988.

The political institutions that have evolved since the constitution are a complex mix of consensual rules that seek to enhance representativeness and majoritarian rules that pursue governability and accountability at some expense to fairness and representation (Lijphart 1999; Powell 2000). Electoral institutions, for example, allow for the representation of diverse interests in the political game but are often blamed for encouraging levels of fragmentation and decentralization that can complicate the policy-making process (Ames 1995a, 1995b). The 1988 Constitution maintained several features from the earlier democratic period, such as a president; proportional representation (PR); an open list for the legislative electoral system; a fragmented party system; federalism; and an independent judiciary.

Presidents and state governors are elected via two-round majoritarian rule. Whereas presidential candidates compete for votes in the entire national territory, electoral districts for governors are limited to the state territory. The presidential and gubernatorial term of office is four years, and presidents and governors are allowed to run for reelection consecutively just once. Senators are also elected by majoritarian rule, but in a single round, and their electoral district is the state territory. The senatorial term is eight years in office. National and state legislators run in an open-list proportional representation system with virtually no national effective threshold, that is, no minimum vote required to win a seat. Legislators compete for votes in the entire state territory, and the district magnitude varies from one state to the next. The largest state, São Paulo, has district magnitude equal to seventy for the Chamber of Deputies, and the smaller states have district magnitude equal to eight. There is no term limit for any legislative position, and the term of office is four years. Open-list PR leads to party fragmentation and encourages voters to support candidates based on personal qualities and activities. It also encourages individual legislators to cultivate direct relationships with local constituencies rather than relationships through national parties.

Brazil is a federal system with twenty-six states plus a federal district, which holds the capital city, Brasília. Each state has its own state constitution and a state assembly. The federal system has contributed toward making Brazil's party system among the most fragmented in the world, contributing to the decentralization of power and to a reduction in governmental effectiveness.

The 1988 Constitution delegated extensive and unprecedented powers to the judiciary and to other organizations such as the Court of Accounts (Tribunais de Contas) and the Office of the Public Prosecutor (Ministério Público). The country also has an extremely investigative Federal Police (Polícia Federal) and a very independent and combative media. This web of accountability institutions plays a key role in monitoring and constraining other political branches, especially the powerful executive.

Notwithstanding the tendency for gridlock and control, Brazil has managed to cope with the decentralizing nature of its consensual institutions, largely by relying on the centralizing powers of its majoritarian institutions. Though presidential regimes with multiple parties have often been prone to institutional gridlock, in Brazil the constitutional powers of the president centralize power, providing decisiveness and governability. The legislative powers of the president include decree and veto powers, the right to introduce new legislation, permission to request urgency time limits on certain bills, and discretionary powers over budget appropriation. Legislative rules and norms determine the agenda of Congress and influence the behavior of legislators in a way that promotes governability.

Despite strong presidential powers, it is important to keep in mind that the institutional setting that emerged from the 1988 Constitution was a consequence of legislative choice. The legislature delegated considerable power to the executive, including the power of unilaterally executing the budget. The underlying rationale was to prevent institutional instability and gridlock between Congress and the executive, which was prevalent in the previous period of democratic rule (from 1946 to 1964). The majority of legislators learned from the twenty-two years of dictatorship that an institutionally weak president could not last without some sort of governing capacity to enforce his agenda. Legislators decided not to change the electoral rules—that is, not to reform the open-list PR system in the new constitution because it would create too much uncertainty with respect to their own electoral survival—but they also opted to transfer institutional power to the executive to ensure governability.

The most important consequence of the institutional design is that most elected presidents since 1988 have been able to build reasonably stable post-electoral majority coalitions within Congress and have experienced relatively strong party discipline within the presidential governing coalition, along with a high level of governability. In fact, Brazil has not yet faced a truly divided government under the current set of political institutions. This is not coincidental, given the institutional powers and resources held and selectively distributed by the executive. The combination of provisional decree, vetoes, urgency petitions, and budget dominance provides the executive with an impressive set of instruments for imposing its own legislative priorities on the agenda of Congress.

This disproportionate share of power of the executive, together with other features of the political system, such as the large number of weakly institutionalized parties and perverse incentives due to campaign finance, has often led to calls for political reform. Yet, thus far, all initiatives toward wholesale changes in political institutions have foundered, except for very minor tweaks, indicating that with all its pros and cons the current system is likely to remain the rules by which the political game is played in Brazil in the foreseeable future.

CHAPTER 3

From Disorder to Growth and Back:
The Military Regime (1964–1984)

IN 1964, A MILITARY COUP INTERRUPTED THE DEMOCRATIC INTERREGNUM that Brazil had witnessed since 1946. The 1946–1964 period was a tumultuous time as the country simultaneously went through the growing pains of industrialization and of democracy. The state was the dominant organization, and the economy was fairly closed. The electorate consisted of only 18 percent of the population. The dominant network, who enjoyed rents, consisted of industrialists in protected sectors; bankers who shared seigniorage gains with the state; and regional (more so than national) politicians. The fiscal basis of the state was narrow and depended on the inflation tax and increasingly on compulsory savings mechanisms that the developmental state created. Declining economic performance led to increasing inflationary pressures, prompting an escalation of redistributive demands from those outside the dominant network. The outcomes from this closed order were increasingly at odds with expectations from the dominant network but did not lead to an abandonment of the belief in developmentalism to shape institutions. Developmentalism actually achieved its apex under authoritarian rule. GDP growth was highly volatile and inflation high (27 percent yearly average). By the early 1960s, inflation grew to 64 percent and growth slowed to under 1 percent, prompting a crisis with the military mounting a successful coup in 1964.

FROM CHAOS TO A SHORT PERIOD OF ORDER

Though the average level of GDP growth was high in this early period (6.9 percent from 1946 to 1964), it was also extremely volatile and accompanied by recurring inflation (26.8 percent yearly average). The year before the coup, GDP growth was 0.6 percent and inflation 64.3 percent, respectively, the lowest and highest values for the period 1946–1964. Industrial policy consisted of an overvalued exchange rate, which discouraged foreign investment, and high tariffs, which protected the national industry.

Similarly, the political front was marked by polarization and decision paralysis as well as rampant populism, clientelism, and electoral fraud, all in a highly unequal, poor, and uneducated society with several rural conflicts for land reform. The populist coalition that governed Brazil for almost the entire democratic period of 1946–1964 (except for a seven-month interlude in 1961) lacked partisan support and agenda-setting powers in Congress and had few constitutionally derived powers to assure governability. The president did not have the prerogative of permanent or temporary decrees; could not initiate new legislation or propose changes to the constitution; could not discharge bills from gatekeeping committees; did not have the right to craft the budget; and could not withhold legislators' amendments to the budget (Figueiredo and Limongi 2006). The executive's role was limited to enacting or vetoing new laws devised by the legislature. This constitutional design, which combined multiparty fragmentation with a powerless president, produced an environment prone to political instability, gridlock, and lack of political coordination. No single party was able to hold the majority of seats in Congress, nor was government able to build or sustain a postelectoral majority coalition. Minority governments were the norm, not the exception. Additionally, the main political parties in that period—Social Democratic Party (PSD), União Democrática Nacional (UDN), and Brazilian Labor Party (PTB)—presented very low levels of party discipline (Amorim Neto and Santos 2001). It was not a coincidence that during this democratic phase Brazil experienced much political turbulence: several failed military coups; a president who committed suicide after being involved in a frustrated effort to assassinate his major opponent; a coup inside of another coup to assure the inauguration of this president's successor; a president who resigned; his vice president assuming power only under a negotiated regime change to a parliamentary system; and finally the democratic breakdown in 1964 that recentralized the political game.

Without agenda-setting powers, Brazilian presidents frequently fell hostage to a fragmented and polarized Congress, leading this period to be dominated by recurring gridlock and legislative paralysis. Figure 3.1 shows that from 1946 to 1964, most laws originated from Congress rather than the executive, a pattern that was dramatically reversed after 1964 and would not return even after redemocratization, as we shall see in forthcoming chapters.

The military regime was a reaction to disorder and uncertainty. At first, the agenda of the military was not clear. Would they persist in the pursuit of economic growth through the same state-led protectionist development model that had come to dominate Brazil since the 1930s? Or, would the priority be stabilization and fiscal discipline? Would political participation be allowed and dissension tolerated? How much influence would Congress retain? In the early years of military rule, uncertainty shrouded these questions in large part because of lack of political cohesion within

Figure 3.1. Percentage of bills enacted by proponents in Brazil (1946–1985). Source: Data provided by Pessanha (1997); figure created by the authors.

the military, which had several factions with distinct economic and political agendas.

Several distinct features of the Brazilian military regime enhanced this uncertainty vis-à-vis other authoritarian Latin American counterparts: first, initially the military rulers retained many democratic institutions, such as the constitution, political parties, elections for states and *municípios* (counties), and a functioning Congress. That is, the military kept many features of political life relatively intact. Second, the armed forces also decided to preserve the basic components of the pre-1964 liberal democratic constitution, suggesting that they did not have the intention, at least in the beginning, of staying indefinitely in power. Furthermore, the military regime in Brazil was not centered around a personalistic leader or traditional caudillo, but rather on an institutionalized collective junta with some degree of alternation of power among different factions within the military. As a consequence, the five different administrations in twenty-one years of military rule presented considerably more variation than is typically the case with military regimes that are anchored on a single individual or tight-knit group.

At the outset of the military period, two different sets of beliefs about what kind of economic policies the regime should pursue prevailed within the military factions: developmentalism and economic liberalism. The belief in liberalism had roots in the pre-1930 commodity-export era, and the belief in developmentalism originated with state-led industrialization beginning in the 1930s.

In Brazil, economic liberalism evolved into a very different notion than the original economic liberalism that arose in Europe, where it was essentially an ideology of a rising bourgeois against privileges from the rurally based aristocracy (Bresser-Pereira 1984). In Brazil, on the other hand, economic liberalism was essentially the ideology *of* the rural aristocracy, along with agricultural exporters, importers of manufactured products, and the more traditional urban middle classes. These social and economic sectors opposed policies that protected the emerging industrial sector at their expense by restricting trade and manipulating exchange rates. They saw Brazil's comparative advantage lying in agriculture and free trade as the best way to pursue growth and development. The agricultural business sector espoused the belief in liberalism and the UDN defended their interests in Congress.

The belief in *developmentalism* started after the 1930 revolution but intensified in the early 1950s Vargas era. This belief formed the basis of the Import Substitution Industrialization (ISI) model driven by state-led industrialization associated with foreign indebtedness and populist incorporation of diverse sectors of the society, in particular workers and middle classes. Both sets of beliefs had their proponents in the early stages of the military regime. After a brief foray with liberalism based on macroeconomic adjustments as the main belief, and stagnation the result that emerged from those policies in the short-run, the tide turned to the belief in developmentalism, which became the driving force behind institutions and policies through the majority of the military rule. Developmentalism established growth, economic might, and industrial progress as imperatives, leaving issues of democracy and combating inequality and poverty as secondary and subservient objectives.

Although the military had a common enemy in the threat of communism, they were far from united, and it is possible to identify at least four divergent internal factions: (1) soft-liners (or *sorbonistas*, since their main leaders had been trained at the Ecole Superieure de Guerre in France, at the Army Command and General Staff College in Fort Leavenworth, Kansas, and at the Superior War College in Brazil), (2) hard-liners, (3) developmentalists, and (4) techno-bureaucrats.

The sorbonistas were not only politically moderate and economically liberal but also espoused a quick return to democracy. This is one of the reasons why the military retained the democratic Constitution of 1946 and the electoral calendar (for mayors, in March 1965; for governors, in October 1965; and for the presidency, in February 1967). The sorbonistas planned to reestablish democracy after cleaning up the country against the imminent risk of socialist alternatives and against the nationalist state-led development model installed by previous administrations relying on populist coalitions.

The internal faction of hard-liners did not have a clear-cut economic agenda. Rather, they were mostly concerned with preserving internal security and social/political order as well as forestalling the rise of communist ideologies in Brazil. They were not particularly committed to democratic procedures or to returning power to a different civilian political elite.

The developmentalist faction within the army, on the other hand, was fully committed to an agenda of nationalist development of industry, yet not through the same populist variants of policies used in the pre-1964 period. They believed that, after restoring the country's fiscal health, the state should play a key role with large-scale intervention and participation in the economy.

Finally, the fourth military faction, techno-bureaucrats, was mostly composed of top-ranking officials who supported the unity of the army around bureaucratic and hierarchical principles and in favor of the interests of the military corporation such as higher salary, perks, and better work conditions.

Initially, the sorbonistas, under the leadership of General Humberto Castelo Branco, controlled the "revolutionary" government from 1964 to 1967 with the support of the military and civilian political elites, including the governors of some of the major states. This first administration followed an economic agenda fundamentally oriented toward economic stabilization and fiscal discipline, frustrating the expectations of the national industrial elite, which was eager for expansionist economic policies, subsidies, and external borrowing. In 1964, the Brazilian economy had stagnant GDP growth, annual inflation above 100 percent, no access to external credit, lack of international credibility, and a foreign debt of about US\$3 billion. The economic team, coordinated by Roberto Campos and Octavio Bulhões, two outspoken advocates of vigorous anti-inflation measures, followed an orthodox prescription aimed at restricting excess demand, high public debt, excessive credit for the private sector, and high salaries, which together were seen as the main sources of persistent inflation. The government launched the Economic Action Program (PAEG), which was the most comprehensive stabilization plan put in place in Brazil. According to R. Cardoso (2013), the PAEG had three targets: (1) to lift restrictions on balance of payments, (2) to control inflation, and (3) to develop institutional conditions favorable to economic growth after a return to monetary stability.

The administration created new institutions in order to pursue the agenda of economic adjustment. However, the measures were not a consequence of a well-thought-out institutional blueprint but rather aimed at dealing with specific problems. A few days after the coup, the military decreed the Institutional Act (IA) #1, which provided institutional conditions for the executive to overcome the lack of powers in dealing with Congress under divided government. Institutional Act #1 granted the executive the power to submit constitutional amendments and exclusive powers to propose expenditures. Institutional Act #1 denied legislators the ability to increase expenditures on any bill proposed by the president. In another measure aimed at recentralizing the fiscal game, the government prohibited state governments from issuing new bonds to cover state budget deficits without federal authorization.

As Brazil did not have a proper Central Bank or the administrative capacity to coordinate fiscal and monetary policies, the government created several administrative and economic organizations to increase state capacity in these areas. The government created the National Monetary Council to coordinate fiscal and monetary policy and in 1965 created a Central Bank. To address the large public deficits that were one of the important determinants of inflation, the government took special measures to put in order the accounts of state-owned enterprises, in particular those in the railroad, shipping, and oil industries.

The new administration greatly increased tax revenues. Brazil did not have instruments or mechanisms to adjust late payments to inflation. The government established an inflation indexation system to halt the erosion of the real value of taxes. With taxes indexed, taxpayers no longer had incentives to delay payments. Very soon, the government applied indexing to several credit and financial operations including indexed government bond and mortgage contracts within the newly created National Housing Bank (BNH). Indexation quickly became a fundamental instrument of economic policy because of the significant tax revenues it generated. The government also implemented a number of legal measures to take control of wage policy so as to keep wages from rising faster than inflation, not only for public servants but for the private sector as well.

From Order to Unsustainable Growth

In less than one year, the situation of the Brazilian economy improved dramatically. As a consequence of higher tax revenues and a drastic decrease in public expenditure, the public deficit, which was 4.2 percent of GDP in 1963, declined to 3.2 percent and 1.6 percent in 1964 and 1965, respectively. Although inflation was still high, it was cut in half. Personnel expenditures in the public sector declined as well. These results enabled the government to renegotiate the external debt with the IMF and foreign banks, which helped the country regain external credibility, which in turn led to a new influx of foreign investments (US$222 million from the United States and US$650 million from USAID (United States Agency for International Development). In February 1965, the World Bank announced a new set of loans, and the IMF announced a new standby agreement of US$126 million.

Although the anti-inflation program was partially successful, the stabilization of the economy also led to a slowdown of the economy with a 5 percent drop in national industrial production. Naturally, economic stabilization was much criticized by the domestic industrial interests that resented the withdrawal of subsidies, especially those in São Paulo who felt deeply the slowdown of the economy. The political vulnerability of the first military government became apparent with the electoral defeat in the gubernatorial elections of 1965 of its candidates in five states, especially in Rio de Janeiro and Minas Gerais. The electoral defeat caused great distress among the hard-liners and tipped the balance in their favor. Hard-liners criticized the decision of the sorbonistas to maintain the electoral calendar instead of simply appointing the new governors indirectly.

Realizing that the stabilization of the economy would take longer than originally planned and under pressure from hard-liners and developmentalists, Castelo Branco issued a congressional amendment that extended his own term in power until March 15, 1967. This decision led to the loss of political support from prominent UDN (conservative) politicians and from important governors who were potential candidates for the presidency in the upcoming election, all of whom strongly opposed the program of economic stabilization.

As a response to the adverse electoral result in the gubernatorial elections, and with the support of the techno-bureaucrats and national developmentalists groups, Castelo Branco unilaterally decreed Institutional Act #2, which, among other things, abolished all existing political parties and instituted the provisions for the formation of a two-party system, establishing them as the only legal ones: Aliança Renovadora Nacional (ARENA), supporting the military regime; and Movimento Democrático Brasileiro (MDB), representing the opposition.[1] Through this maneuver, the military regime assured a stable parliamentary majority supporting the government in both houses, leaving to the opposition party a minority role. This biased two-party system would last until 1979, when multiple parties would finally be reestablished.

Institutional Act #2 also reshaped executive-legislative relations by transferring to the executive formerly legislative initiatives in budgetary matters, and enabling the president to request the urgency (discharge) procedures of forty-five days in each house (or thirty days for both houses

---

1 Interestingly, although IA #2 decreed the two-party system in Brazil, it preserved the open-list proportional representation electoral rules, which in principle favors the development of a multiparty system.

in a joint session) to all bills initiated by the executive. If a bill was not approved or voted within this period, it would automatically become law. Later, party fidelity was also introduced to make sure that ARENA members would not vote against its party leader's orientation. As a consequence of these institutional changes, Congress approved the overwhelming majority of bills introduced by the executive, thus overcoming the decision-making paralysis of the pre-1964 Congress.

In February 1966, the military tightened its grip on the electoral process through IA #3, which introduced indirect elections for the presidency, governorships, and mayors. Although Castelo attempted to stay in power for a longer period (his term was extended for one extra year), he turned out to be a reactive and weak lame-duck president. In March 1967, Castelo's minister of war, Costa e Silva, representing the conservative hard-liners, became the next Brazilian president. The loss of political rights to the electorate prompted social protests and subsequent military repression.

In many ways, the first military administration was a lost window of opportunity in which Brazil could have broken away from the dominant developmentalist beliefs that had dominated since the 1950s. As should have been expected, the sorbonistas suffered from the overwhelming political unpopularity of attempting to control inflation through fiscal discipline and austerity. In addition, political contingencies associated with electoral setbacks while pursuing the unpopular anti-inflation program increased interfactional tensions and competition within the military regime itself. Lacking political support for the orthodox stabilization and fiscal measures, Castelo's administration came to a melancholic end. Having lost the battle and as a final way to consolidate his achievements and tie the hands of his successor, Castelo Branco issued IA #4 to reconvene Congress for an extraordinary session to approve a new constitution in 1967. By replacing all the institutional acts with a new constitution, Castelo Branco attempted to weaken the hand of the developmentalists and hard-liners. The new constitution reproduced the basic principles of representative democracy present in the Constitution of 1946, while at the same time retaining all unilateral mechanisms that had been instituted through IA #2, thus institutionalizing the means for a strong executive.

The "election" of Costa e Silva inaugurated a new cycle of the military regime with a distinct dominant network supporting his government and a new set of political and economic policies. Instead of emphasizing inflation control, fiscal discipline, and international credibility with foreign investors, Costa e Silva implemented a set of policies that aimed at pleasing sectors of the domestic business that had felt betrayed by the previous administration's orthodoxy. Although the hard-liners did not have a clear economic agenda, conservative nationalist and developmentalist ideologies influenced them. The Costa e Silva administration advocated economic development pursued under state planning and intervention following the ISI model, with fewer concerns over inflation control.

While Castelo Branco's government diagnosed inflationary pressures as a demand-induced problem, the new economic team saw inflation as being mostly cost induced. Therefore, the great majority of economic policies and initiatives stimulated, rather than limited, demand. For example, the new faction reformulated wage policy to make up for the wage losses due to the indexation of the previous period. In the same vein, the administration provided more access to credit to stimulate demand. The government's goal sought expansionist development without inflationary pressures. In many ways, these new policies benefited from the financial and fiscal reforms implemented under the first administration, especially the reduction of the deficits of the government.

Consistent with the diagnosis that inflation was cost-induced, in 1968, the Costa e Silva administration imposed strict controls over industrial costs and the prices of final products under the newly established Interministerial Price Council (CIP). CIP oversight of the domestic industry took the form of extremely active price interventions and the imposition of tough penalties for violations. During the initial economic boom, the strategy contributed to moderate price increases, and inflation fell 25 percent in 1968. Except for the problem of income distribution, the economic performance of the new military faction was excellent, with stabilization of inflation at around 20 percent and with GDP growth at 11 percent. The striking growth was a consequence of the growth of national industry led by passenger vehicles, chemicals, electrical equipment, and construction. Bresser-Pereira (1984) notes that the basic force behind this new economic expansion was the middle classes' increased capacity to purchase consumer goods, especially automobiles, as well as the availability of large-scale consumer credit.

> Foreign borrowing was critical to Brazil's economic and political development after 1967. . . . The overwhelming majority of the borrowing went, directly or indirectly, to boost production of basic industrial products. . . . In principle, the system was magical: foreign finance boosted industrial production, and enough of this production was exported to cover interest and principal payments. (Frieden 1987: 95–96)

Additionally, during the relative prosperity of the borrowing boom, Brazil pursued state intervention policies that helped to cement the alliance between the national industrial interests and the military.

Despite the good economic performance, the regime became more repressive and concentrated even more power with IA #5, which further empowered the executive to dictate emergency measures at his own discretion. Different from its predecessors, the fifth act bore no expiration date. Although it did not abolish the 1967 Constitution, it allowed the executive to suspend activities of Congress and habeas corpus indefinitely, allowing the government to rule by decree. Torture became the dominant modus operandi of the new military faction. It was perhaps the inevitable next step in the general direction of concentrating all power in the executive. Concentration allowed, for example, a tax reform that reduced from 20 to 12 percent the share of the main federally collected taxes transferred to the states and counties (including urban areas) without any opposition from subnational units. With the new economic prosperity and less redistribution to subnational units, the tax revenue of the federal government increased considerably.

Institutional Act #5 provided unprecedented governability, but at the same time it rapidly increased the degree of popular discontent. Dissatisfaction with the growing repressive nature of the system led to strikes by workers, student protests, and the early signs of what would over time grow into a strong reaction against authoritarian rule. Confronted with these manifestations, the military regime fought back with increasingly repressive measures. The tension reached its climax in August 1968 when President Costa e Silva suffered a stroke. The Constitution of 1967 stipulated that the vice president should replace the president in case of incapacitation of the president. But, the council of military ministers decided to keep the presidency under their control and chose General Emilio Medici as the new president: "not because he or his military electors thought he had the vision or the knowledge a president needed, but because he was the only four-star general who could stop the army from tearing itself apart" (Skidmore 1988: 105).

The Medici administration was a continuation of the dominant network composed of the nationalist and developmentalist factions of the military, but now with a strategic alliance with techno-bureaucrats, along with increased repression. The important distinction of this administration was a much greater level of delegation to bureaucrats, who were insulated from political pressures. Congress played a minimal role in policy making. For example, prior to Medici, in 1967 Congress initiated 44,485 amendments to the national budget and approved 39,248. In 1973, legislators introduced only 4,110 amendments and approved only 17 (Martínez-Lara 1996).

To insulate the technocratic autonomy, the government relied heavily on repression and censorship, on the one hand and, on the other, provided autonomy to techno-bureaucrats (notoriously Delfim Neto) to manage the economic policies pursuing a strategy of accelerated industrialization. The techno-bureaucrats' control of the National Monetary Council allowed them to filter demands from different sectors of the economy as well as decide which groups and sectors benefited from state economic policies. The government secured the support of the cadre of top bureaucratic professionals, public managers, and technocrats by substantial increases in salaries. The Medici administration delegated issues related to noneconomic or domestic policy making to the National Security Council and all political matters to the chief of civilian affairs.

The belief in developmentalism reached its apogee from 1967 to 1973. The combination of economic growth with a strong repressive authoritarian regime led to political stability and weakness of opposition with acquiescence achieved via repression. High growth rates undermined criticism of the prevailing economic model. Economic policy rested on a combination of state intervention and the inclusion and protection of selected sectors of the national economy in the pursuit of industrial development and economic might. The nationalist approach to development was combined with the patriotic appeal of supporting the domestic industrial sector. Skidmore (1988: 110) summarizes this period as follows: "the hard-line military needed the technocrats to make the economy work. The technocrats needed the military to stay in power. The high growth rate in turn gave legitimacy to the authoritarian system."

THE MIRACLE FADES

The Brazilian Miracle of high growth was short-lived and ended in early 1973 with an oil shock that brought external indebtedness and rekindled inflation. Instead of adjusting to the new reality by slowing down the economy, the government chose to go ahead with import substitution in the hope of reducing Brazilian dependence on imported products. The strategy still retained substantial economic growth (6–7 percent a year) but at the expense of increased public spending, unbalanced government accounts, foreign debt, and inflation.

Income inequality reemerged as a key problem as a consequence of accelerated growth without explicit concerns for income distribution. The belief in economic development as an imperative relegated any concern with equity to the sidelines. The tendency for income concentration resulted from the nature of Brazilian industrialization: capital-intensive and technologically sophisticated goods intended for consumption by a small minority of the population in the upper and middle classes, part of the dominant network (A. Castro 1994). The close association of the Brazilian business elites to the authoritarian rulers and the mutual benefits generated by the regime for members of the dominant network sustained the belief in ISI leading to growth with little care for redistribution.

Despite its successful reliance on repression and economic growth, the political alliance formed by hard-liners, national business elites, and technocrats lost control of Medici's succession in 1974. This seems odd, given that the government ended its term apparently stronger than at any time since 1964: the economy was booming and armed threats from the left no longer existed. Some factions of hard-liners tried to prolong Medici's term, yet the president decided to stick to the preestablished timetable. Soft-liners, captained by General Golbery do Couto e Silva, advocated the need for liberalization and the return to rule of law, with a gradual elimination of the arbitrary and repressive nature of the regime.

General Ernesto Geisel, a soft-liner closely identified with Castelo Branco and president of Petrobrás, the massive state-owned oil company, won the nomination of the government party in 1973. Geisel's brother, Orlando Geisel, who was minister of the army, neutralized the opposition by hard-liners. In addition, a very carefully orchestrated campaign by the moderate faction within the military led Ernesto Geisel to be chosen by almost unanimous decision in the army.

Similar to Castelo Branco in 1964, Geisel started his administration offering clear signs that the goal of his government was to lead Brazil to a return to democracy; however, different from Castelo Branco, the return would be at a "slow, gradual, and secure" pace, under the control of the governing party. Geisel balanced opening up politically and initiating the transition to democracy with guarantees, while at the same time appeasing the hard-liners who continued to worry about threats from the left. The transition to democracy became viable through the design of an electoral game that was simultaneously in the interest of both the military government and the opposition (Lamounier 1989). It may seem contradictory, but the majority of the opposition was willing to play this game. Unlike the redemocratization in Argentina, Portugal, or Greece, where collapse of the military regime triggered the transition to democracy, in Brazil the process was endogenous and gradualist, in which the maintenance of the electoral calendar played a key role in the opening process.

To be credible, Geisel carried out elections for Congress and state legislatures in November 1974 with fewer restrictions and less censorship. The government showed commitment to a clean, open, and fair electoral process, allowing even candidates from the opposition to have free access to radio and television for the first time. However, the results of the 1974 election surprised the government. The opposition almost doubled its representation in the lower house of Congress, jumping from 87 to 165 seats, out of 364 seats. The results in the Senate accorded with those in the Chamber of Deputies, the opposition-held seats increasing from 7 to 23. However, the party representing the military government, ARENA, still held the majority of the seats in the Senate. The elections for state legislatures also led to striking defeats to the military government. The opposition gained control of six states, including the powerful states of São Paulo, Rio Grande do Sul, and Rio de Janeiro. Similar to what had happened with Castelo Branco's electoral defeat in the gubernatorial election of 1965, the consistent electoral success of the opposition threatened Geisel's view of gradual liberalization. Nevertheless, President Geisel moved quickly to affirm the results of the election. In practical terms, however, the opposition regained the power of blocking constitutional amendments only because the overwhelming legislative power remained in the hands of the executive.

Afraid of facing another electoral defeat in the upcoming election for governors in 1978, the government exercised the dictatorial powers of the fifth act and closed Congress in 1977, once again using as pretext the refusal by the opposition to support a government bill to reform the judiciary. Geisel then announced a series of constitutional changes, which became known as the "April Package," clearly designed to provide electoral advantages to the military. The package postponed the direct gubernatorial election from 1978 to 1982; established that one-third of the Senate be elected indirectly; altered the composition of the electoral college; and changed the rules for amending the constitution to a simple majority instead of the former two-thirds majority.

Even with these and other arbitrary measures, the opposition continued to play along with the military. At the end of 1978, President Geisel repealed IA #5, depriving the president the authority to declare a constitutional recess, remove congressmen, or strip citizens of their rights. The decision reaffirmed Geisel's personal power and control over the army, and it further legitimized the process of political opening. Next, Geisel initiated negotiations for an amnesty law, which restored political rights to politicians and a pardon to members of the military faction involved in torture and repression.[2] At this time, the president also reestablished the freedom of the press.

Geisel's political similarities to the Castelo administration did not carry over to economic policy. Geisel retained a belief in developmentalism. In 1976, the government launched the second National Development Plan (PND II),[3] establishing a target rate of 10 percent growth a year, led by intermediate industrial products and capital goods. The strategy sought to take advantage of the great international liquidity of petrodollars to finance ambitious programs of investments led by state enterprises in the areas of energy (hydroelectric, with power plants like Itaipu; ethanol based; and nuclear), metallurgy, petrochemical, industrial goods, and infrastructure for transportation.

2 Pardons are an important mechanism to prompt society to be forward looking. Chile and South Africa also gave pardons to repressive factions.
3 An earlier PND had been implemented 1972–1974.

Geisel's plans failed to materialize, in part because the international economic environment deteriorated further in the late 1970s with the second oil shock, which led to massive increases in the value of imports. Unfazed, the government maintained the policy of pursuing accelerated growth without further concerns for inflation, which shot from 15 to 35 percent. The easy availability of foreign capital allowed Geisel to pursue his strategy, but it ran the country deeper into debt. Geisel undertook a new vigorous wave of import substitution. Now, the government extended the dominant network to include producers of sugarcane and ethanol, steel, iron, cellulose, petrochemicals, and other raw materials. The government directly and heavily invested in electricity, transportation, and communication. In addition, the government used fiscal credits and tax incentives to stimulate the private sector and state-owned enterprises (SOEs) to pursue other import substitution projects. The nature and technological characteristics of these new import substitution projects required further investment, leading to an increase in the external debt and extra pressure on inflation. It was during the Geisel administration that state intervention in the economy, in the form of direct ownership of SOEs, reached a historical peak. As a consequence of the investments associated with the PND II, gross capital formation by federal SOEs jumped to 4.3 percent of GDP or 16.3 percent of the total fixed capital formation in 1975 (Musacchio and Lazzarini 2014).

In 1978, Geisel managed to appoint as his successor General João Figueiredo, the former head of the Intelligence Service Agency. The new administration showed great continuity with its predecessor, reappointing Mario Henrique Simonsen, the finance minister of Geisel, to become a new "super-minister" for economic policy. To deal with rising foreign indebtedness, an overheated economy, and an inflation rate of 40 percent, Simonsen pushed to slow down the economy with a Five-Year Plan. The strategy made Simonsen extremely vulnerable both within the government as well as among the national business community, who refused to accept that the economic miracle was over. Simonsen resigned after five months. Figueiredo brought back Delfim Neto, the developmentalist techno-bureaucrat from the early Miracle Years. Neto promptly returned to ISI policies, satisfying both the expansionist aisles of government and the national business community.

BACK TO DISORDER

In the early 1980s, intensifying import substitution proved extremely costly to Brazil. As the international crisis spread to Brazil, unemployment increased and rates of GDP per capita turned negative. The economic downturn had its biggest impact in the industrial and durable goods sectors, located in the main urban areas of the country. With the Mexican default in 1982, the economic situation worsened, as markets anticipated a subsequent Brazilian default. Brazil went to the IMF, who lent money and facilitated access to international private banks. But, when Brazil failed to meet the initial targets established by the IMF, the IMF halted disbursements.

The economic recession shattered the belief in ISI leading to growth. The military lost the support of powerful segments of the domestic economy that had previously been part of the dominant network. The core of the country's business community (the national industrial bourgeoisie) abandoned the military and joined other dissenting groups, including industrial workers, the middle class, and intellectuals, in expressing growing discontent against the regime. In the absence of the economic miracle, the previous network fell apart, and with it dissolved the overarching belief in developmentalism.

Prominently, the *Manifesto dos Oito* (Manifesto of the Eight), which was publicized in 1978, articulated the dissatisfaction among the "young Turks" who took over the leadership of the Federation of the Industries of the State of São Paulo (FIESP).[4] In the manifesto, they criticized both the exclusionary nature of the regime and the increasing state regulation of the economy under Geisel. Amid a wave of strikes, they pressed for the political opening of the regime and for reforming capital-labor relations.

The transition to democracy in Brazil forced the national business community elites to rethink their political activities and reorganize themselves for articulating focused political influence (Payne 1994). Despite the incentive, no cohesive business organization emerged in Brazil, but only rather ineffective and informal lobbying by individuals or small groups (Schneider 1998).

In 1979, prior to the deep recession, the administration restored the multiparty system. The soft-liner strategists realized that the two-party system was no longer capable of preserving the legislative majority supporting the military regime. On the contrary, it electorally consolidated the opposition under the big partisan MDB umbrella that was about to win control of not only Congress but also state assemblies and many municipal governments in the upcoming general elections. To avoid this massive defeat, the alternative was to fragment the opposition by reestablishing a restricted (no Marxist parties allowed) multiparty system with the emergence of several new parties, especially on the center and left of the ideological spectrum. This decision pleased segments of the opposition

---

4 Interestingly, the leader of the young Turks, Dilson Funaro, was appointed finance minister and president of BNDES during the first democratic government in Brazil (see Cruz 1995).

and factions that would no longer have to squeeze under the MDB partisan umbrella. This military strategy of preserving open-list proportional representation without restricting the number of political parties proved successful with the creation of several new political parties, including the Workers' Party (PT), founded by unionists, intellectuals, and members of the church under the leadership of Luiz Inácio Lula da Silva.

In addition to this radical change in the party system, the government required a straight ticket (all votes to one party) for all elected positions available in Congress. The outcome of the election of November 1982 confirmed the multiparty strategy. The combined opposition parties managed to win a slight majority of 240 to 235 seats in the House, but in the Senate ARENA (the military party) enjoyed a comfortable majority of 46 to 23. In the electoral college, which would be responsible for choosing the next president, ARENA retained the majority of 359 to 321. Nevertheless, the 1982 election represented a turning point in the process of democratization because it marked the end of the government's control of the congressional agenda. In addition, the opposition managed to win ten subnational governments, including the most economically powerful states: São Paulo, Rio de Janeiro, and Minas Gerais.

The electoral success of 1982 emboldened the opposition to propose in 1983 a constitutional amendment to restore the direct presidential election in November 1984. However, no political force in Congress had the two-thirds majority necessary to reform the constitution. To forestall the indirect election through the electoral college, the opposition launched a national campaign in favor of direct elections "now"—*Diretas Já*, which mobilized the entire nation and is still the largest popular movement ever seen in Brazil. Despite its success in motivating the population, the movement did not succeed, as the amendment to the constitution fell short by 22 votes of the required two-thirds threshold in the Chamber of Deputies. The remaining alternative was to find a candidate capable of attracting the support of sectors of the dissenting group within the government party, who split and formed a new party called the Liberal Front Party (PFL). To be successful in the electoral college, the Democratic Alliance was formed, with Tancredo Neves from the Brazilian Democratic Movement Party (PMDB) as the candidate for the presidency, and José Sarney, representing the PFL, as the candidate for the vice presidency. The Democratic Alliance's ticket obtained an overwhelming majority of 480 out of 686 votes in the electoral college in January 1985, putting an end to twenty-one years of military rule in Brazil.

The newly elected president inspired hope and enthusiasm among the population, recapturing the spirit of the campaign for direct elections. Dramatically, however, he was hospitalized before his inauguration with a serious abdominal infection and died five weeks later. The death of

Tancredo shocked Brazil, as expectations ran high of him truly moving Brazil to become more inclusive. Change required firm leadership, which Tancredo may have possessed. The electorate expected Tancredo to implement an agenda of political and economic reforms capable of leading the country to economic growth, inflation control, income redistribution, and social inclusion.

Disappointment turned to despair as the presidency fell to José Sarney, a conservative and oligarchical politician who had been closely associated with the previous authoritarian regime. Redemocratization thus began under considerable uncertainty.

The Decline of Developmentalism

The rise and fall of military rule represents a full cycle in the framework discussed in chapter 2. The cycle began when the uncertainty and poor economic performance of the previous period (1946–1964) ushered in a military coup with a new dominant network that followed a new belief of developmentalism. For a period in the late 1960s to early 1970s, the institutional changes delivered strong economic growth, so that the outcomes matched the expectations of developmentalist beliefs. The positive economic results compensated for the authoritarian and repressive nature of the regime (at least for some). But as economic growth proved unsustainable after 1974, the belief in developmentalism increasingly seemed an inappropriate interpretation of how the world really works. The next ten years (1975–1985) represent a long and gradual transition to a new cycle in the framework. Declining but still relatively high growth rates in the mid-1970s protracted the transition.

The military blamed external shocks for the disappointing economic results. At first, this view seemed plausible, but it held less purchase over time as economic performance continued to deteriorate in the late 1970s and early 1980s. "Young Turks" at FIESP replaced the old guard, and the new business community became increasingly critical of statism and supported the transition to democracy. The two decades of military rule illustrate that a window of opportunity in which the old belief is discarded and a new belief emerges can sometimes be long and protracted.

CHAPTER 4

Transition to Democracy and the Belief in Social Inclusion (1985–1993)

A New Belief Emerges

The 1980s are known as the lost decade in Brazil. Statistics tell the story. Average real GDP per capita growth fell from 9.4 percent per year in the 1970s to 3.0 percent per year in the 1980s. Annual average inflation increased an order of magnitude across decades, from 40 percent in the 1970s to 430 percent in the 1980s. The Gini coefficient increased from 0.57 in 1980 to 0.64 in 1991 (Barros and Mendonça 1994), showing that inequality worsened during this period despite the move from dictatorship to democracy. Even poverty, which had fallen dramatically from 68 percent of households below the poverty line in 1970 to 39 percent in 1980, failed to show any sustained improvement and stood at 36 percent in 1990. Although there were undeniable improvements in democracy, the impeachment of President Collor in 1992, the first directly elected president in three decades, raised questions about the political stability of the fledgling democracy.

With the advantage of hindsight, we see that some important elements of the transformation that would take place in Brazil after 1994 (described in chapters 5 and 6) originated and started to evolve during the period 1985–1993. In particular, the belief in social inclusion emerged with the demise of the military cycle and became established in the mid-1980s. Similar rhetoric arose about social inclusion across much of Latin America, but its substance varied enormously. The new dominant network shaped the "flavor" of social inclusion in Brazil. The "opening up" brought to the fore of the dominant network a "big center" of political parties, along with national and foreign banks, state-owned enterprises, trade unions, and a rising agribusiness sector.

The belief in social inclusion led to demands for a new constitution. The constitution did not impose beliefs from the top down but rather expressed a latent belief held by many. The interplay of changes in beliefs and constitutional change ultimately shaped the outcomes we discuss in chapters 5 and 6. The Constitution of Brazil was aspirational in that it contained considerable hopes for reform. Redistribution was a central aspirational hope. The income distribution in Brazil ranked as the world's second most unequal, and so calls for redistribution were no surprise (Ferreira et al. 2008).

The immediate consequence of the belief in social inclusion was a disastrous hyperinflationary process that quickly dispelled the hope of regaining the glory years of the Brazilian miracle (1968–1973). Hyperinflation resulted from the nature of the dominant network, which lacked leadership. The dominant network was merely a tacit agreement among all groups that each should receive something and that policies should be socially inclusive even for those outside of the dominant network (e.g., the poor). Indeed, the emphasis in inclusion and correcting past injustices without attention to fiscal restraints not only allowed all manner of private interests to pursue their own ends but ultimately failed to improve the lot of the poor, who were most vulnerable to the nefarious consequences of inflation. In the late 1980s and early 1990s, inflation over 1,000 percent per year wreaked havoc on the daily lives of individuals, firms, and government. Given the damage of inflation, it is remarkable that the dominant network never abandoned the belief in social inclusion. In the next chapter, we describe how the belief in social inclusion remained strong in the next period, though was subservient to fiscal and monetary orthodoxy.

THE TRANSITION TO DEMOCRACY

In the previous chapter, we described how the transition to democracy in Brazil, ushering in a period known as the New Republic (1988–1994), neither came about by rupture nor through direct elections, but through a voluntary, albeit protracted and negotiated, restitution of power to civilian hands.[1] The first civilian government after twenty-one years of authoritarian regime came to power in Brazil under great pressure for greater political and social inclusion. The results of the agreements brokered by the military government ushered in a very heterogeneous dominant network: politically important was the coalition known as the Democratic Alliance, under the leadership of Tancredo Neves, of the Brazilian Democratic Movement Party (PMDB) and the Liberal Front Party (PFL). Most business interests and trade unions aligned with the political coalition.

Tancredo won the (indirect) first election in 1984 but took ill and died on the eve of his inauguration. The shock shook the nation to its core,

---

[1] This is consistent with the North, Wallis, and Weingast (2009) and Wallis (2014) views about dominant networks among the elite and contrasts with the notion that redistributional conflicts between elites and masses set in motion the dynamics as proposed by Acemoglu and Robinson (2006). We return to this point in chapter 7.

fed conspiracy theories about interest groups impeding the return to democracy, and introduced massive uncertainty about the future. Furthermore, it raised doubts about the capacity of the new civilian government to deliver an inclusive agenda under the leadership of Vice President José Sarney, a conservative political figure with very different credentials from Tancredo's. Sarney's past involvement with the pro-regime Aliança Renovadora Nacional (ARENA) party during the military period raised doubts about his suitability as an agent of change in a process that intended to break so clearly from the past.

Sarney lacked political legitimacy, making the transition to the first civilian government vulnerable to pressure for immediate structural changes not only in the economic and political spheres but also in social policies and inclusion. The notion prevailed that the new government had to make good on a social debt toward those who had been excluded from the "economic miracle" of the previous decade. Sarney responded to the inclusionary pressures by adopting the motto *Tudo Pelo Social* (everything for the social good) as the top priority of his administration.

The political manifesto of the Tancredo/Sarney campaign in 1984, known as the "Commitment to the Nation," reflected the aspiration of an inclusive and comprehensive agenda for change. With regard to social policies, the manifesto listed as goals resolving income inequalities; implementing emergency measures against hunger and unemployment; revising wage policy and eliminating wage controls; and guaranteeing the autonomy of labor organizations. The political agenda of the manifesto was equally overambitious: restoring direct suffrage for the president and all mayors of city capitals; convening a Constituent Assembly; restoring the independence of the judiciary and legislative branches; strengthening of the country's federal structure, with effective financial and political autonomy of states and municipalities; and allowing the unfettered formation of new political parties. Finally, the economic agenda included resuming economic growth; rescheduling foreign debt; fighting inflation; implementing tax reform; correcting regional inequalities; and supporting free enterprise with special emphasis on small to medium-sized national firms.

The all-encompassing nature of the inclusive agenda generated extremely high expectations and soon revealed the limits of the heterogeneous coalition, combined with a politically vulnerable president. To demonstrate goodwill and that his government would act in a democratic fashion, President Sarney opted not to use his unilateral decree and urgency powers until a new constitution was written and approved. Congress duly stepped in to fill the power vacuum. Sarney also maintained the cabinet chosen by Tancredo Neves. The decisions sent contradictory signals to the public about government policies. The president promised to address the country's difficult economic and social agenda. The minister of planning, João Sayad, pressured for a heterodox economic policy, supporting Sarney's promise, but the minister of finance, Francisco Dornelles, put forward an orthodox approach through domestic fiscal and monetary austerity, establishing a 10 percent cut in public spending, a two-month suspension of all government bank lending, and a one-year freeze of all public sector hiring. After twenty-one years of dictatorship, Congress received the announcement of such orthodox and austere policies with disappointment. They wanted to demonstrate to their constituents, especially prior to the November 1986 elections, that they were responsive to the expectation of voters for social inclusion. According to the *Folha de São Paulo* (January 14, 1986), only 20 percent of legislators declared support for Sarney's administration, 56 percent remained politically neutral, and 25 percent were openly hostile.

As a consequence, Sarney announced that the government would still strive to meet its foreign debt commitments, but not at the expenses of social deprivation at home. Addressing social needs with only modest economic growth meant adding fuel to the already inflationary fire of 200 percent in 1985. Roaring inflation prompted citizens to construct their daily lives in ways to minimize the costs of inflation. The wealthy accessed overnight money market accounts, but the poor suffered enormously. In a struggle to impose his political leadership, Sarney replaced the orthodox minister of finance with an active businessman of the Federation of the Industries of the State of São Paulo (FIESP) who favored growth over fiscal austerity and who had been very critical of the demands for adjustment by the IMF.

In an attempt to quell inflation, Sarney enacted by decree the heterodox *Plano Cruzado* in early 1986. Initially, the plan appeared to work and halted the falling popularity of the president and his governing coalition. The *Cruzado Plan* froze prices, which over time led to shortages from excess demand.

The upcoming general election of November 1986, which would also elect the legislators who would draft the new constitution, made it politically expedient to postpone the realignment of prices. The political success of the *Cruzado Plan* paid off by generating a massive victory for the PMDB, which won all but one race for governorships, as well as the majority of the Chamber of Deputies (53 percent) and of the Senate (63 percent). It was the largest electoral victory to date by a political party in Brazil's proportional representation multiparty system, whose nature normally tends toward fragmentation.

Shortly after the election, the government implemented price adjustments to address the shortages of goods. The impact of the adjustment package, named *Cruzado Plan II*, on the president's authority and popularity was very negative. The optimism generated by the first *Cruzado Plan* transformed into disillusionment as voters felt cheated with *Cruzado II*. The political capital of Sarney eroded quickly, and he no longer managed to unify the Democratic Alliance coalition.

To make matters worse, Brazil did not meet the payments on its debt to private creditors and declared insolvency. Brazil also declared a unilateral partial moratorium on its foreign debt interest payments. The country's default was a historical watershed: in a televised pronouncement in February 1987, Sarney announced the government's decision, playing down its long-lasting consequences. The moratorium was but the first sign of significant flaws in the development model pursued by previous governments, and it would be followed by hyperinflation and fiscal collapse.

In the subsequent years, Brazil tried a series of other economic plans: the *Bresser Plan* in 1987; the "rice and beans policy" in 1988; the *Summer Plan* in 1989; the *Collor Plan* in 1990; and the *Collor Plan II* in 1991.[2] The sequence of frustrating failures induced a fatigue with government stabilization policy among the population and initiated a quickly declining trend in the hope and optimism toward the country's new democratic situation.

Meanwhile, Congress voted for and the president approved a series of measures aimed at restoring democratic institutions: the restoration of direct presidential elections; the right to vote for illiterates; legalization of all political parties including the Communist Party; and direct elections of mayors for all cities. The full restoration of democratic institutions was the most consensual agenda of the Sarney government. The military government in 1982 allowed direct elections for governors. This gave governors considerable political clout because of their legitimate election, though it made President Sarney more vulnerable. At this time, states collected the "state" tax directly, which gave governors considerable influence on spending and influenced the careers of legislators in a gubernatorial coattails effect (Samuels 2000).

Faced with the demands of civil society and a lack of funding due to the national fiscal crisis, the elected governors financed their programs and policies by issuing bonds and debentures from the state treasuries, state enterprises, and especially through state banks that acted as de facto issuers of money because the central bank generally monetized the debts of politically powerful states. This was done with few concerns for the solvency of states. The behavior "was encouraged by the certainty that in the end, [the states] would be rescued by the federal government. Brazilian cooperative federalism suffered from serious moral hazard" (Gama Neto 2011).

In this scenario of political disarray and economic turmoil, the government initiated a process of drafting a new constitution. The general

2 We elaborate on these plans later in the chapter.

disillusionment with the government led political players from the governing coalition as well as from the opposition to allocate their political energy to the new Constituent Assembly. The process of drafting the constitution, the final charter itself, and the subsequent amendments provides important insights into the beliefs underpinning institutional change.

Codifying Beliefs: The Constitution of 1988

Reporting the promulgation of Brazil's new constitution, the *New York Times* posed the fundamental question for Brazil: "how to put the Constitution into operation in a country with rampant corruption, runaway inflation and vast social inequality?"[3] With the benefit of hindsight, the country has been highly successful since 1993: hyperinflation has been eliminated, inequality lessened, and corruption reduced.

Earlier, we referred to the constitution as a watershed. Brazil's "Machiavellian moment"[4] lasted at least a decade. The long "constitutional moment" from 1987 to 1997 was a critical transition in which the nation confronted its "constitutional quandaries" (Schofield 2006: 1). First, a new core belief in social inclusion solidified, and later, during the constitutional reforms in the mid-1990s, the belief in fiscally sustained inclusion and an open economy emerged.

Constitutional amendments followed the hyperinflation and fiscal crisis, which resulted ultimately from the implementation of the 1988 charter, shattering the existing statist views. The whole process entailed extensive political squabbling and bargaining. The convoluted and erratic pace of subsequent amendments resulted from actors facing high levels of uncertainty about the link between institutions and outcomes.

In what follows, we will expand on three points. First, the initial Constitution of 1988 embodied the beliefs about a new social contract. The process was messy and full of ugly compromises, as there was no template. The constitution also incorporated old beliefs that led to an inconsistent and contradictory text. Second, the very constitution-making

---

3 "Brazil Complete New Constitution," *New York Times*, September 3, 1988, http://www.nytimes.com/1988/09/03/world/brazil-complete-new-constitution.html.
4 We borrow the expression from Pocock (1975), who used it to denote a moment when a new republic first confronts the problem of maintaining the stability of its ideals and institutions. For our purposes, the new Brazilian Constitution is not the one approved in 1988, but the current charter that incorporates the extensive amendments of its articles on the role of the state in the economy passed in 1995–1997. None of the sixty-six amendments approved between 1998 and 2014 significantly altered any of these articles. Thus, the current constitution may be viewed as the "political charter" approved in 1988 and the "economic charter" passed in 1995–1997.

process was unprecedentedly inclusive and participatory, reinforcing the beliefs that it reflected. Third, the constitution—as amended in 1995–1997—fundamentally altered the subsequent path of Brazil.

Several provisions had massive short-term consequences and are best conceptualized as an endogenous shock: the reduction of the voting age to sixteen and the elimination of the ban on illiterates opened political participation to millions of individuals who had hitherto been excluded.[5] Similarly, the extension of basic education and universal health care to all citizens, regardless of previous contributory history, and the equalization of the value of rural and urban benefits had major immediate impacts in terms of both citizenship and fiscal expenditures. These are the foundations of "dissipative inclusion," which we discuss in detail later in the chapter.

The beliefs among the dominant network in participatory democracy, rule of law, and social inclusion underpinned the beginning of the constitutional process. The constitution embodied the new beliefs, but also some old beliefs remained salient, for example, the role of the state in the economy. Ultimately, after a few years, the constitutional status quo led to rounds of hyperinflation and to new updated beliefs among those in power about the importance of macro stability and fiscal sustainability. In the wake of the constitutional reform process started during Cardoso's first administration (1995–1998), the government eliminated much of the constitution's statist provisions but left the core set of individual and collective rights, along with the clauses pertaining to separation of powers and rule of law, unscathed. This means that part of the set of beliefs formed during the transition to democracy in the late 1970s and 1980s took root and evolved over time leading to changes in the constitution. The economic beliefs—those on how the economy works—however, evolved in a different direction. As discussed thoroughly in chapter 5, the dominant network changed their beliefs in light of poor economic outcomes, particularly the hyperinflations in the early 1990s. Indeed, the hyperinflationary crises led to the recognition by the dominant network that the old closed economy no longer functioned and Brazil needed a break with the past.

Importantly, the views on the importance of rule of law have old roots, reflecting liberal republican concerns about separation of powers and presidential abuse that emerged in the nineteenth and early twentieth centuries. The beliefs in rule of law and social inclusion are the *core beliefs* of the new constitutional charter (Greif 2006; Schofield 2006).[6] The

---

5 These constitutional provisions were enacted in 1985 as amendments to the 1969 Constitution decreed by the military and subsequently incorporated to the charter of 1988.
6 The belief in rule of law dates back to republican concerns of the late nineteenth and early twentieth centuries. The belief in social inclusion hearkens back to the Vargas years from 1930 to 1945.

set of beliefs finally adopted at the end of the decade-long "constitutional moment" centered on the notion that social rights had to be reconciled with the fiscal constitution.

The military years forged the beliefs about democracy that undergirded the constitution-making process.[7] Lamounier expressed his first-hand experience from participating in the committee that drafted the first blueprint.

> The regime created by the constitution of 1946 was—and still is today—, viewed as elitist, socially irresponsible and open to populist manipulation. During the authoritarian period, from 1964 to 1985, a new concept of democracy flourished, most notably among the grass-roots and those groups linked to religious movements. The basic principle is that the new democracy has to be substantive and participatory rather than exclusively "representative", in the conventional usage of the term. (Souza and Lamounier 1989: 31)[8]

The constitutional convention redesigned political institutions, but there was some continuity in some basic constitutional structures. Electoral rules, federalism, and the presidential system remained unaltered in broad terms. Nonetheless, the new constitution delegated extensive powers to the president while significantly strengthening checks and balances. The key challenge for the Constituent Assembly members was how to reconcile the need to constrain a powerful executive while preventing political instability and guaranteeing that the president could implement his agenda.[9]

THE CONSTITUTION-MAKING PROCESS

In 2014, the Constitution of 1988 is still widely viewed as a historical landmark. With 245 articles, the Brazilian Constitution is one of the world's longest and most detailed constitutions. In addition to provisions dealing with separation of powers and individual rights and guarantees,

7 In terms of current debates in political theory, these concerns are consistent with the so-called republicanism and its emphasis on political participation and active citizenship rather than a return to direct democracy.

8 A majority defeated a dissenting view represented by a group of conservative legislators in the vote on the legal definition of the Representative Republic of Brazil where the people are represented indirectly.

9 The concern for constraining a powerful executive while preventing gridlock followed from the experiences of the First or Old Republic (1891–1930) and the Estado Novo (1937–1945). The concern with efficiency and stability emerged from experiences of the populist democratic period (1946–1964).

the constitution contains numerous articles pertaining to public policy issues. Not surprisingly, it has been termed a "code," a "constitutional monstrosity," and an "ugly compromise" (see Howard 1996; Reich 1998; Sartori 1994). "Like a cathedral originally constructed as a hotel, the new Constitution is structurally flawed" (Rosenn 1990: 779). The constitution required enactment of some 285 ordinary statutes and 41 complementary laws in order to make its provisions effective. The unwieldy nature of the constitution resulted from a need for the Constituent Assembly to complete a constitution, which was possible only by postponing the details to future legislation (Rosenn 1990: 778). Its very provisional and contingent nature generated a "constitutional" culture solidifying social inclusion: The constitution was the product of an extensive bargaining process and therefore contains numerous technical flaws and inconsistencies as well as concessions:

> The constitution of 1988 is not the ideal constitution of any single group. Maybe its virtues are precisely its very flaws, imperfections that result from its delayed, controversial, and convoluted constitution-making process, which was the work of intense popular participation, of the contradictions of Brazilian society, and by the same token of much negotiation.[10]

An "ugly" but functional "compromise," the constitution became the focal point of myriad interest groups in a context characterized by strong political fragmentation. A strong presidential system was one of the few elements that was not controversial and yet had huge downstream effects, enabling Cardoso to initiate the "critical transition."

The constitution-making process bore the imprints of two key episodes from the earlier democratization process: the failure of the campaign for direct elections (*Diretas Já*) for president, the largest mass movement in Brazilian history; and the death of the indirectly elected Tancredo Neves on the eve of his inauguration as president, and the subsequent inauguration of José Sarney, a conservative provincial politician closely associated with the former regime. Severing the links with the past became the paramount task.

Notably, the constitution-making process entailed vesting the ordinary legislature, elected in 1982 (senators) and 1986 (federal deputies), with the powers to draft a new constitution, as opposed to a separate Constituent Assembly. Although many political actors supported the idea of amending the 1946 Constitution—maintaining some articles introduced

---

10 The quote is from the constitutional scholar Afonso da Silva (2002: 238). Other scholars, including Martínez-Lara (1996) and Reich (1998), share this general interpretation about the constitution.

by the military's Constitution of 1967—the proposal for an entirely new charter gained force after massive popular mobilization for an independent drafting body. With the passage of Amendment 26 to the Constitution of 1967, the current legislative body became simultaneously involved in a two-level game of bargaining over ordinary legislative matters and over constitutional issues.

The drafting process entailed massive popular participation involving thousands of working groups all over the country in a host of different types of organizations including universities, firms, neighborhood organizations, churches, recreational institutions, and business associations.[11] Grassroots organizations presented a total of 188 popular amendments containing more than 12 million signatures (Pilatti 2008).

The drafting process involved interest groups in many ways. Some provided advocacy services whereas others extensively monitored the voting behavior of participants. The absence of a strong hegemonic actor in the process—the president was relatively weak and the party system fragmented—allowed for extensive lobbying activities by interest groups. Volatile coalitions formed and disappeared swiftly: "these coalitions were not by any means consistent and stable. They had to be shaped, and reshaped, according to the issue at hand, involving re-alignments article by article and sometimes word by word" (Martínez-Lara 1996: 196).

The constitution-making process spanned nineteen months, making the Brazilian Constituent Assembly one of the longest in history. The long time frame of the drafting process provided ample opportunity for interest groups to exert influence in the decision making of the Constituent Assembly. The lengthy constitutional assemblies led to a long charter but, more importantly, raised the stakes of the constitutional game.[12] Text specificity implies that every single organized interest has a stake in the constitution, thus contributing to the endurance of its core set of values and principles and relative effectiveness in many issue areas (Elkins, Ginsburg, and Melton 2009: 86–87).

---

11 Martínez-Lara (1996: 196–97) points out: "In their attempt to influence the decision-making, these groups showed a high level of organizational sophistication, using all types of available methods: direct influence in the selection of candidates responsive to their demands, the use of all forms of media communication as well as more direct methods, such as rallies and demonstrations." The media offered extensive support for the creation of groups and presentation of proposals by collecting and sending the proposals to the Constituent Assembly. The *Globo* media conglomerate ran spots encouraging the population to submit proposals. Citizens sent more than 72,000 individual proposals to the Constituent Assembly secretariat (Montclaire et al. 1991). See also the handbook on how to participate in the drafting process by Herkenhoff (1986).

12 Sixty percent of the legislators polled at the beginning of the drafting process said that they "preferred a short text" (Martínez-Lara 1996: 72).

The level of popular and interest group participation, the highly decentralized format adopted for the works, and the duration of the drafting process all contributed to make the text an inchoate collage of proposals, some of which displayed inconsistencies.

> The Brazilian constitutional convention was characterized by extraordinary public involvement, including the submission of citizen proposals. . . . The Brazilian charter is an unwieldy document to be sure, but a highly public one in its origin and provisions. Already, it has endured significantly longer than has the typical Latin American constitution. (Elkins, Ginsburg, and Melton 2009: 79)

Notwithstanding its numerous technical flaws, it constituted a focal point for the actors involved in the transition process.[13] It strengthened the belief that a change in the rules of the game required bargaining and compromise in Congress. This meant that violent or arbitrary means were no longer acceptable as instruments of change. The choice of flexible amendment rules made possible active amendment activity aimed at eliminating problematic provisions and adapting the text to new circumstances.[14] The massive participation in the constitutional process reflected the dominant beliefs in democracy and social inclusion. The protracted constitution-making process and its highly participatory nature further reinforced these beliefs.

The constitution drafting in Brazil should be assessed against the backdrop of alternative scenarios. The negotiation process could have turned into gridlock and eventually result in the perpetuation of the old regime in different forms or lead to a fully fledged authoritarian solution. Another scenario is cycling and a protracted process without agreement on a set of institutional proposals (Reich 1998). The open-ended character of the document led Rosenn (1990) to refer to Brazil's "transient constitutionalism." Unlike classical constitutions that provide a stable framework for the rules of the game, the Brazilian charter provided a stable focal point but without clear rules because of the numerous inconsistencies. Constitutional politics in Brazil in the 1990s and 2000s took on the form normatively advanced by scholars such as Holmes and Sunstein (1995): a long and detailed charter, which was a product of intense bargaining and participation, with permissible rules of amendment, precluding the entrenchment of provisions in a context of high uncertainty and

---

13 On constitutions as a focal point, see Hadfield and Weingast (2014a) and more generally Hadfield and Weingast (2014b).
14 Amendments to the constitution require approval by a qualified majority of three-fifths of the legislators in two rounds of vote in the two houses. See also chapter 5 on the Cardoso years.

contingent compromises. With Congress at the center of the bargaining process, democratic politics had legitimacy. The alternative of a shorter constitution with strict amendment rules would have resulted in a larger role for the Supreme Court.[15]

The decision-making process in the Constituent Assembly was indeed remarkably decentralized and conflict-ridden (Praça and Noronha 2012; Melo 2013). The first draft received 1,636 amendments. The initial process was unworkable, so Congress rebooted the process with twenty-four thematic committees. Congress established an integration committee made up of forty-nine legislators—chosen in observance of the seat shares of each party—to review and integrate the draft chapters and sections into a complete working draft (*substitutivo*), which was then discussed and voted on by the full assembly membership. At this stage, Congress voted on the 200 popular amendments submitted, and the process became more centralized.[16] The subcommittee and (thematic) committee work entailed 182 public hearings—and considerable amendment activity. The committees reviewed and amended the work of the subcommittees.[17]

The integration committee produced two substitutivos, named *Cabral 1* and *Cabral 2*, respectively, the second following after general dissatisfaction with *Cabral 1*. Aptly nicknamed the "*Frankenstein* project," *Cabral 1* contained 501 articles along with numerous detailed provisions (Martínez-Lara 1996: 109–10). In the second substitutivo, congressmen proposed 20,790 amendments, as well as accepting 83 popular amendments, which restored some of the dirigiste and protective provisions of the initial drafts. The resulting text reflected the nationalist and statist preferences of the presiding commission, which controlled all assignments of the rapporteur. This draft text—known as project A—prompted a reaction on the part of conservative forces within the assembly, leading to a mobilization to change the amendment rules to be used in the final vote on the draft.[18] The immediate justification was the explosive number of more than eight thousand *destaques*—specific amendments to a title or chapter to be voted separately. A cross-party coalition of conservative legislators—nicknamed the *Centrão* (big center)—mobilized legislators to pass a proposal stipulating that the destaques apply to whole chapters

15 As suggested in Knight (2001), who explores the trade-offs involved in the choice of detailed constitutions, amendment rules, and the scope of constitutional interpretation.
16 For the following details, we rely on Martínez-Lara (1996).
17 Congress addressed 14,000 amendments in two rounds. In turn, the subcommittee and committees received 6,360 amendments.
18 The argument that the preferences of the presiding committee were significantly to the left of the floor median is contested in D. Medeiros (2012), who argues that the choice of system of government was the divisive issue prompting the reaction.

and rest on a simple majority of votes.[19] The procedures allowed the Centrão to overcome collective-action problems of sustaining a majority (280 legislators) in key votes.

The Centrão faced collective-action problems and was more effective as a veto player against the numerous proposals of trade unions and civic organizations than as a proactive group (D. Medeiros 2012). The choice of the system of government and land reform most concerned the interests of the Centrão.

The final document represented the outcome of intense bargaining and accommodation as well as the short-term balance of power between the Democratic Alliance and the conservative political forces at specific vote opportunities. As a consequence, the final document represented a hodge-podge of liberal, statist, developmentalist, and social-democratic views, though with an overall left-wing slant. A number of *idées forces* prevailed, including a strong rejection of authoritarianism and endorsement of democratic principles, including both direct and representative democracy models; a remarkable affirmation of individual and collective rights; a vigorous defense of the rule of law and separation of powers; and last but not least, a strong bias toward decentralization, politically, administratively, and fiscally.

The most important electoral changes in the constitution included reaffirming the right to vote for illiterates, earlier promulgated as Amendment 25 (of May 15, 1985) to the 1967 Constitution; and lowering the voting age from eighteen to sixteen. The changes in the electoral rules resulted from the belief in social inclusion held by the dominant network rather than by mass mobilization.

Emblematic of the centrality of individual and collective rights and guarantees in the constitution was the inclusion of a chapter devoted to these issues in the first part of the constitutional text, instead of putting it at the end as in all previous constitutions. The overarching concern about the disrespect for the law during the military rule prompted the drafters to hardwire rights in the constitution, rather than ordinary legislation.

> Many of the new Constitution's provisions represent significant liberal or progressive advancements, particularly with regard to protection of individual rights and expansion of the rights of the working class. Article 5 protects a large number of individual and collective rights. This enormous article appears to protect virtually every form of known human right. (Rosenn 1990: 789)

19 The core group of legislators who formed the Centrão came from the Brazilian Labor Party (PTB), PFL, Partido Democrático Social (PDS), Christian Democratic Party (PDC), Liberal Party (PL), and a right-wing group of more than one hundred legislators from the PMDB.

Another important change was in procedures for protecting constitutional and legal rights, which previously were woefully inadequate.[20]

The new constitution also significantly strengthened the prerogatives in budgetary matters and oversight for the legislature. The judiciary branch, in turn, acquired new powers, and the constitution dramatically streamlined and empowered both the public prosecutor's office and the court of accounts. The constitution also significantly extended judicial review. Before 1988, decisions by the Supreme Court in representation actions had *erga omnes* effects, but only the attorney general had standing to bring such an action. The new constitution extended standing rights in the hands of many: the president of the Republic; the executive committees of the Senate, Chamber of Deputies, or state legislatures; governors of states; the Federal Council of the Brazilian Bar Association; any political party represented in Congress; and any syndical confederation or national class entity.[21]

By virtual unanimity, the Constituent Assembly approved universalistic provisions calling for meritocratic hiring in the public sector as well as uniform entitlements and social security benefits for both urban and rural populations. The most contentious issues in the Constituent Assembly debates involved land reform; industrial/labor relations and labor legislation; the role of the military (including amnesty for political crimes); market protection for national firms and state monopolies; and the paramount issues surrounding the system of government, for example, presidential versus parliamentary. President Sarney wished to depart with the legacy of securing a strong presidential system. By mobilizing pork and public sector jobs, Sarney attracted legislators to reject the semi-presidentialist formula approved in the various early drafts from the commission of notables (the Afonso Arinos Commission). A strong presidential system also had the support of the military, and the final draft gave extensive powers to the president along with a five-year term.

The military wielded some veto power over security issues—rejecting the creation of a defense ministry headed by a civilian. The military also weighed in on other issues: prohibiting the right to strike in essential services, and the expropriation of land in productive areas. Along with the system of government, land reform was another contentious issue and the one that galvanized the work of the Centrão. Again, the veto power of the Centrão mattered. The Centrão blocked proposals for land

---

20 Despite the vicissitudes of the implementation of these rights, they are not mere rhetorical elements. As we show in chapters 5 and 6, they have played a crucial and increasingly determining role in public life.

21 The constitution renamed the existing representation the *Acão Direta de Constitucionalidade* (direct action of unconstitutionality).

expropriation of productive farms as well as more radical redistributive proposals, such as compensation of landowners with government bonds. Importantly, this was the area where the redistributive threat in a highly unequal society was strongest and the potential use of violence loomed large. More aggressive land reform provisions in the constitution would undoubtedly have prompted greater rural violence in subsequent years.

Although the Centrão presented some pro-market amendments, it was primarily interested in opposing the demands of trade unions and leftist parties, in particular the most openly radical and socialist proposals for agrarian reform. On a number of occasions, however, the Centrão adopted a conservative programmatic stance. On the vote on Article 1 of the Constitution, the Centrão opposed the constitutional definition of the Brazilian polity as a legal democratic state based on the principle that "all power emanates from the people, who exercise it by means of elected representatives or directly, as provided by this Constitution." It proposed a motion defending a minimalist definition by eliminating the expression "or directly," signaling a programmatic stance on representative democracy.

The constitution-making process entailed consensus on Import Substitution Industrialization (ISI) and nationalism among progressive and conservative factions. Many of the Centrão members aligned with leftist parties around the preferential treatment of Brazilian firms and state monopolies of mineral resources and oil. Leftist interests "confirmed their veto power and displayed some proactive behavior only when they joined forces with established conservative interests" (Pilatti 2008: 263).

The key ISI tenets first acquired constitutional status with the enactment of the Constitution of 1934 and reaffirmed in the Constitution of 1946. The 1934 Constitution called for the nationalization of mineral assets, oil, gas, and telecommunications, as well as of the insurance and savings and loans sectors. In addition, the former constitutions approved an array of provisions calling for preferential treatment for Brazilian firms.[22] The first draft of the constitution included measures to nationalize foreign-owned firms; to limit and to require public disclosure of all sums transferred abroad as royalties, profits, interest, and payments for use of technology; and to prohibit transfer to foreigners of all lands containing mineral resources. Once in control, the Centrão softened the more nationalist provisions contained in the earlier draft. Nonetheless, the constitution as enacted contained a large set of protectionist and dirigiste measures. These included the banning of foreign-owned companies from exploring for or extracting minerals; and the reaffirmation of

22 The definition of a Brazilian firm appeared for the first time in 1969 in Amendment 1 to the Constitution of 1967.

mineral deposits and hydroelectric sites as the property of the federal government.[23] Foreign firms engaged in mining, mineral exploration, or production of hydroelectric power in Brazil had four years to either give up effective control or industrialize their mineral output in Brazil. A constitutional provision barred foreign oil companies (then engaging in oil exploration through risk contracts with Petrobrás) from future operations.[24] A provision also prohibited foreign capital from operating in health care.

The constitution also codified the central tenets of ISI in myriad ordinary laws and materialized in an array of organizations both within and outside the state. The corporatist system of industrial labor relations that was put in place in the 1930s was part and parcel of ISI. Unions (worker and employer) enjoyed a monopoly of representation within territorial jurisdictions. The constitution mandated a compulsory annual contribution equivalent to one day of work to unions and labor courts, which mediated disputes and held discretionary power.[25] Business consisted of exporters and domestic firms. Domestic firms lobbied for and succeeded in embedding in the constitution a definition of Brazilian firms: "a firm whose effective control is permanently under the title, either directly or indirectly, of individuals resident and domiciled in Brazil or entities of domestic public law." Domestic firms received protective tariffs and the maintenance of existing monopolies as well as the extension of monopolies to new areas such as telecommunications and mining. But labor interests defeated business in its attempt to resist the expansion of social security benefits and protective labor legislation.

The constitution altered in fundamental ways how the government addressed social rights and redistributive issues. The scope of the changes is impressive and amounts to rewriting the social contract in Brazil: "Article 6 declares that education, health, labor, leisure, security, social security, protection of maternity and infancy, and assistance of the unprotected are social rights. Article 7 contains 34 subsections that read like a miniature, progressive labor code" (Rosenn 1990: 791). Article 7 stipulated a 120-day maternity leave as well as an (unspecified) right to paternity leave; an eight-hour day—six hours in uninterrupted shifts—plus a forty-four-hour workweek; a flat minimum wage equaling a minimum salary for all pecuniary pension benefits; the right to strike, constitutionally guaranteed except in the case of essential services. In addition, Article 7 also freed the creation, internal organization, and functioning of unions from public

---

23 Mineral exploration and mining is restricted to Brazilian individuals or firms with national capital who obtain authorization or a concession from the federal government.
24 Of the seventy-two exploratory contracts in force when this provision was enacted, only one resulted in a viable oil discovery.
25 The system survives to the time of this writing.

control.[26] Importantly for its impact on the budget, a new provision mandated the equalization of rural and urban social security benefits.

The losers from the constitution-making process consisted of an unholy alliance of pro-market/liberal forces and leftist groups who managed to secure that the constitution be subjected to a full revision in 1993. Business elites and liberal groups viewed the future revision as a window of opportunity for dismantling the statist elements in the constitution. However, the revision was a fiasco because of the eruption of a major budget scandal involving key legislators, and to the lukewarm support—or in many cases even veiled resistance—it received from President Itamar Franco (Melo 2002).

As a fiscal constitution, the Brazilian Constitution proved onerous. It massively expanded social rights and entitlements. The equalization of rural and urban social security benefits entailed a large fiscal burden because all existing and future rural pensioners would be entitled to a full minimum pension (equal to a minimum salary). The constitution granted public sector employees the status of civil servants, thus entitling them to a full replacement rate (100 percent) for their current salaries, as opposed to private sector pensions whose limit was set to a ceiling independent of current wage. The creation of the SUS (Unified Health System), entitling all citizens to a comprehensive array of health benefits independent of past contributions, came with a huge price tag. Importantly, the constitution mandated fiscal decentralization, which meant that the states and counties gained a larger share of the revenue pie, to the detriment of central government. Equally important was the rejection of privatization in favor of state-owned enterprises. Decentralization later delayed the adoption of effective fiscal and monetary policies to stabilize the currency. Hyperinflations and fiscal crises during the Sarney (1985–1989) and Collor (1990–1992) administrations shattered the remaining beliefs in developmentalism and social inclusion without fiscal boundaries. The hyperinflation crises provided a window of opportunity for leadership. Cardoso stepped into the leadership role and produced among the dominant network an updated set of beliefs—in fiscally sound social inclusion.

THE CONSTITUTION'S DELEGATION OF POWERS TO THE PRESIDENT

Foreigners who study Brazil today usually do so from the standpoint of her economic situation. Brazilians themselves do so. And both Brazilians and foreigners are baffled. Their studies lead them to no definite

26 The institutionalized labor elites that emerged during the Vargas Era pressured for these changes. However, the new labor unionism, which emerged in the late 1970s and which Lula symbolized, advanced a much stronger notion of union autonomy from the state.

conclusions and they fall back on grandiloquent, albeit sincere phrase about the Great Future of Brazil. But when things are continuously not well with a country of Brazil's formidable resources, there must be some causal factor that is constant to account for that phenomenon. High import duties, export taxes . . . , excessive borrowing valorization schemes, lack of continuity in the policy of public administration, social disturbances and revolutions—all these and other influences may be invoked to account for dislocation of trade and financial difficulties. *But they are not prime causes and in themselves they explain nothing. The origins of Brazil's troubles are to be sought in the defect of the political regime.* (Hambloch 1936: 1; emphasis added)

The drafters of the charter shared Hambloch's concern with the defects of the political regime. In particular, the Centrão worried about the role of the executive branch in the political system. The dominant network wanted to rein in the executive branch following two decades of military rule but also cared about governability. This explains one of their most important decisions, which prima facie seems paradoxical: the strengthening of presidential powers. The Constitution of 1988 delegated extensive powers to presidents, while at the same time considerably strengthening the checks and balances in the political system. The collective decision was the upshot of a set of beliefs resulting from the experiences of democracy in the 1940s and 1950s followed by twenty-one years of military rule.

During the democratic interregnum prior to the military regime, presidents lacked coordinating capacity. A lack of coordination brought instability. Both the Constitutions of 1934 and 1946 aimed at reining in presidential power and, as a result, created a weak presidency. In 1988, part of the set of beliefs informing constitutional choices about the role of the president was a mirror image of that underlying the choices in 1934 and 1946, to the extent that they aimed at introducing checks on the executive and constraining its action. But, more importantly, the framers also responded to the lack of governability during the democratic years of 1946 to 1964 and granted significant agenda-setting powers to the president to prevent gridlock.

The Constitution of 1988 vested the presidents with a number of agenda powers including the power to issue *medidas provisórias* (decrees with immediate legal effects); exclusive initiative of laws in budgetary matters limiting the ability of legislators interfering in the budgetary process; and procedural advantages such as the power to label a bill "urgent" (thereby granting it priority consideration in the legislative agenda). Still, the constitution contained a web of checks and balances constraining the president. Post-1988, successful presidents engaged in extensive bargaining with political partners in the coalition in order to control the agenda. In addition, "pork for policy" games (see chapter 5) became an integral part of presidential power.

The constitution considerably strengthened checks and balances and the rule of law. It granted autonomous status to the Ministério Público (MP) (public prosecutors' office), which some regard as the fourth branch of government (Kerche 2007).[27] The model adopted in Brazil is distinct from its counterparts elsewhere around the world because it combines a wide variety of instruments to defend collective rights with high levels of institutional independence (Arantes 2002, 2004). As in most countries, the MP prosecutes, in the name of the state, those who commit crimes. However, in Brazil, the MP has taken on an additional role in public policy making. The change began in 1985 when the government created a legal instrument known as the "public civil suit" (ação civil pública). It authorized the MP to take to court any person or entity for harm done to the environment, consumer rights, or the artistic, cultural, historical, tourist, or landscape patrimony of the nation.[28] The 1988 Constitution amplified the scope of the MP to "promote civil inquiries and public civil suits for the protection of public and social patrimony, of the environment and of other diffuse and collective interests." This article allowed the public ministry to take into its jurisdiction the monitoring of all public policy because any act of public policy making can be construed to affect "diffuse and collective interests." In effect, the constitution stipulated that social conflicts that previously would have been mediated only in the political arena could now also be brought to the judicial arena. Clearly, simply establishing a new role for the MP in the constitution would be innocuous if not accompanied by other provisions that granted the MP the conditions necessary to carry out that role. The constitution provided independence, resources, and legal instruments. Whereas before the constitution the MP was part of the executive power, the new charter made the MP autonomous, not only in terms of insulation from interference by the other powers but also in terms of budgets, which are hardwired and automatic. The only prerogative of the president is to choose the head of the federal public ministry from one of its members at the start of the term, being immovable thereafter. The independence extends to the level of the individual prosecutors. Becoming a MP is transparent but difficult and carries considerable prestige: a public exam open to all citizens with the necessary qualifications, though vacancies often remain unfilled because of the difficulty of the exam.

27 Prosecutors have the last word on whether criminal charges are filed, with the exception of those rare cases in which Brazilian law permits civil prosecution. In those cases, the prosecutor acts as custos legis and ensures that justice is delivered. They also have exclusive standing in all public civil actions that involve diffuse collective interests (Arantes 2002).

28 This discussion on the Ministério Público is from Mueller (2010).

The 1988 Constitution establishes that prosecutors cannot be fired, transferred, or have their salaries reduced. In addition, each prosecutor is independent within the profession, being immune from internal pressure as in effect there is only administrative and not functional hierarchy (Arantes 1999: 90). Salaries are among the highest in the country for public sector jobs, and as a consequence they attract highly competent people. In addition to resources, the MP possesses a set of powerful legal and judicial instruments. The first of these is the "Adjustment of Conduct" warrant, through which they can request that an individual, firm, or governmental entity cease or change a certain behavior or be prosecuted. In practice, this instrument has been a credible threat as it can impose significant costs even if the case is struck down in court.

The constitution also considerably strengthened the judicial branch. It fortified judicial review and granted rights of standing to a host of actors such as national associations, governors, political parties, and the Brazilian Bar Association, among others. The constitution also delegated a set of new powers to accountability agencies in charge of monitoring and auditing public expenditures. The Tribunal de Contas da União (National Tribunal of Accounts), in turn, had its status changed: it acquired new powers and prerogatives and much greater functional, financial, and administrative autonomy.[29] The constitution also mandated that Congress appoint six of the nine justices to the Tribunal de Contas da União (previously the president had the prerogative of selecting all members). Furthermore, legislative oversight became more robust.

Overall, the Constitution of 1988 strengthened the belief in social inclusion that undergirded the foundation for the subsequent institutional deepening that took place in the 1990s and 2000s. The constitution has been extensively amended since its enactment, reflecting changing beliefs not only about the economic role of the state but also about the constitutional structure. The decade-long constitutional moment ended with a consensus within the dominant network on fiscally sound social inclusion and powerful presidents operating in a constrained institutional environment. The constitution has become a focal point of Brazilian democracy. By playing this role, it legitimized procedure over substance, which is an essential part of democratic life.

BACK TO UNCERTAINTY AND CHAOS

The Constituent Assembly met amid deteriorating economic conditions. In this section, we provide a narrative of the process of the descent into chaos. Interestingly, the peak of hyperinflation occurred eighteen months

---

29 Similar changes occurred at the subnational level in Brazil (see Melo and Pereira 2013).

after the enactment of the constitution. We document the failed attempts at fighting inflation: the *Cruzado Plans I* and *II*, the *Bresser Plan*, and the *Summer Plan*. The *Collor Plan* is analyzed in the next subsection along with a broader discussion of the Collor administration.

Failures of the Brazilian Economic Plans before the Real

The early years after redemocratization brought about increased inflationary pressures, leading to the introduction of the *Plano Cruzado* by decree in February 1986. The main elements of this heterodox anti-inflation plan included freezing prices, wages, and exchange rates; and monetary reform. The plan initially achieved both its economic and political objectives: it tamed inflation (the monthly inflation rate, as measured by the general price index, declined from 22 percent in February 1986 to –1 percent in March). The overall level of economic activity accelerated. Industrial production increased 8.6 percent in the first quarter of 1986 from the corresponding period in 1985, and increased 10.6 and 11.7 percent in the second and third quarters, respectively. During the first few months following the *Cruzado Plan*, external accounts also remained strong. "Superficially, it seemed that Brazil had accomplished the trick of running solid external accounts and maintaining spectacular growth with rising real wages, diminishing unemployment, and insignificant inflation" (Baer and Beckerman 1989: 42). Moreover, the *Cruzado Plan* relieved the central bank from continuously operating the overnight market so as to assure liquidity.

The *Cruzado Plan*, designed to reduce inflation via a combination of price and wage freezes, boosted the president's falling popularity, calmed down political criticism, and reunified the Democratic Alliance. However, the increase in real income, which was implicit in the price freeze, quickly led to explosive demand for consumer goods, which overheated the entire economy. By sharply increasing real wages and freezing real prices from one day to the next, the government in fact decreed a massive income recomposition. Because the immediate consequence was to shift income toward low-income citizens, the rate of savings diminished dramatically. Aggregate demand rose sharply and rapidly pressured aggregate supply. Capacity utilization reached record levels, and demand for labor, particularly skilled workers and executives, pushed wages up further. The business sector reacted by reducing supply and intensifying political pressure for compensation.

Despite the successful start, the *Cruzado Plan* quickly turned sour (Fishlow 2011).[30] The *Cruzado Plan* failed by the end of 1986 as inflation

---

30 From the mid-1980s and into the 1990s, institutional reform advanced in tandem with efforts toward controlling inflation. Albert Fishlow recounts the challenges rampant inflation threw at policy makers and the various programs aimed at stabilizing the macro

revived, external accounts collapsed, and real growth sagged (Baer and Beckerman 1989). The plan was fatally flawed from the outset by having incorporated a substantial wage increase. Things got worse owing to the persistent public sector deficit combined with the relatively low exchange value of the Cruzado by the time it was launched. The poor execution of the plan also played an important role in its failure. The plan froze prices in disequilibrium far too long, and monetary policy was far too loose.

As time passed, political and electoral criteria dominated economic concerns because Sarney's popularity rested on the price freeze. The upcoming general election placed enormous pressure on Sarney to postpone realigning prices and adjustments. "Zero inflation" soon became the mantra to win the upcoming election. The plan succeeded politically, but the shortage of goods and a thriving black market cast a shadow over the sustainability of keeping inflation at bay. A week after the election, Sarney implemented *Cruzado II*, which increased taxes and realigned prices for middle-class consumer products (e.g., automobile prices up 80 percent, public utilities up 35 percent, and alcoholic beverages up 100 percent). Cooling consumption and restoring external accounts motivated *Cruzado II*. Rather than saving, consumers diverted their expenditure to other goods. The government adjusted the official exchange rate by mini-devaluations. Given the great uncertainty in the business community, the premium of the dollar in the black market stood at around 100 percent at the end of 1986. Inflation revived in the wake of *Cruzado II*. Inflation rose 8 percent in December 1986; 18 percent in January 1987; 14 percent in March; 19 percent in April; and 26 percent in May. By the middle of 1987, the yearly rate of inflation ran more than 1,000 percent. International reserves plummeted, and Brazil declared a unilateral partial moratorium on its foreign debt interest payments on February 1987.

The general mood of optimism generated by the *Cruzado Plan I* transformed to disillusionment as voters felt they had been cheated with *Cruzado II*, designed before the election but made public only afterward. Society felt that the whole stabilization plan was a crude political manipulation. Sarney's popularity sank, and he was no longer capable of unifying the Democratic Alliance coalition. The government appeared to be as vacillating, manipulative, and deceptive as the preceding military regime.

In April 1987, Luiz Carlos Bresser-Pereira replaced Dilson Funaro as minister of finance. Bresser introduced another heterodox plan called the *Bresser Plan*, set new prices and another initial wage freeze, this time

---

economy. The country went through a number of economic programs and different currencies, but until the *Real Plan*, with only limited success. Taming inflation could not have been achieved without a commitment to a balanced fiscal policy, and Fishlow discusses the relevant problems on that front.

with caps to be readjusted every three months. The *Bresser Plan* included a trigger mechanism for automatic wage increases and a target interest rate above inflation in a desperate attempt to prevent overheating the economy. According to Bresser-Pereira (1984) himself, the objective of his emergency plan was to reduce inflation to about 10 percent by the end of the year; to stem the depreciation of wages; to avoid recession; to reverse the international financial crisis; and to restructure the balance of payments. However, the strategy of freezing wages and prices once again quickly proved incapable of containing inflation. This was in large part due to the continued deficit spending by the government. Finance Minister Bresser-Pereira left office after failing to secure from Sarney a promise of larger fiscal revenues essential for successful price stabilization. His successor, Mailson da Nobrega, eschewed the now discredited policy of trying to freeze prices by edict and instead adopted a more modest day-to-day effort to control prices and public spending, known as the *Rice and Beans Plan* (which in Portuguese has the same meaning as the expression *plain vanilla*; that is, contrary to the others it was an orthodox plan). But by mid-1988, the economy was once again in crisis, with inflation running at 81 percent a month by March 1990; investment slowing; GDP growth at barely 1 percent; and unemployment on the rise.

Mailson da Nobrega followed the *Rice and Beans Plan* with the *Summer Plan*, once again desperately freezing prices and wages, and introducing a new currency, the Cruzado Novo. The *Summer Plan* was a shabby copy of its predecessors and collapsed quickly. The stamina of the government to propose new plans died, and Sarney's term ended on a melancholy note. The attention of the public focused on the first direct presidential election in almost thirty years, which was held on October 15, 1989. Fernando Collor de Melo, a little-known politician, considered by many an outsider, beat Luiz Inácio Lula da Silva (Lula) with a strong political platform against big government and for modernization of the national economy.

The Collor Government: Great Hope, Huge Disappointment

The inauguration of Fernando Collor generated great expectations and hope. Collor began his term in 1990 with a 70 percent approval rating. The electorate hoped for a definitive solution to hyperinflation; an end to endemic corruption; and renewed economic development through a liberal agenda of opening up the economy. When Collor took office in March 1990, inflation stood at a monthly rate of 81 percent. Even the gains in social and political inclusion brought little solace to the poor or the middle classes in the midst of this inflationary havoc.

In Collor's words, there was "only one rifle with one bullet" to kill inflation; that is, there was no room for trial and error. As if predicting how erratic his administration was going to be, or maybe forgetting his own rhetorical image, Collor gave the only gun with a sole bullet to an inexperienced shooter. He appointed a relatively unknown economist, Zelia Cardoso de Mello, as minister of finance, who promised to kill the monster by implementing a new heterodox economic shock plan formally entitled *New Brazil Plan* but popularly known as the *Collor Plan*.

The heart of the *Collor Plan* was opening and liberalizing the economy along with reducing government expenditures. As part of the plan, Collor initiated a new Industrial and Foreign Trade Policy (PICE) program, which raised real wages and promoted economic openness and trade liberalization (Villela 1997). PICE included a gradual reduction of tariffs (with protection of certain industries); an export financing mechanism through the creation of a Foreign Trade Bank; a reduction in customs duties; antidumping provisions; and government support for high-tech sectors. Three programs would assist the implementation of the PICE: (1) the Program of Industrial Competitiveness (PCI), (2) the Brazilian Program of Quality and Productivity (PBQP), and (3) the Program of Support to the Improvement of the Technological Capability of Industry (PACTI).

Formally, PICE had seemingly contradictory goals: the intention was to stimulate the entry of foreign companies while increasing local innovation (Villela 1997). The measures produced contradictory effects: local production saw improvements in quality and productivity in face of foreign competition; but PICE simultaneously curbed domestic innovation following from unrestricted competition from imported technology.

The Collor administration also launched the National Development Plan (PND). No previous administration attempted large privatizations. PND slated sixty-eight companies for privatization. Unlike traditional privatization programs that sought to finance a government's deficit, the PND aimed at reducing the public debt. Instead of currency, many investors used government bonds to pay for public companies. Between 1990 and 1992, PND privatized eighteen companies worth US$4 billion, mostly in the steel, fertilizer, and petrochemical sectors. The PND also terminated several government monopolies whose negative social impact was expected to be countered by increased competition.

The public viewed the *Collor Plan* with suspicion, which turned to resentment when the administration imposed a freeze on bank assets over US$1,300. Citizens felt betrayed when they could not access their money. Freezing liquid assets led to a dramatic fall in consumer spending and, as a result, reduced inflation rates substantially, from more than 70 percent per month in January to 10 percent per month in the following months. As inflation fell, business enthusiastically backed the *Collor Plan*. In a survey conducted by the Estado de São Paulo with forty big and midsize businesses in seven cities, the overwhelming majority demonstrated great optimism about the plan. As in the earlier initial support for the *Cruzado Plan* in 1986, the business community accepted sacrifice as long as the state fulfilled its obligations, especially the need for permanent deficit-reducing measures.

However, by December, when inflation rebounded to 20 percent per month, concerns about the success of the plan mounted, and business support deteriorated. The failure of the *Collor Plan* to control inflation led to a sharp decline in presidential support by the public as well as within Congress. A number of works critical of the program appeared shortly after its implementation: Longo (1992) criticized the fiscal imbalances; and Simonsen (1991) objected to its technical details. Critics feared that if the government did not reduce expenditures or raise revenues quickly that they would have to resort to borrowing on the external market at exorbitant interest rates to compensate investors for the possibility of a new moratorium.

Not only was the implementation messy, but the theory behind the plan was questionable (Carvalho 2003). Furthermore, the government lost credibility by reneging on commitments. The short-term gain in cash flow soon turned into an explosive growth of internal debt and higher inflation. The prognosis of the critics proved correct: by the time the government released the frozen Cruzados eighteen months later, Brazil had reverted back to hyperinflation. The *Collor Plan* was an abject failure.

Faced with deteriorating economic conditions, the government announced *Plano Collor II* in December 1990, which had a similar initial price freeze but emphasized better management tools for deficits along with budget cuts for state enterprises. The administration hoped that one more price shock would rid the economy of inflation. *Collor II*, like its predecessor, failed. Collor blamed the business community for rising inflation and attacked the auto and pharmaceutical industries in particular for raising prices. Collor apparently mistook his initial popularity and success at reducing inflation as a pass to rule without orchestrating political support in Congress. Collor chose to develop direct connections with voters instead of coordinating via a coalition (Kernell 1997). By early 1992, Collor had little support with the public at large, the business community, or Congress.

A political bombshell hit Collor in May 1992, when Pedro Collor (the president's younger brother) accused President Collor of involvement in an influence-peddling scheme allegedly run by his former campaign treasurer, Paulo César Farias. In response, the Federal Police and Congress began independent investigations. On August 26, 1992, Congress released its final inquiry report, concluding there was evidence that Fernando Collor had personal expenses paid by money raised by Paulo César Farias. The president of the Brazilian Bar Association and the president of the

Brazilian Press Association formally accused President Collor of having committed crimes of responsibility (the Brazilian equivalent of "high crimes and misdemeanors") warranting the removal of Collor from office per the constitutional and legal norms regulating impeachment proceedings. In response, the Chamber of Deputies (the lower house of Congress) initiated impeachment proceedings. On September 29, 1992, the deputies voted overwhelmingly (441–38) in favor of the impeachment of President Collor.

Facing almost certain conviction and removal from office by the Senate, Collor resigned on December 29, 1992, during the end of proceedings in the Senate. The Senate adjourned, and the full Congress met in a joint session to take formal notice of the resignation, proclaim the office of president vacant, and then swear in the vice president, Itamar Franco, as president, as stipulated by the constitution.

Itamar Franco, a quirky and relatively marginal political figure, succeeded Collor in office, inaugurating a salvation government. With the exception of the PT, which preferred not to occupy formal positions in the government, all other political parties became part of the governing coalition of Itamar. The decision by Itamar to reestablish the coalition-based presidentialism rebuilt bridges between the executive and legislative branches.

By the time of his inauguration, inflation was 4 percent a day and Itamar changed his finance minister three times in his first four months before appointing his then chancellor and foreign minister, Fernando Henrique Cardoso, as finance minister in May 1993. Cardoso recruited a team of prominent economists, mostly from the Department of Economics of the Catholic University of Rio de Janeiro, to prepare a new economic plan (called the *Real Plan*). The implementation of the *Real Plan* was gradual and transparent, and its success was realized quickly and increased with time. Annual inflation fell from the four-digit level in 1994 to less than 5 percent in 1998. For the first time in decades, Brazil experienced sustainable price stability and encouraging GDP growth, averaging 4 percent a year from 1994 to 1997.

As a consequence of the mounting success of the *Real Plan*, Cardoso resigned as finance minister in April 1994 and ran for president in the upcoming October election. Cardoso had considerable support: President Itamar; the Brazilian Social Democracy Party (PSDB) (Cardoso's party); an electoral coalition including the PFL; and a group of prominent PMDB legislators. But Cardoso ran against a strong contender: popular front-runner Luiz Inácio Lula da Silva from the Workers' Party (PT). Lula ran on a platform of aggressive social reforms and denounced the *Real Plan* as one more economic plan doomed to fail. Beating the odds, Brazil elected Cardoso as president.

CHAPTER 5

Cardoso Seizes a Window of Opportunity (1993–2002)

> It ought to be remembered that there is nothing more difficult to take in hand, more perilous to conduct, or more uncertain in its success, than to take the lead in the introduction of a new order of things.
>
> Because the innovator has for enemies all those who have done well under the old conditions, and lukewarm defenders in those who may do well under the new. This coolness arises . . . partly from the incredulity of men, who do not readily believe in new things until they have had a long experience of them.
>
> —Nicolló Machiavelli, *The Prince* ([1532] 1998, 23)

> You can't inflate your troubles away or allow mountains of debt to build up. . . . Building prosperity requires caution and patience. It requires time. Populism is a shortcut that doesn't work.
>
> —Fernando Henrique Cardoso (2006, 679)

FERNANDO HENRIQUE CARDOSO SEIZED A WINDOW OF OPPORTUNITY TO move Brazil toward a more open society, both politically and economically. This was not an easy task, and, as discussed in the introduction, Brazil was an unlikely candidate for massive institutional change. Cardoso and his economic team changed the trajectory of Brazilian development by exercising leadership in a cognitive and coordinative way. In part owing to its continental size, the country was inward looking and was one of the few countries that could boast high and relatively sustained growth rates during the Import Substitution Industrialization (ISI) in the postwar period. The country's relative success with the ISI model became an obstacle for change. Under the inherited shadow of hyperinflation and economic stagnation, Cardoso guided the dominant network to a restructuring of beliefs from the past, deep-seated illiberal beliefs. "Antiliberal ideas such as corporatism, import substituting industrialization, dependency theories, and structuralism have held a sturdier hegemony in

Brazil than in most other developing countries" (Schneider 1992: 235). The 1988 Constitution of Brazil encapsulated these beliefs and over time acquired legitimacy. In addition, because democracy, along with social inclusion as discussed in chapter 4, preceded market reforms, the special interests that could oppose change had to be convinced that massive changes would be beneficial. This took place gradually and required sustained leadership and institutional deepening. The course taken was not preordained but evolved in the face of obstacles and opportunities.

The exhaustion of the ISI model and hyperinflation shattered the beliefs of the dominant network. Because outcomes did not match expectations, a window of opportunity arose, which Cardoso exploited. Our framework expects punctuated changes to be followed by a deepening in beliefs and institutions. The process was nonlinear and messy: as the Cardoso administration implemented trade liberalization and privatization policies and achieved monetary stabilization, firms redeployed assets in new entrepreneurial activities, and the groups in the dominant network who supported Cardoso increased as they updated their beliefs. Bankers, industrialists who benefitted from the previous order but now came to recognize its exhaustion, the middle classes, the expanding service sector businesses, and the media were crucial members of the new dominant network. In turn, hyperinflation and the experience as consumers crucially influenced the beliefs of citizens. An accumulation of incremental changes associated with the experience of monetary stability, social inclusion, and enhanced consumption engendered ultimately a process of punctuated change. Institutional deepening requires multiple loops around the circuit to shape and solidify beliefs among the dominant network. Through iterative changes in outcomes, institutional deepening solidifies core beliefs.

The process of the critical transition implied coordination and extensive political bargaining to overcome collective-action problems and smooth the up-front costs involved. The impact of the changes varied significantly across the sectors, and therefore the types of political bargaining also varied, and there were setbacks in negotiations. Our framework expects that after a big change, to stay the course with a reinforcement of beliefs and institutions is just as critical for completing a transition. The successful stabilization plan required not just the *Plano Real* but institutional deepening: the constitution was extensively amended to assure that stabilization was not transitory. We expect leaders to catalyze changes in the country's course and shifts of beliefs. In this section, we show that Cardoso used a set of instruments that was crucial for making institutional change viable. A strong president armed with a suitable toolkit, which included "pork for policy" instruments, was crucial for ensuring the legislative approval of a vast agenda of institutional change in a fragmented polity.

The emerging belief system was an amalgamation of competing beliefs, and we find that leadership played a role in this process. Over time, the population at large, as well as politicians of all stripes and economic factions, updated their beliefs, generating extensive support for a process of institutional deepening based on fiscally sound social inclusion.

THE REAL PLAN

The window of opportunity for Cardoso when he was appointed finance minister arose because of the failure of prior stabilization plans, and the weakness of President Itamar Franco, who succeeded after the impeachment of President Collor. Previous stabilization plans involved a combination of wage and price freezes; oftentimes sprung on the public—*Cruzado I and II Plans* (both in 1986) and *Collor Plans* (1990–1991). Cardoso's focus as a finance minister was macroeconomic stabilization rather than the wider reform agenda that he advanced as president. In his term as finance minister, Cardoso did not get involved in the controversy around trade liberalization or privatization but capitalized on the liberal trade path embarked on by President Collor. However, the fight against inflation had as one of its key anchors the inflow of imports to drive down domestic prices.

The popular appeal of the *Real Plan* introduced in February 1994 was twofold:[1] the quelling of inflation was the biggest anxiety affecting a majority of the population; and the design of the plan was relatively simple and transparent. For Cardoso's team, it was apparent that fiscal deficits were a major component of inflation because of monetization of the deficits by the Central Bank. The economic team composed of Gustavo Franco, Pedro Malan, and Pérsio Arida, among others, had learned from past failures as well as from foreign models. In the context of the early 1990s, the successful stabilization plans included those of Israel and Argentina.[2] At the time, Argentina's convertibility program (1991) was the international showcase of a successful stabilization program. As a model, the Argentinean program involved the creation of a currency board and the dollarization of the economy, which in turn entailed important political costs because of the symbolic loss of national sovereignty. While Argentina seemed to prove that

1 The new currency was introduced in July 1, 1994, following a schedule envisaged in Provisional Measure 434 of February 1994, the legal instrument that officially launched the *Real Plan*.
2 Michael Bruno, as the World Bank's chief economist and the architect of Israel's 1985 stabilization plan, was a constant touchstone for the economists involved with the Brazilian stabilization program (see Prado 2005: 128; Williamson 1985; and Arida 1986, which contains an article by Bruno).

a solution to hyperinflation existed, there was great uncertainty among Brazilian policy makers about the benefits of a full dollarization, because of the political costs and the associated inflexibility.[3]

Cardoso's economic team looked backward and forward when advancing the *Real Plan*. They needed to tame inflation, which had reached 2,000 percent in the annualized period prior to June 1994, but also anticipated the long-term benefits of stabilization if they could stay the course with institutional deepening. The key issue was how to make the plan politically viable in the context of strong aversion to authoritarian solutions that involved not only temporary confiscation of assets, as in the *Collor Plan*, but also emergency measures calling for the freezing of prices and wages. Voters' rising aversion to policy surprises was well understood by the reformers.

Deindexation was the crucial issue area because of the potential disruption of the welfare of citizens in the short term. It was to be achieved via voluntary mechanisms. In practice, this involved a strategy of voluntary conversion of all contracts to a new monetary system—the URV—that would finally be replaced by a new currency.[4] Cardoso and his economic team devised a public campaign centered on the notion of "no shocks, transparency, and voluntary participation."[5] Cardoso's motto was: "Everything that will be done has to be transparent so that people believe in what is being done." Despite transparency, the uncertainty level surrounding the fate of the *Real Plan* was considerable. As one of the most influential economic journalists in Brazil argued: "The Real Plan was extracted by forceps. Nobody believed in it. Neither the government, politicians, business, trade unions, the IMF or the rich countries' governments. Even the inner circle of economists doubted that it could succeed" (Prado 2005: 204).

---

3 Dollarization and a currency board were advocated because they provided a credible commitment against political interference.

4 The only compulsory element was the prohibition of indexation in contracts with less than one year. URV was the acronym for Unidade Real de Valor, which was not an actual currency that could be used for paying bills or taxes. Rather, it was a reference of monetary value to be used in contracts. When it was created, it was valued 647.50 Cruzeiros Reais. Every day, the Central Bank would set the URV's value. So there might occur inflation in Cruzeiros Reais, but prices in URV would be fixed until the definitive creation of the new currency, the Real.

5 Cited in Prado (2005: 73). Elsewhere, Cardoso noted that the new democratic Brazil required a different modus operandi: "nothing will be secretive. We would anticipate the main steps and show that it would be a process not a miraculous act. Therefore, there was a need to deal with time and make people part of the process. There were risks: should the media not help in the explanations, should we not be capable of a certain didacticism, if disbelief won before the currency change we would have lost the war. *I chose to run the risk and not embark on a technocratic plan*" (Prado 2005: 175; emphasis added).

In part because Cardoso was finance minister and not president, there was significant uncertainty surrounding the government's commitment to the *Real Plan*. President Itamar favored a price freeze and doubted that the *Real Plan* would work. Industrial sector interests offered resistance because of the plan's redistributional consequences, particularly as a result of the use of trade liberalization as a currency stabilizer. Exporters worried about uncertainty in exchange rate policy. Public sector employees and the salaried in general worried about the impact of deindexation. Resistance from seemingly obvious losers from the *Real Plan* included public sector employees and public sector contractors as well as the interests associated with the ISI state development. Gustavo Franco, one of the architects of the *Real Plan* and the president of the Central Bank (1993–1999), noted publicly that "inflation had friends in high places." This is an accurate characterization: many economic agents benefitted from inflation.

In 1993, the year preceding the introduction of the new currency, the inflation rate had reached 2,477 percent. When it was introduced, inflation fell to 950 percent, to reach 10 percent in 1996 and 5 percent in 1997. Inflation aversion in Brazil was inversely correlated with its intensity (Kaplan 2013: 289). Though the public at large would benefit from taming inflation, the cards seemed stacked against the *Real Plan*: the IMF refused to officially support the plan; the World Bank expressed skepticism on several occasions; and the US government refused to grant a zero coupon bond loan to back the plan. Many politicians from Cardoso's own party, such as the powerful governor of São Paulo, argued that the plan had major problems but agreed to support this "adventure into the abyss."[6]

To the surprise of many, the *Real Plan* started to work and, once working, deepened beliefs about the *Real Plan* actually breaking the back of inflation. A crucial element of the success of the *Real Plan* was the approval of the Fundo Social de Emergência (FSE) in February 1994. FSE was a stabilization fund created by de-earmarking 20 percent of all revenue sources. The FSE was crucial in the short term because—as the failed *Cruzado Plan* had made clear—an enormous revenue gap would be immediately generated as a result of the elimination of seigniorage gains under zero inflation.[7] The FSE was the first crucial test for the Cardoso team and

---

6 Mario Covas cited in Prado (2005). An additional source of uncertainty was the judicial system—a major potential veto gate over many initiatives—and legal complexities associated with the labyrinth of indexes used in the country.

7 Gustavo Franco (1995: 5; emphasis added), in retrospect, argued that "the destruction of earmarking was a crucial necessity for the restoration of fiscal governance in Brazil, and this was precisely the one measure considered *necessary* for a safe start to the stabilization program. This was accomplished by the passing of the constitutional amendment establishing the social emergency fund, early in 1994."

the first measure aimed at overhauling fiscal federalism. This crucial measure in the government's fiscal reform was passed when the government enjoyed a slim majority of 53 percent. As Cardoso pointed out, it was much more difficult to pass this amendment than subsequent amendments involving the extension of its provisions or on related topics.[8]

The popularity of the *Real Plan* continued to grow when Cardoso resigned his post as finance minister to run for president as the PSDB candidate.[9] More importantly, by passing the FSE, the coalition PSDB-PMDB-PFL forged in 1993–1994 showed its strength. Shepherding the amendment package in Congress was a crucial test for relations between the executive and the legislative branches under the framework of the new constitution. The FSE is also testimony to the "art of policy making" in that it emerged over time after Cardoso and his team recognized the importance of taming inflation. The next question was how? This demonstrates the dynamic of leadership in making the *Real Plan* a success.

Public sentiment toward reforms was deeply marked by Collor's aborted initiatives in the area of trade liberalization and reform of the state. The fact that Collor had been elected points to the fact that his appeal for a move away from the ISI economic model had resonated in Brazilian society. The task was to separate Collor's message from his patrimonialist political practices (see F. Cardoso 2010: 160). For die-hard proponents of ISI, organized in associations such as IEDI, it became increasingly clear that change would have to come from a much more robust modernization project.[10] The reformers could foresee many of the downstream consequences of their strategies, but they faced a collective-action problem and needed strong coordination.

Three key elements undergirded the *Real Plan*:

> i) a fiscal strategy centered on the approval of the Constitutional Amendment creating the Social Emergency Fund, while other reforms were enacted through a prolonged period of time; ii) a monetary reform process to take place during a few months of voluntary adoption of a new unit of account later to become the national currency; and iii) a big bang approach towards opening the economy with aggressive trade liberalization and a new foreign exchange policy. (Franco 1995: 1)

The big bang approach suggested by Franco is a misnomer. While there was indeed a plan for a massive initiative of constitutional change, the

---

8 A constitutional amendment was required because the FSE altered some constitutional rules regarding the distribution of tax revenues to municipalities and states. In practice, it was tantamount to a strong centralization of fiscal authority.

9 The parties referred to in the text are: PSDB—Brazilian Social Democracy Party; PMDB—Brazilian Democratic Movement Party; and PFL—Liberal Front Party.

10 IEDI is the acronym for the business think tank, Instituto para o Estudo do Desenvolvimento Industrial.

process was widely negotiated and protracted. Even the initial set of constitutional amendments was extensively discussed in Congress. Importantly, while these negotiations involved concessions and pork, the core of the initiatives was not significantly altered or watered down.

The reform coalition was not only looking backward but also looking forward and had to face the up-front costs entailed by all these measures. Fernando H. Cardoso (2006: 483) aptly captured the backward-looking approach on the part of opposing interests: "It's understandable that when facing innovative proposals the first reaction is to look at them using the rear window. When they are looked from the viewpoint of business as usual innovations tend to be negatively evaluated."

Another crucial test for Cardoso's new government was Congress's approval of an increase in the monthly minimum wage (set at US$100 in March 1995). Cardoso vetoed the bill amid massive protests, signaling his firm commitment to fiscal responsibility. In a context of high uncertainty, reputation building was a key element in Cardoso's strategy.

EARLY INSTITUTIONAL DEEPENING: CONSTITUTIONAL AMENDMENTS

The stability of the Real depended on controlling fiscal expenditures as well as controlling the money stock. With Gustavo Franco at the helm of the Central Bank, the monetary side was covered, but much expenditure was hardwired into the constitution. As a result, early on in his presidency, Cardoso proposed several constitutional amendments and had a hard time getting them approved, because amending the constitution required two rounds of votes in each house of Congress and approval by three-fifths of the number of congressmen.[11]

Cardoso and his team went to work on amendments shortly after his inauguration in January 1995. Cardoso sent Congress seventeen proposals for constitutional amendments. This constitutional big bang signals Cardoso's sense that the short-term success of the Real represented the window of opportunity for comprehensive institutional change. Importantly, and somehow paradoxically, this strategy reflected extensive negotiations, and the proposals were approved swiftly by large majorities, except for the amendments dealing with taxation and social security.[12]

---

11 As noted earlier, while Cardoso was finance minister, his economic team managed to pass the FSE, but they had hoped for more: hard budget constraints, administrative reforms, and reform of the pension system (Franco 1999). But without the support of President Itamar, the amendments never got off the ground.

12 Social security involved "acquired rights" and had concentrated costs, in addition to high transition costs, whereas taxation involved controversial federalist issues. These features complicated the negotiations of these reforms.

It was also necessary to signal Cardoso's commitment to fiscal reform, at the same time that the monetary stabilization was being implemented. However, Cardoso was also looking forward to the long-term consequences of institutional change. By proposing a big set of constitutional changes, Cardoso sent a signal to business elites of a credible commitment to reforms, which was crucial to buy limited business support for the *Real Plan*. To pass the amendments so early on in his tenure required leadership: knowing what to do and how to do it.

To pass his amendments, Cardoso engaged in pork for policy with his legislature. Pork for policy entailed the president using his large arsenal of patronage and presidential powers—including decrees—to "buy" votes, most often on constitutional issues, but also to dampen criticism.[13] This pattern evolved and became highly institutionalized over time following the reorganization of the presidency under two terms of Cardoso.[14] The constitutional structure that emerged from the Constitution of 1988 is a hybrid of majoritarian and separation of powers features. It combines federalism, a strong judiciary, and a fragmented party system (which is a product of open-list proportional representation) with a powerful president with strong reactive and proactive powers (veto powers and agenda powers, which includes the ability to issue provisional legal measures with immediate force of law). Coalition management, via strategic allocation of cabinet portfolio, pork, and policy concessions (Pereira, Power, and Raile 2011), was an essential ingredient in making credible political deals.

The emerging consensus on the virtues of an open economy undergirded Cardoso's economic team. The new government's "mental model" built not only on recurrent past failures but also on other successful role models of developing economies such as Chile. The failure of the ISI's model resulted primarily from institutional features associated with developmentalist beliefs. These included state-owned enterprises enjoying monopolistic control over sectors, protective tariffs and subsidies, and public finance institutions designed to capture the inflation tax (Calomiris and Haber 2014: chap. 13). The new economic team did not devise any brilliant novel plan but simply absorbed the cumulative experience with failed plans as well as lessons from other countries that were undergoing similar problems. The set of policies to avoid and those that worked were common knowledge among the economists on Cardoso's

---

13 For a formal presentation of the pork for policy game in Brazilian politics, along with a narrative of its use to pass parts of the pension reform, see Alston and Mueller (2006).
14 Its survival under the two terms of Lula and the term of Dilma underscores its importance in the country's new institutional dynamics. It entails both the exchange of pork for policy votes as well as the strategic appointment of cabinet positions. Neither Lula nor Dilma matched the skill of Cardoso.

team who received their PhDs at world-class schools. But, the problem at hand was not primarily epistemic; it involved leadership and heresthetics. Cardoso took on the leadership role to embark on an ambitious program of wholesale institutional change. Hyperinflation and economic underperformance shattered existing beliefs on ISI, and the ensuing uncertainty opened space for leadership. While uncertainty about the distributional consequences of reform may inhibit support for reform *by the interests affected by change*, as suggested by Fernandez and Rodrik (1991), it also undermines existing beliefs (Przeworski 1991), creating space for credible proposals by political entrepreneurs.[15]

The Cardoso government prioritized the amendments pertaining to the economy, only later to seek passage of amendments in the difficult and complex areas of taxation, social security, and state reform. The first reforms stipulated the elimination of the state monopolies in the areas of oil and energy (Amendment 9), mineral resources, telecommunications (Amendment 8), coastal shipping (Amendment 7), and cooking gas distribution (Amendment 5). The concept of national enterprise, which was central to the ISI, was also redefined, and its amplified meaning included all registered firms that operated in the national territory (Amendment 6),[16] and foreign firms were allowed to operate in the area of insurance, reinsurance, and social security (Amendment 13).

The constitutional big bang reform was the biggest test for the government coalition. Despite the institutional hurdles and the amount of redistribution the amendments entailed, Congress approved all but one amendment—tax reform, which was actually never put to a vote. Two factors help explain the fate of the tax reform proposal: (1) risk aversion about any negative impact of the reform on revenue generation and (2) uncertainty about the short-term impact concerning losses and gains, particularly on the distributional effects of the reform of consumption taxes for the states. The government ended up preferring the status quo of a highly extractive and inefficient tax system to an improved system with uncertain revenue outcomes (Melo 2002; Melo, Pereira, and Souza 2010). The fate of tax reform reflects the lexicographic priority of revenue generation for currency stabilization over other issues in the agenda.

---

15 The role of uncertainty in enhancing the ability of actors to introduce change is a traditional analytical point in political economy, which can be dated back to Marx's analysis of the "relative autonomy of the state" in *The Eighteenth Brumaire of Louis Bonaparte* ([1852] 1963).

16 Article 171 of the Constitution of 1988 stipulated strict provisions defining a "Brazilian company with national capital." The amendment replaced this definition with the concept of a Brazilian company as those firms organized according to Brazilian law and with headquarters in Brazil, independent of the origins of capital or requirements regarding the status of ownership.

It was the Achilles' heel for government's reform credibility among business interests.

The massive institutional change that followed in the wake of the constitutional amendments paved the way for the privatization of the large state-owned enterprises in public utilities: telecommunications (the Telebrás holding) and electricity distributors (Eletrobrás), with total sales in excess of US$110 billion among the two companies. At this time, it was one of the largest privatization programs in the world. Following utilities, the government sold the world's largest iron ore company—the Companhia Vale do Rio Doce—in 1997. The sale of Companhia Vale do Rio Doce signaled the demise of the ISI era. Between 1990 and 2002, the government privatized 165 enterprises, obtaining total revenues of around US$87 billion, which helped reduce public debt by an amount equivalent to 8 percent of GDP (Musacchio and Lazzarini 2014). Importantly, the massive privatization program did not transfer ownership outright to the private sector. Musacchio and Lazzarini (2014) show that the Brazilian government retained significant minority equity positions in a variety of firms using the investment arm of its development bank, the BNDES. Retaining a significant minority stake provided credible commitment to investors that the government would not expropriate their profits through excessive regulation or taxes.[17] In addition to providing finance and minority equity, BNDES played a key coordination role. The model used in this privatization wave ushered in what those authors call the model of "leviathan as a minority investor."[18] This large-scale change of property rights and the massive institutional change that the Cardoso administration shepherded greatly transformed the nature of capitalism in Brazil.

After the approval of the amendments directly associated with the privatization process, the government moved toward other issue areas, but very cautiously. Indeed, the more controversial reform areas of pensions and taxes awaited Cardoso's second term. In the case of pension reforms, the issue of acquired rights represented an additional complication as it involved a clash between belief in inclusion, which was encapsulated in the 1988 Constitution, and belief in fiscal sustainability.

Two factors in coalition management proved essential to guarantee the implementation of the government agenda: first, engaging in pork for policy games, involving execution of budget amendments, concession of

17 See Levy and Spiller (1996) for a general application of credible commitment to the telecommunications industry across several developing countries.
18 Musacchio and Lazzarini (2014: 273) claim that this model of state capitalism entails less agency losses and exhibits less political intervention than the model of full ownership during the military governments.

BNDES loans, and patronage; the second strategy involved assignment of portfolio positions to coalition partners (Amorim Neto 2002). Presidential success in Brazil has come to be associated empirically with these two factors along with the strong agenda powers enjoyed by presidents. In Brazil, a budget is passed along with amendments, but the amendments are executed only if the president deems them fiscally sound. This gives the president enormous leverage over Congress. Indeed, the approval of budget amendments originating from members of the governing coalition was crucial to guarantee support for the government agenda, but it was not consolidated until the middle of Cardoso's first term of office. Importantly, pork for policy games were kept under control, and part of Cardoso's leadership role involved not allowing them to undermine the core logic of government. In other words, these exchanges involved extensive gains from trade that made the transition process viable.

Presidential preponderance in executive-legislative relations was also made possible by the approval of the constitutional amendment allowing reelection of incumbents for one term of office. The government spent enormous political capital in the approval of Amendment 16 to the constitution (June 1997). It was another instance of Cardoso withstanding up-front costs for long-term benefits. But it also relied on the support of governors and mayors, who would themselves benefit from the reelection rule.

COALITION MANAGEMENT UNDER CARDOSO

> The greatest political question was, indeed, the allocation of the ministerial posts.
>
> —F. Cardoso (2006: 269)

Executive-legislative relations in Brazil changed dramatically under Cardoso. Strategy in coalition management in the 1990s contrasted markedly with that of previous presidents. Although Cardoso's party, the PSDB, was the second largest party, it refrained from holding the presidencies of the Chamber of Deputies and Senate, opting instead to support candidates from the coalition partners.[19] The coalition enjoyed sizable majorities in

19 The only exception in this political equilibrium came toward the end of Cardoso's second term, when his party supported the successful bid of Aecio Neves for the presidency of the Chamber of Deputies, which led to the exit of the PSDB's main partner, the PFL in 2002, and to a minority government. Coalition management remained crucial for successive presidents, and problems in this area plagued the administration of Lula, as we shall see in chapter 6.

the Chamber of Deputies, ranging from a maximum of 76 percent to a minimum of 62 percent of seats in the period from April 1996 to March 2002. Importantly, between January 1995 and March 2002, the average proportionality rate in the distribution of ministerial portfolio and the power share of coalition allies in Congress was 63 percent, the highest in any period from Collor to Sarney.[20] As a result, the coalition remained remarkably stable. Indeed, the core of the coalition, which comprised three parties—PFL, PSDB, and PMDB—remained cohesive except for Cardoso's last year in government, when the PFL left the coalition.

Coalitional management under Cardoso also entailed an insulation of the government strategic core, which included not only the ministries and agencies in charge of finance, budget, and planning, but also those in the social sectors (Melo 2005). In short, Cardoso allocated the most important ministries to allies on whom he could depend. For example, Pedro Malan was Cardoso's finance minister for two terms. Historically, the social sector had been part of patronage games. For the key ministries of the social sectors—the Ministries of Education and Health, in particular—Cardoso appointed high-profile individuals from his inner circle, including José Serra (mayor of São Paulo) and Paulo Renato Souza (an economics professor). The pork for policy game was circumscribed to the fringe of the state machinery, particularly in the cash-stripped ministries for regional development, as well as transportation and mines and energy, which had lost most of their parastatals—and consequently political power—in the wake of the privatization process. This strategy prevented the deterioration of the pork for policy game into systemic patronage and clientelism. While pork for policy is not unique to the Brazilian context, it is not universally found in Latin America, as the Argentina case discussed in chapter 7 shows. Pork for policy in a window of opportunity (engendered by shattered beliefs in the benefits of a closed economy) with a clear sense of direction toward structural change is unique. Institutional deepening sustained by beliefs consistent with the new institutions triggered a transition process.

ASSERTING FISCAL CONTROL OVER STATES

The massive institutional change that occurred in the 1990s also included a structural transformation in the country's intergovernmental relations and fiscal federalism, and in the relationships between the central

20 The proportionality rate refers to the difference between the share of seats held by a party and the party's corresponding share in the ministerial portfolio. For an extended analysis of proportionality in presidential cabinets in Brazil, see Amorim Neto (2002).

government and the states. Whereas at the beginning of the decade the country was characterized by a centrifugal dynamics, at the end it was marked by a strong centripetal movement toward the center. Decentralization was part and parcel of the beliefs encapsulated in the Constitution of 1988. But the chaotic situation of the states in the early 1990s shattered the notion that the states could behave responsibly.

Indeed, in this transitional phase, the federal government revamped intergovernmental relations as part and parcel of the process of institutional change. Two contextual factors shaped the relationship between the federal executive and subnational interests. The first was the impact of the new constitution on intergovernmental relations. The other was the impact of the stabilization program on state finances.

The timing and sequence of events in the transition to democracy in Brazil in the 1980s converted state governors to "barons of the federation" (Abrucio 1998), as they enjoyed virtual veto powers in many issue areas. As discussed in chapter 3, the military government restored direct elections for governors in 1982 while the first direct presidential election took place much later, in 1989. Legitimized by popular elections, the new governors of the largest states—in particular those of São Paulo, Minas Gerais, Rio Grande do Sul, Rio de Janeiro, and Bahia—became the key negotiators in the transition to civilian rule. Their legitimacy in the context of a weak president guaranteed the prominence of subnational and regional interests in the constitution-making process. Consequently, under the new constitution, the states and municipalities saw their taxing powers increase and their share of the general revenue spike, without a corresponding rise in functional competencies. The states increased expenditures even more than their revenues increased. The resulting vertical fiscal imbalance led to mounting debts by the states. By 1993, the states functioned under a soft budget constraint because there were no effective tools by which the federal government could impose fiscal discipline on the states.

The reassertion of the central government's fiscal authority was one of the daunting challenges for the new government. Again, the years that followed the implementation of the *Real Plan* provided a key reform window because the elimination of inflation undermined the material basis of the political survival of many governors. Cardoso exploited the sudden vulnerability of the "barons" by implementing an array of deals redefining the rules of the subnational fiscal game (Melo, Pereira, and Souza 2010).

As the first step in the revamping of Brazilian fiscal federalism in the 1990s, Cardoso proposed a constitutional amendment allowing the federal government to confiscate current state revenue in case subnational state-owned enterprises (utilities and other companies) defaulted on their debt.[21] Approved as Amendment 3 to the constitution, the measure led to the rescheduling of a total of US$34 billion of debt of the states. The second stage in the revamping of Brazilian fiscal federalism took place shortly after the implementation of the *Real Plan* in 1994. The states' finances went bust as a result of the plan. The end of inflation made it clear that an estimated 20 to 40 percent of the states' revenue was generated through float (interests from overnight financial operations with current accounts balances).

Cardoso implemented his second package to bail out the states with much stricter conditionalities. These included the imposition of targets for the primary fiscal account and a ceiling for personnel expenditures set at 60 percent, as well as privatization of utilities. The federal government also resorted to a strategy of stick and carrot, offering incentives (e.g., anticipation of revenue from future privatization of state utilities controlled by state governments). Indeed, between 1997 and 2000, states privatized twenty-four utilities. In addition, following PROES (Program of Reduction of the State Participation in Banking Activity), twenty-three state banks were either privatized or closed. These measures, however, did not prevent further fiscal misbehavior, and, in 1997, Cardoso imposed another package on the states where debt refinancing took place against the proceeds from future privatization of state banks and energy utilities. These measures led to a massive privatization operation: thirty state banks and twenty electricity distributors were privatized. In the case of banks, some were federalized or converted into second-tier financial houses. In total, in Cardoso's first term of office, the government privatized or intervened in 190 financial entities (Franco 1999: 278).

STAYING THE COURSE AGAINST THE EARLY OPPOSITION TO THE *REAL PLAN*

As interest rates rose to fight inflation, the interests associated with ISI escalated their pressure on the new government.[22] However, as Bacha, the

---

21 The current constitution allowed for withholdings in case of default by state authorities (*autarquias*) and public bodies, not banks, sanitation companies, electricity generators, and the like.

22 In 1995, Mercosur introduced a common external tariff in Brazil. The prior tariff schedule determined by law in 1957 remained in operation for thirty years, until its first reform in 1987, and second change in 1991 under Collor (Baumann 2002). During those three decades, a tariff policy council granted provisional modifications in the nominal tariff rates. The tariff council was composed of representatives from several government agencies and business interests. Power to determine tariff levels or dispensation from tariffs was concentrated in the hands of business. Collor abolished the Tariff Council in 1990, after which point tariffs were in the hands of the executive.

Ministry of Finance's most senior policy advisor, put it during the heat of the reactions to the *Plano Real*: "business should learn how to live in a world of stability. . . . When government determines interest rates, those that raise wages and need operating capital will go bust because *current monetary policy is no longer determined by FIESP* (The Federation of the Industries of the State of São Paulo)" (Bacha cited in Prado 2005: 314). The opposition from the industrial elite reached its peak in the period 1996–1998 after inflation had already been reduced but interest rates remained high. Business complained about an asymmetry in the pace of institutional changes associated with lowering the *Custo Brasil*—the high costs of doing business in Brazil because of high interest rates, taxes, pro-labor legislation, and trade liberalization. The business interests had a fair objection; they disproportionately bore the initial costs of the *Real Plan*. The asymmetry resulted partly from the inherent nature of the measures associated with the dismantling of a closed economy and stabilizing the economy, on the one hand, and those measures required to change the tax system and labor legislation, on the other. Stabilizing the monetary system, in principle, could be accomplished with unilateral measures from the executive, while changing taxes or revising labor laws required changes in the constitution, which necessitated complex bargaining between the executive and legislative branches. As a result, opening the internal market to international competition in a context in which domestic firms continued to operate with high costs and regulations elicited considerable criticism.

Business was adamantly against the slow pace in lowering interest rates and pressed for immediate reductions in the basic rate as well as tax reforms. As Fernando H. Cardoso (2006: 249) put it: "Business associations, particularly FIESP and IEDI, along with members of the opposition maintained this view. Their criticism was based on '*Delenda FHC*' [Fernando Henrique Cardoso]: if the measures are from the government, they are by definition bad." Cardoso was suspicious of business criticism: "I was critical of the business community's criticisms: were they longing for a 'national-statist' model, rather than a developmentalist one, that required economic dirigisme, and who knows, special treatment to sectors or even individual firms, by virtue of protectionism and subsidized loans from BNDES?" The FIESP, in 1996, organized a massive street demonstration— the "March toward Brasília"—in the Ministerial Mall in Brasília demanding the approval of constitutional reforms. However, one year later, in its 1997 annual report, it gloomily concluded, "hardly anything changed since then . . . the entrepreneurial mobilization led to almost nothing."[23]

23 FIESP (1997: 14), "Depois de um ano, País ainda espera." Schneider (1997–1998: 95) described the event in graphic terms: "In May 1996 Brazil's National Confederation of Industry (CNI) convened a meeting of industrialists in Brasília for a mass show of unity

The asymmetry in the pace of change in reducing the Custo Brasil and the other issues in the reform agenda explains only part of the conflictual pattern of interactions between the business community and the Cardoso government. The most contentious issues involved the fixed exchange rate regime and high interest rates. Discontentment could very easily lead to the formation of alternative coalitions (Kingstone 1999). On the left, the Workers' Party (PT) made its appeal based more on effective policy to protect domestic industry. Although it accepted the need for a market opening, the PT argued in similar terms as the business community. The surge in imports had hit key sectors of the economy including textiles, auto parts, and capital goods, and many firms went out of business or were acquired by foreign competitors.[24] Though both labor and business saw harm from opening up the economy, they could never form a coalition because part of the central complaint of business was the extant pro-labor legislation in Brazil. High interest rates were not a concern of the Left.

Cardoso reacted to business criticism both with public criticism of their corporatist nature and with an array of compensatory measures. These were extensive and were part of an evolving pork for policy game, which has become a key feature of coalitional politics in Brazil since Cardoso. To appease business and labor demands, Cardoso countered with extended subsidized credit lines from BNDES to industrial sectors. In the steel sector alone, BNDES directed some US$14 billion in loans between 1994 and 2001.

Second, Cardoso created a number of special programs designed to help industry modernize and compete. The special program for the auto industry was the most visible. Facing a wave of disinvestment in the sector and indications of relocation of plants to Argentina, the government slashed tariffs in the auto parts industry, introduced extraordinary tariffs of up to 70 percent on cars and trucks, and extended favored credit lines. This special regime was successfully negotiated with Argentina and placated much of the ire in the sector. The Cardoso administration also

---

and focused lobbying in favor of constitutional reform. Industrialists large and small heeded the call. Nearly three thousand of them from all over Brazil chartered planes and packed shuttles. Fortified by a morning of speeches demanding constitutional reforms, the industrialists fanned out over Brasília in the afternoon to argue their case to members of the national congress. As if to demonstrate that it could not be intimidated, however, Congress chose that very afternoon to vote down a reform proposal backed by business. By the end of that year, it was clear that business had made little progress in pushing several amendments it supported."

24 There was great outcry when a foreign competitor acquired national champions. This was the case, for example, of Metal Leve, the only domestic manufacturing firm with a significant presence in the United States, which was acquired by a foreign competitor.

extended favors to the textile industry, which included vigorous action against dumping, a complaint long held by the industry.

Third, following a series of setbacks in approving a constitutional amendment on tax reform, Cardoso introduced a system of fiscal credits that compensated exporters for payments of the state VAT (value added tax) and payroll taxes (*pis-pasep* and *cofins*). Finally in 1999, as a symbolic gesture to business, Cardoso created a new ministry—the Ministry of Production.[25]

Writing in 1997, Kingstone (1999: 223) argued, "Cardoso's efforts through late 1996 to placate the business community seemed to effectively reduce the level of visible frustration." However, the government continued to rely on a combination of high real interest rates and an overvalued currency to maintain the stability of the Real. Business criticism of his government therefore continued as the Asian crisis (1997) set in, which prompted a bump up of interest rates. Fernando H. Cardoso (2006: 410) recognized the reaction to his government's policies: "The political climate deteriorated. Some industrialists such as those from the FIESP that asked for immediate changes in the exchange rate regime with utmost urgency kept on complaining. They wanted lower interest rates."

As stabilization proceeded and trade liberalization deepened, the process gained momentum as some economic actors realized the possibilities of using their assets more profitably in more open markets or exploring mergers and association with foreign firms, as well as the benefit from a stable currency. In other words, as economic stabilization proceeded, new economic actors developed a stake in the reform process and formed a constituency that did not exist before. However, they faced a strategic dilemma. If the *Real Plan* failed, a bank that had bet on its success by building a loan portfolio would have to scramble to reestablish its float business and abandon its strategy of profit making by lending. For the banking industry as a whole, this was not trivial. It was a watershed in the history of industry of an entire sector that flourished under the ISI regime. Calomiris and Haber put it graphically:

> The vast differences in Brazil's political institutions before and after 1989 gave rise to dramatic changes in the banking system. Prior to 1989, the Game of Bank Bargains in Brazil produced . . . a banking system designed to extract an inflation tax whose revenues were divided between the government and the banks. There was nothing subtle about the Brazilian inflation tax: at its peak, the annual transfer

25 Cardoso appointed Celso Lafer, a prominent member of a family of São Paulo's industrialists, as the ministry head. He was later replaced by Clovis Correia and Alcides Tapias, former CEOs of Villares (an equipment giant) and Camargo Correia (then the country's largest construction firm), respectively.

from the holders of cash and checking account balances to the government and the banks was an amazing 8 percent of GDP. (Calomiris and Haber 2014: 416–17)

Many banks actively participated in the privatization process and therefore became committed to the success of the reform process. Calomiris and Haber (2014: 440) cite Banco Itaú as an example of a large Brazilian bank grappling with this strategic dilemma. As these authors argue: "In the end, *Banco Itaú* bet in favor of the *Real Plan* and was rewarded by being able to play a major role in the expansion of the Brazilian banking business."[26] Bankers faced a dilemma: either to cooperate with the new government expecting that the transition to a new system would be completed successfully or stick to the status quo of high inflation and accumulated signs of its unsustainability. The banking sector gradually updated their beliefs in light of the evidence about the unsustainability of the status quo, and this reached a tipping point.

As firms redeployed assets to new opportunities, they raised their stakes in the success of the plan. Privatization and trade liberalization opened economic opportunities for firms in various sectors. As these businesses flourished, the entrepreneurs updated their beliefs on the open economy. Once price stability set in and Cardoso gained credibility as a reformer, industrial firms began adjusting rapidly. This choice of strategy was not always the preferred outcome. However, as Kingstone (1999) noted, once firms did adjust, they set in motion a process that locked them into a particular adjustment course that depended on continuation of the reforms. In the auto industry, the sheer size of investments that both the assemblers and the parts producers undertook (nearly US$6 billion between 1991 and 1996) made the sector dependent on the continuing success in implementing reforms in Brazil.

In turn, citizens also benefitted from the plan and from the market reforms. Most obviously, they benefitted from low inflation, particularly the poor and middle classes, who were more penalized under high inflation. More importantly, they also benefitted from reforms in the short term on several dimensions. First, their real incomes rose, and so did employment. Second, as consumers, citizens gained enormously from trade liberalization as the prices of tradable goods fell sharply. The spectacular expansion of basic services such as telephone lines and access to imports generated strong support to liberalization among citizens, particularly low-income groups (although price hikes led to discontentment). As

---

26 *Banco Itaú* had already been burned by its bet in favor of a previous inflation reform (the *Cruzado Plan* of 1986) and had suffered large losses when it proved unsuccessful (Calomiris and Haber 2014).

Baker (2005) argues, consumption-based processes are at the basis of the formation of favorable beliefs about trade reform.

Changes brought about by trade reform in terms of availability, quality, and affordability of goods and services provided a firsthand experience that shaped beliefs in crucial ways. Baker (2009) marshals public opinion data from Brazil in the 1990s and 2000s to show that most Brazilian citizens are enthusiastic about globalization because it has lowered the prices of many consumer goods and services while improving their variety and quality. Of the array of reforms implemented by Cardoso, only privatization in areas such as utilities has caused discontent because it has raised prices for services. He finds that "the safest overall conclusion is that more than two-thirds of Brazilians persistently supported free trade in the fifteen years following the implementation of Collor's trade liberalization measures. . . . As with trade liberalization, most Brazilians approved of foreign investment, with pro-trade majorities ranging from 54% to 72%" (Baker 2009: 198).

Importantly, Baker (2009) found no wealth effects in attitudes toward reforms among respondents to extensive surveys. Both elites and poor groups exhibited similar assessment toward reforms, a finding he attributes to their experience as consumers. In terms of our framework, the discredit of ISI among the dominant network (in particular, bankers and industrialists who benefitted from the system in the past) triggered a reform process whose outcomes prompted citizens to endorse reforms. This runs counter to the notion that elites mechanically shape mass beliefs and is consistent with the argument in chapter 2 that citizens' concrete experience with high inflation in the previous decade and with the new tangible benefits of trade liberalization in the mid-1990s helped solidify a new set of beliefs about the benefits of price stability and an open economy.[27] Thus, criticisms of job losses due to technological modernization were soon eclipsed as jobs were created as a result of service expansion.[28] Importantly, the visibility and salience of privatization and trade liberalization declined after 1998, as shown in Baker (2009).[29] In other words,

---

27 This is consistent with our claim in chapter 2 that repeated action consistent with the beliefs crystallizes the new equilibrium. Citizens' quotidian practices reinforce their beliefs about the superiority of an open economy.

28 Utility rates soared to very high levels and have remained an important negative issue, but this was felt much later in 2000.

29 "To report one measure of salience, Brazil's leading newspaper (*Folha de São Paulo*) had over 3,200 stories per year that mentioned privatization in 1997 and 1998, and in Cardoso's second term the paper published 1,700 stories on the topic per year. In Lula's first three years, however, it averaged only 550 stories on privatization per year. Moreover, between 1997 and 2001, the paper published 3,900 stories per year that mentioned some

there appears to have occurred an important structural change in attitudes toward the developmentalist model.[30]

SUSTAINING STABILITY IN THE FACE OF EXTERNAL SHOCKS

The Real suffered following the Russian crisis in 1998, prompting the government to raise interests rates further amid great uncertainty surrounding the sustainability of the stability plan. High interest rates led to a sharp increase in the net public debt, which rose from 28 percent of GDP in 1994 to 43 percent in 1998. Privatization was critical in attracting considerable foreign direct investment but was not sufficient to offset the effects of high interest rates. By 1999, the public debt reached 50 percent of GDP amid turbulence in international markets associated with the Russian and Asian crises. Debt service in 1999 as a percentage of exports surpassed 120 percent, up from 30 percent in 1994.

The cycle of reforms had been only partially completed, and at the end of 1998, a parametric reform in the pension system was finally approved. The key issue was, however, the exchange rate that had been set at parity with the dollar within an implicit narrow band. The Russian crisis cost more than US$70 billion to the country's foreign exchange reserves in a sustained effort to defend the currency. An emergency fiscal agreement with the IMF guaranteed a bailout package of an unprecedented US$40 billion to the country. Four years into the *Real Plan*, there remained uncertainty among many, but Cardoso stayed the course and convinced others in power that Brazil was committed to keeping inflation at bay.

The only option to domestic inflation was devaluation, but Cardoso delayed the devaluation because of the enormous reputational impact that it would have caused in his chances of reelection. After the elections, it became clear that the Real was facing a major crisis. Most countries "shoot the messenger," and Brazil was no exception. Gustavo Franco, the president of the Central Bank and one of Cardoso's closest advisors, resigned. The run against the Real cost US$20 billion in a few weeks, and interest rates reached 70 percent, leading the government to abandon its defense of the Real. Cardoso and his economic team allowed the Real to float in January 1999. After some volatility, the Real stabilized. The costs of the devaluation turned out to be much less than expected, and much of the revenue needed to ensure fiscal stability was generated via a

aspect of globalization besides the FTAA, but between 2002 and 2005 the average per year dropped by 33%" (Baker 2009: 190).

30 Under Dilma there has been a resurgence of developmentalism, but this has prompted significant reactions and criticism, as discussed in chapter 6.

massive expansion of taxes of 10 percentage points of GDP in the period 1994–2002. The fact that the free floating of the currency stabilized at a lower level following a few weeks was evidence that Brazil had made important strides in the transition to an open economy. At the end of the Cardoso era, foreign trade reached 31 percent of GDP (a figure two and a half times that of 1989), and the country ran increasing trade surpluses and a primary surplus of 3 percent of GDP.

Cardoso's Second Term: Combining Macro Orthodoxy with Social Inclusion

The reelection of Cardoso is testimony to the internalization by the public at large of the belief in "the fear of inflation." Cardoso ran his electoral campaign as the symbol of the fight against inflation. This occurred despite large redistributive costs and modest economic growth. Cardoso and his team never deviated from their belief in the fear of inflation as uniting the country, but they also recognized the need to extend social benefits when fiscally sound. After the resignation of Gustavo Franco, Cardoso replaced Franco with Arminio Fraga, a Princeton-trained PhD economist who believed in sound monetary policy like Franco. Symbolically, Franco's resignation might be interpreted as a defeat of the stabilization plan. However, the quick stabilization of the Real testified to world markets that Brazil was serious in its efforts toward macro stability and transitioning to more open markets. Foreign trade continued to increase, and the country consistently ran trade surpluses as well as primary surpluses. As a result, old business industrialists who were weaned on ISI remained opposed to the high interest rates and high taxes necessary to maintain the value of the Real. But, there was a new entrepreneurship within Brazil supporting Cardoso both on the economic and political fronts.

Toward the end of Cardoso's first term, a constitutional amendment was approved to improve primary education. Amendment 14 called for the creation of a fund—FUNDEF (Fund for the Maintenance and Development of Basic Teaching)—to encourage more enrollment and better wages for teachers. Despite the dismal quality of education overall, the fund led to the near universalization of coverage of basic education. Early in his second term, Cardoso embarked on further constitutional reforms; this time in the area of social inclusion. Cardoso had managed to approve a constitutional amendment in the area of pensions in 1998 (Amendment 20). The process was protracted, and a cautious and incremental path was taken. In the area of social security, the government failed to pass specific provisions of the reform package, the taxation of pensioners, which resurfaced in 1999. The government did succeed on several fronts, but it took a series of bills with considerable pork to sway the passage (Alston and Mueller 2006; Melo 2004). The reform was parametric and did not call for the overhaul of the system.[31] But it made progress in eliminating privileges benefitting specific occupational categories and introduced measures that improved the intergenerational equity in the system. More importantly, however, was a host of infraconstitutional changes that guaranteed the expansion of noncontributory pensions within the social security systems.

On social inclusion generally, the government managed to approve two constitutional amendments. The first was the amendment of December 2000, which created the Fund for Poverty Eradication. Following the intense mobilization around poverty alleviation, a Congressional Special Committee was set up in 1999. The poverty issue was highly politicized and led to several legislative proposals for hardwiring antipoverty funds.[32] The committee prepared a constitutional amendment creating the Poverty Fund. The original proposal contained several sources of revenue for the fund, including a tax on individual wealth and assets, which had been proposed by Cardoso while a senator. The proposal—which became Amendment 31—was approved in a compromise. The government endorsed the committee's proposal and accepted that an increase in the tax rate would be earmarked for the fund. The second constitutional amendment was Amendment 29 of September 2000, which stipulated minimum values for investments in the health sector for the three tiers of government. These two innovations had a common denominator: ensuring a more efficient use of existing resources in a context of hard budget constraints while marginally funneling new resources. The government targeted dissipation and misuse of funds by municipalities and states.

Per capita social spending expanded during Cardoso's term in office while the tax burden rose significantly. Per capita social spending increased from US$707 in 1993, to US$944 in 1998, to reach US$994

31 Two factors inhibited a transition to a fully funded system, or even significantly lowering the introduction of a ceiling in the generous public sector system: (1) the prohibitive transition costs estimated by various sources at 3 percent of GDP (Brazil had the highest implicit pension debt in Latin America) and (2) risk aversion in a context of turbulent international markets. Policy makers in the Ministry of Finance and the Central Bank warned Cardoso about the fiscal costs involved in such circumstances. This led Cardoso to go for a parametric reform along the lines of that pursued in European countries, such as Italy and Sweden, from which it copied the model of notional accounts to introduce the "fator previdenciário." (a rule automatically adjusting pensions to life expectancy) (see Melo 2004).

32 Consistent with current beliefs on social inclusion, the committee was entitled "Committee for the Study of the structural and conjunctural causes of social inequality and for presenting legislative solutions to eradicate poverty and social marginalization and for the reduction of regional and social inequality."

in 2002.[33] The expansion of entitlements in the 1990s led to an increase in the share of social security in public expenditures. At the same time, the government created an array of social assistance initiatives, including a conditional cash transfer program (the *Bolsa Escola*) that was up scaled and converted into the *Bolsa Família* program under the Lula government. The increasingly difficult fiscal situation toward the end led to the political insulation of social programs, which crowded out investments in infrastructure (Alston et al. 2010). This was consistent with a near consensus that social spending should be insulated from austerity measures.

Importantly, fiscal orthodoxy prevailed, and Brazil learned how to respond to strong redistributive pressures arising from vast inequalities by massively expanding indirect taxation under Cardoso (a trend that continued at a slower pace under Lula). This is no trivial achievement considering that the inflation tax provided an average of 8 percent of GDP prior to 1994, roughly equivalent to the increase in the tax burden under Cardoso. Equally important: this was accomplished without resistance and capital flight.

THE REASSERTION OF PRESIDENTIAL FISCAL AUTHORITY

The last chapter in the process by which the federal government managed to rein in subnational fiscal behavior was the default of the government of the state of Minas Gerais in 1999. Alleging at the time of his inauguration that the state was bankrupt, the newly elected state governor (former president) Itamar Franco declared a default on the state's debt of US$13 billion to the federal government. The default triggered a decline in the Real, and stock prices fell.

As a result, there was a showdown between Cardoso and Itamar. Itamar's default on the state debt in early 1999 reached the headlines in the international press. But all state debt had already been transferred to the federal government. States had to pay an up-front fee (made possible by the privatization of state utilities and banks) and pay up to 13 to 15 percent of their net revenues to the federal government, every year, as service of the debt. Following the enactment of the laws pertaining to the renegotiation of states' debt, the federal government withheld constitutionally mandated transfers in the full amount of the default payments. There was no gain by defaulting, only reputation costs. Pundits failed to notice that Brazil had changed. After Cardoso won the battle against Itamar, he won the fiscal war with the approval of the Fiscal Responsibility Law in May

33 In US$ of 2005. www.cepalstat.org.

2000. Only then did the World Bank and the IMF herald this law as the capstone in assuring fiscal responsibility, at least while Cardoso was still at the helm.

Conclusions

Brazil entering into a virtuous path toward an open access society cannot be seen as inexorable. The outcome is best viewed as a contingent dynamic process of belief change and leadership, shaped by an array of factors. Many alternative coalitions could have emerged, and many outcomes would have been far from what actually transpired. Cardoso and his team faced great uncertainty and had to constantly adapt. They looked backward in a problem-solving fashion but also looked at the potential downstream benefits. Leadership was required because of the considerable up-front costs and coordination problems. As discussed in chapter 2, when the new beliefs are locked in, leadership is no longer necessary, and the institutional dynamics enter into an autopilot mode. This happened toward the end of Cardoso's second term in office, when citizens, politicians, and business organizations adopted the belief of fear of inflation along with belief in social inclusion. Crucial for this change was the ever-widening group of organizations with a stake in the status quo of fiscal and monetary orthodoxy. For example, rather than sticking to the old regime of rent seeking, firms redeployed their assets in new profitable ways. Importantly, new firms in areas that were opened up as a result of institutional reforms—for example, foreign firms in mobile telephone services or oil—were incorporated into the dominant network. Citizens as consumers updated their beliefs in the benefits of liberalization and price stability. Citizens' aversion to inflation and economic elites' failure fatigue following six failed economic stabilization programs set the stage for the exercise of leadership.

Uncertainty permeated the whole transition process, and a number of factors helped to make Cardoso's reform commitments credible, particularly the *Real Plan*. They included a number of contextual factors—Itamar Franco's weakness as president, an orchestrated coalition government, and the approval of the constitutional amendment allowing the reelection of presidents. This was crucial because of the uncertainty surrounding Cardoso's successor's commitment and ability to sustain the reform path. A strong president rather than a lame duck was able to engage in pork for policy games backed by a newly articulated pattern of coalition management and introduce a host of compensatory measures that did not compromise the overarching goal of maintaining the stability of the currency and the lexicographic priority of revenue generation while increasing policies embracing social inclusion.

A key factor in the transition was leadership, which was reflected in Cardoso's decision to take significant risks and to bear major up-front costs associated with the Real and the constitutional reforms. The technology to fight inflation, in the wake of the Argentinean and Israeli experiences, was common knowledge among economic experts; discontentment with ISI was high, suggesting a bias away from the status quo; and citizens' aversion to price instability was already deeply ingrained in popular beliefs. The problem was not epistemic or one of cognitive dissonance as suggested in technocratic approaches to development. Coordination failures, uncertainty, and commitment problems plagued reform efforts. The level of uncertainty surrounding the *Real Plan* was extremely high for most of Cardoso's two terms in office. Even the IMF and the World Bank were critical of the stabilization plan. As discussed in this chapter, Cardoso engaged in pork for policy games that guaranteed that his reform agenda was implemented. In many issue areas, he realized that the political costs involved were prohibitive and retreated. However, by providing a focal point in the reform agenda, in which currency stabilization and the fiscal imperative were lexicographically superior in relation to all the other issues in the reform agenda, the executive leadership played a crucial coordinating role.

CHAPTER 6

Deepening Beliefs and Institutional Change (2002–2014)

> Regimes and dynasties rise and fall, relative prices adjust, climates fluctuate, neighboring competitors appear and disappear, and boundaries and borders shift. . . . Out of these shifting patterns, societies occasionally produce arrangements with a better chance of initiating the transition to open access. Historically in the West, societies in Athenian Greece, Republican Rome, and the Renaissance city-states of Northern Italy appear to have been on the doorstep of the transition, although all three failed to produce open access societies.
>
> —North, Wallis, and Weingast (2009: 150)

> Perhaps making growth happen is ultimately beyond our control. Maybe all that happens is that something goes right for once . . . and then that sparks growth somewhere else in the economy, and so on. Perhaps, we will never learn where it will start or what will make it continue. The best we can do in that world is to hold the fort till that initial spark arrives.
>
> —Banerjee (2008: 15)

THE UNCERTAIN TRANSITION

In mid-April of 2002, the unthinkable had become highly likely. Opinion polls started indicating the probable victory of the left-wing candidate of the Workers' Party, Luiz Inácio Lula da Silva, a former metallurgical worker turned union leader, turned politician. Lula had already run for and lost the three previous presidential elections (1989, 1994, and 1998) and had at many times seemed past his political prime. And yet, in his fourth run for the presidency, after decades as a main leader of the opposition, things started to change. With the currency crisis of 1999 and the economic downturn caused by the massive energy crisis of 2001, unemployment and inflation had started to rise, leading to a collapse of Cardoso's popularity. As a lame duck, owing to term limits for the

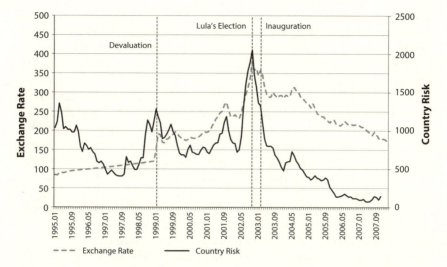

Figure 6.1. Country risk, exchange rate, and commodity prices for Brazil. Sources: Country Risk—C-Bond spread over US Treasury bonds for January 1995 to December 2005 and Bonus Global República spread for January 2006 to November 2007 (Valor Economico at Ipeadata). Exchange rate in R$ cents/US$ (Gazeta Mercantil at Ipeadata). Commodity Non-fuel Price Index, 2005 = 100, includes Food and Beverages and Industrial Inputs Price Indexes (IMF, http://www.imf .org/external/np/res/commod/index.aspx).

executive posts, Cardoso eschewed resorting to populism and maintained the policy of stringent primary surpluses. Together with the choice of a less than charismatic successor as presidential candidate, these circumstances led to the scenario where for the first time in Brazilian history a left-wing party was set to take the presidency. The markets' reaction to this realization was a 150 percent jump of the country risk and a devaluation of the Real from 2.3 R$/US$ in early April to 3.9 R$/US$ in mid-October (see figure 6.1).

Markets had many reasons to be nervous. The newfound order since the *Real Plan* had brought profound changes to the country, but together with the benefits from openness and stability, many problems persisted, and new hardships had appeared. The discontent that was being expressed in the polls could be the indication of a new window of opportunity facing the country, with a new dominant network, new beliefs, new institutions, and new uncertain outcomes. Given the nature of the opposition that the Workers' Party (PT) and Lula himself had systematically exerted during the Cardoso presidencies—to the *Real Plan*, to the Fiscal Responsibility Law, and to practically every other attempt at reform—it was natural to expect that a punctuated change of policy objectives and style were in store. It is true that in June 2002 Lula undertook a "credibility shock" through which the party sought to counter the markets' expectations by making clear commitments that macroeconomic policy would remain austere. They released the *Letter to the Brazilian People* where Lula pledged his firm commitment to maintain the primary fiscal surplus and stated that "the premise of the transition to a new model will naturally be honoring the country's contracts and obligations."[1] But in the middle of an election campaign, this would naturally have seemed as cheap talk or perhaps, given Brazil's history, an attempt to preempt a possible undemocratic turn of events. The fact is that at this point in time there was much uncertainty and good reason to doubt whether the direction and nature of change from the previous years would be sustained. The inability to sustain institutions and policies in continuous cycles of growth and crises are a typical pattern of underdevelopment, so it would be quite natural for Brazil to veer off toward a new uncertain direction at this point.

And yet, despite all odds, what took place was a surprising continuation of what had been put in place by the previous government. Although a new party with different ideological policy preferences was now in power, in essence there was no departure in the nature of policies that were to be pursued or the means through which they were to be sought. The main point in this chapter is that this period saw a deepening of the belief in fiscally sound social inclusion, as well as the strengthening of the institutions that emerged from that belief. Even when new policy objectives and emphases materialized, such as the scaling up of social redistribution, they are more likely explained as a natural evolution from the previous policy direction than a rupture. The international financial crisis of 2007–2008 and the pre-salt oil discoveries in the same period led to the suspension of continuity in macroeconomic management and gave way to a relatively short-lived experiment (2010–2013)—the so-called New Economic Matrix—based on the massive expansion of credit and subsidies, as well as price management and exchange rate interventions. However, the dramatic policy reversal in Dilma's second administration signals the strength of centripetal forces toward fiscally sound social inclusion.

Despite the change in the identity of the group and party in power, there was no fundamental change in the dominant network or in the nature of beliefs and institutions and consequently no change in the overarching objective of policies. The new institutions and constitutional structures that had emerged in the 1980s and 1990s effectively constrained political

1 http://www2.fpa.org.br/carta-ao-povo-brasileiro-por-luiz-inacio-lula-da-silva.

and economic elites in their interaction, ensuring competitive processes in the political and economic arenas. We provide evidence that this continuity is due to the reinforcing nature of beliefs matching expectations within the dynamic of our framework in chapter 2 and not due to a series of alternative explanations such as ideology, preferences, commodity prices, or interest group politics. In many instances, the government tested the boundaries of the policy space defined by the belief in fiscally sound social inclusion and was rebuffed or restrained, so that the general direction of policy in this period is best understood as the product of choice subject to active constraints from beliefs and institutions. It is true that a marked intensification in social redistribution has since been observed, but there was no actual discontinuity in social policy: old programs were merged and scaled up rather than dismantled or created ex nihilo. Unlike the Sarney period of populist inclusion (1985–1989), the new redistribution was to occur within the constraints of macroeconomic policy. It is not difficult to argue the counterfactual case that had another president been elected, redistributive programs would still have expanded significantly.

In the final section of this chapter, we argue that the changes we described in chapters 4, 5, and 6, covering the period since 1985, have in effect been tantamount to a change in the social contract, from an equilibrium characterized by high inequality and low redistribution to one marked by significantly lower inequality and higher openness and redistribution. Although we expect that this new social contract will create an environment conducive to sustained economic growth, we highlight the fact that this has so far been slow to materialize. The process through which greater equality and openness are achieved is inherently disruptive and messy, leading to all sorts of resistance and backlash from those who are harmed by the process, as inevitably happens when there is redistribution. We call this style of development "dissipative inclusion." It is a process through which open access to economic and political markets is achieved through belief-led purposeful policy, but where inefficiencies and dissipation are an integral part of the process. These distortions are not a mere bug in the system that could be eliminated if there were more knowledge or if more effort were made, but rather it is a largely unavoidable side effect that will necessarily arise. What makes dissipative inclusion work is that without the belief in fiscally sound social inclusion, either the policy would not materialize or the costs from the dissipation would overwhelm benefits from the inclusion. What the belief does is to sufficiently tilt the playing field so that the inclusive policy not only gets through the interest-ridden political process that alone it would not manage to survive, but also does so in such a way where the net benefit to society, in terms of openness and eventually growth, will still be positive.

CONTINUITY IN CHANGE

Despite the fear and uncertainty of the electoral period in 2002, as reflected in the country risk index and exchange rate shown in figure 6.1, the market's apprehensions quickly abated. The country risk index started to fall immediately after the election and even before the inauguration, quickly converging toward previous levels as the new government reiterated commitments that its macroeconomic policies would continue along the lines of the previous government. Similarly, the exchange rate retreated from the preelection panic level as the government-elect signaled its intentions of maintaining stable monetary and fiscal policies. An important part of this "credibility shock" was the signing by Cardoso, prior to the transmission of office, of an agreement for a stabilization plan with the IMF that was publicly endorsed by Lula. This was very significant given the historic position by Lula and his party of viewing the IMF as a main culprit for anything bad that ever happened in Brazil. To placate the suspicions of the business elites, Lula invited as his running mate a prominent politician from the conservative Liberal Party. Another signal was the appointment of Henrique Meirelles—a former top executive with Bank of Boston—as head of the Central Bank, an appointment endorsed by Arminio Fraga, the former head of the Central Bank under Cardoso. A smooth transmission of power also was aided by the extraordinary willingness of President Cardoso to appoint seventy key civil servants chosen by president-elect Lula months prior to the change of office.

On the fiscal side, once in office, the Lula government voluntarily raised the primary surplus target accorded with the IMF from 3.75 percent to 4.25 percent. Once again, this was quite unexpected and highly symbolic given the systematic criticism they had maintained against fiscal austerity during their years as the main opposition party. In order to achieve these targets, Lula cut R$14.1 billion from the budget affecting all areas of government, especially social programs. Further evidence of the new government's responsible fiscal stance was the increase of interest rates during the first months in office and cautious reductions thereafter, resisting severe pressure from allies and opposition, as well as business and media, to undertake bolder reductions. Again, this responsible management of interest rates presented a complete about-face for a party that had always decried the perverse effects of high interest rates on economic growth and unemployment.

Further evidence of the government's newfound zeal came when it chose pension and tax reforms as its first major policy objective in Congress. While the previous government had not been successful in passing several urgently needed changes to the pension system, the Workers' Party approved legislation against which they had in the past been the main source of opposition. Once in power, not only did the Lula government reopen pension reform but did so much in the same lines as that of the previous government, approving an important constitutional amendment in the area of social security.[2]

Lula's government not only pursued policies that were similar to those of the previous government but also did so by making use of many of the same governing instruments. This choice represented a departure from everything that Lula and the PT had always preached and created fissures in the party and the governing coalition, antagonizing many of the president's most important supporting groups, such as unions and civil servants. The reform was approved with substantial support from opposition parties in Congress. Even though political institutions had remained basically unchanged, one might have expected the new government to have eschewed what they historically construed as the dirty practices of past governments. The Workers' Party had always questioned the abuse of strong presidential powers through which the executive managed to control the legislative agenda and to a large degree approve all its proposed projects. It was thus expected that the arrival of the Workers' Party to power would dramatically change the nature of the executive-legislative bargaining game. Instead, the new government mimicked their predecessor and adopted essentially the same methods, using the many political currencies (pork) and prerogatives available to the executive to build and manage a supermajority in Congress (Hunter 2010). As would any other party, the Workers' Party promptly drew on those instruments to form a broad and heterogeneous coalition that assured a majority in Congress and high levels of governability.

Current political economy accounts of fiscal behavior in Latin America are consistent with the developments in Brazil but fall short at providing a necessary and sufficient explanation. Inflation aversion and austerity in Brazil is consistent with the received theory: in a globalized world, the threats of exit by mobile capital greatly constrain governments to be fiscally conservative (Boix 2003). Authors such as Kaplan (2013) argue that this constraint is compounded by the transformation of global finance in the last two decades, whereby a decentralized market for sovereign debt bonds replaced banks as sources of revenue. As a consequence, countries see their policy space narrow. In particular, center-left governments are constrained in their ability to respond to redistributive pressures because of the threat of capital flight (Campelo 2011). Received wisdom also suggests that past experiences with inflation have indeed shaped the public

---

2 Three federal deputies and one senator from the PT voted against the amendment, alleging the continuities between the proposal and Cardoso's agenda. They were expelled from the PT and formed a new party, the PSOL (Partido Socialismo e Liberdade).

sentiment against inflation: it casts a long shadow on policy making. The more traumatic such experiences are (such as that of Brazil under Sarney and Collor), the higher the level of inflation aversion (Kaplan 2013). While these developments are consistent with the Brazilian experience, they could not account for the stability of the fiscal outcomes in Brazil, and the observed variation elsewhere. Why hasn't Brazil embarked in fiscally unsustainable redistribution, as countries such as Argentina, Venezuela, or Ecuador have done, if they also benefitted from a boom in commodity exports? Institutional deepening provides the key to understanding the Brazilian case: there has been massive institutional change that both reflects and sustains new beliefs. Note that Brazil was prima facie a candidate for failure because of its unparalleled level of inequality, and consequently its much higher demands for redistribution.

DEEPENING THE SOCIAL CONTRACT

Despite the broad continuity in macroeconomic policy and in the use of strong presidential powers, the Lula government did tighten the focus on social inclusion, redistribution, and fighting inequality. This was not so much a change in course as it was a picking up of the pace of changes that were already in motion, a natural consequence of the belief in social inclusion. Although rhetorical gestures toward redistribution had marked the so-called New Republic since its inception in 1985—the slogan adopted by the Sarney government was *Tudo Pelo Social* (everything for the social good)—Lula converted fighting poverty and inequality into the overwhelming concern of his government, both symbolically and programmatically. His motto was *Um Brasil para Todos* (a Brazil for everyone), and, initially, the centerpiece of his redistributive strategy was the *Fome Zero* (Zero Hunger) program, a social assistance program based on food coupons, and in the wake of the program's fiasco, the *Bolsa Família*, which has since become one of the most lauded conditional cash transfer programs in the world together with Mexico's *Progresa*. Although several other similar programs were already in place prior to the *Bolsa Família*, the important innovation of the Lula government was its massive expansion in terms of beneficiaries while maintaining its fiscal sustainability (it cost 0.4 percent of GDP).

Taken together, the socially inclusive policies since redemocratization in 1985 have effectively led to a change in the social contract in Brazil.[3] This includes the early fiscally unsustainable inclusion and redistribution from 1985 to 1994, together with the social policies subject to a

3 This section draws from Alston et al. (2013).

hard budget constraint in the Cardoso government, and including the intensified social policies in the Lula and Dilma governments. By "social contract," we refer to society's choice of the combination of redistribution and inequality. The prototypical contrast in social contracts is the high inequality–low redistribution contract that characterizes the United States and the low inequality–high redistribution contract that characterizes Scandinavian countries, though a wide variety of idiosyncratic combinations are found across the world. Since 1985, Brazil has shifted from a high inequality–low redistribution social contract to the present lower (albeit still high) inequality–high redistribution contract. In what follows, we provide evidence that what has taken place has been a fundamental transformation in Brazilian society and not a mere drift within the same system. The driving force of this fundamental change is, naturally, the change in beliefs that has taken place over this period, working through the institutions that have emerged as a consequence.

Figures 6.2 and 6.3 show a sharp increase in federal social spending from 1995 to 2009, up 146 percent in real terms and 104 percent in per capita terms (IPEA 2011: 25). As a percentage of GDP, the increase is more modest but still considerable, justifying Brazil to be classified by K. Lindert, Skoufias, and Shapiro (2006: 3) as a "high spender" in the context of Latin American countries and social spending. For the period 1990–2012, Brazil retained the highest social spending overall in Latin America, measured in per capita terms, and at 17 percent is the country with the highest social spending effort (social spending as a share of GDP). Unlike other countries in the region, this expansion is fiscally sustainable because it has been financed by taxes (both indirect taxation and social contributions), not windfall profits.[4]

Basic education spending in Brazil reached 4 percent of GDP, above the OECD average (Bruns, Evans, and Luque 2012). Other impressive gains included improvements in primary school completion rates and preschool coverage. In the period from 1992 to 2009, economic activity among seven- to fifteen-year-olds fell by more than half, from 18 percent to less than 7 percent, while school attendance rose from 85 percent to 98 percent in 2013 (ILO 2011). The system has also become more equitable: The number of years of schooling of children in the bottom quintile of the income distribution has also doubled, from 4 to 8 (Ter-minassian 2013).

---

4 Lustig, Pessino, and Scott (2013: 25) found that Argentina, Uruguay, and Brazil are the countries that achieve more redistribution through fiscal policy in Latin America. However, "Argentina's sharp rise in public spending during the 2000s has been increasingly financed by distortionary taxes and unorthodox revenue-raising mechanisms," which ultimately "may not be fiscally sustainable." This may also be the case of Venezuela and Ecuador (see Cornia 2014: chap. 14).

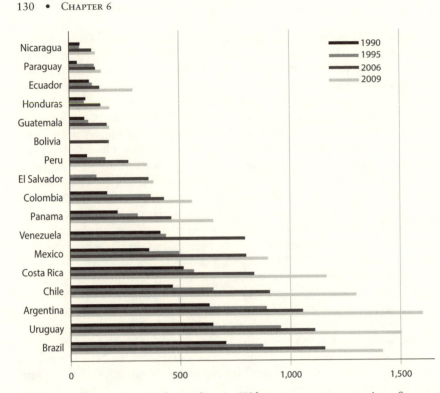

Figure 6.2. Per capita social spending in US$ at constant 2005 prices. Source: http://estadisticas.cepal.org/cepalstat/WEB_CEPALSTAT/Portada.asp?idioma=i.

Partly as a consequence of the need to finance these expenditures in a fiscally sound manner, Brazil has had an extremely high and growing tax burden, especially for a developing country. Out of 179 countries, Brazil ranked as the 33rd highest tax burden in 2012 (34.3 percent of GDP), above countries like Canada (31.3 percent), Japan (28.1 percent), and the United States (26.9 percent) (Heritage Foundation 2012).[5] Compared to other BRIC economies, Brazil's tax burden is approximately double that of India's (16.8 percent) and China's (17.5 percent), yet on par with Russia (34.4 percent). However, while Brazil allocates more than 60 percent of its total government spending to social programs, matching OECD levels, Russia spends only 50 percent (World Bank 2011: 16).

5 Note that the Heritage Foundation data is in percent of GDI (Gross Domestic Income) instead of the more usual percent of GDP (Gross Domestic Product). The fact remains that Brazil has a very high tax burden for a developing country.

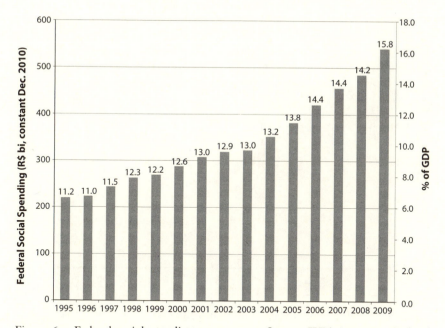

Figure 6.3. Federal social spending, 1995–2010. Source: IPEA (2011: 5). Federal social spending is in constant Reais of December 2010.

Besides direct government expenditure on social programs, Brazil also has heavy pro-social regulation that is indirectly redistributive, such as labor legislation that is strongly biased toward the employee. Perhaps one of the most important redistributive regulations in recent years has been the minimum wage policy. Whereas Ramos and Reis (1995) found very little impact of minimum wage policy on reductions of inequality, more recent studies indicate that at least 35 percent of the fall in inequality by 2005 could be attributed to the minimum wage policy (Saboia 2007). Figure 6.4 shows the real level of the minimum wage in Brazil from 1984 to 2012. Since 2006, the official rule for annually adjusting the minimum wage has been to add the variation of inflation in the preceding year plus the growth of GDP two years back. Following this rule, the increase in 2012 reached an unprecedented 13 percent, owing to the high level of growth in 2010 and the moderately high inflation of 2011. Although this rule has direct and fiscally perverse impacts on government social security spending, it also serves as a floor and a benchmark used by the private sector. The policy incorporated millions of new consumers into the markets for goods and services, including a plethora of durable goods such as automobiles. Increased social spending is fundamentally changing society in novel ways. The *Economist* (2011: 48–50) points out that

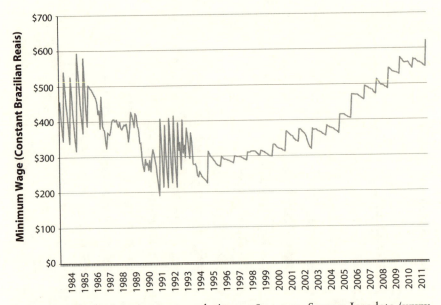

Figure 6.4. Real minimum wage evolution, 1984–2012. Source: Ipeadata (www .ipeadata.gov.br). The values are in constant Brazilian Reais of January 2012. The minimum wage was nationally unified in Brazil in 1984.

Brazil is undergoing a similar transition as Britain in the 1880s, when rising incomes led to a shortage of domestic servants. It cites a study by IPEA (Institute for Applied Economic Research) that found that while in São Paulo from 2008 to 2012 the size of the workforce rose 11 percent and wages 8 percent, the number of domestics fell by 4 percent and their wages rose 21 percent.

Have all these social policies, spending, and regulations had an impact on inequality? Figure 6.5, which shows the evolution of inequality and poverty in Brazil from 1981 to 2009, indicates the answer to this question is definitively "yes." Although we do not present a rigorous analysis that there is direct causation from the social policies to the distinct fall in inequality and poverty since the mid-1990s, there is broad consensus in the literature that the redistributive policies have been effective (Barros and Corseuil 2004; IPEA 2009; Neri 2012). Both poverty and inequality have oscillated in the past in response to shocks and the macroeconomic cycles, yet it is clear in the data that both have been systematically falling since the early 1990s. It bears emphasizing that such a prolonged reduction in equality is unprecedented in Brazilian history. Furthermore, it has persisted throughout a period in which inequality has sharply increased across the world. Latin America was an important exception to this trend. The annual percentage change in Gini in Brazil between 2000 and 2010 was –.07 leading to a reduction in percentage points of –5.4 between 1998 and 2009 (Lustig, Lopez-Calva, and Ortiz-Juarez 2012: 18–19). The annual percentage change in the Gini was higher in Ecuador (–1.47), Argentina (–1.23), Peru (–1.22), Venezuela (–1.21), and Mexico (–1.16). While further reductions in Ecuador, Argentina, and Venezuela seem fiscally unsustainable, the decline of inequality in Mexico is less impressive considering its much lower value for Mexico.

Higgins et al. (2013) present an estimate of the extent of redistribution in Brazil with data for 2009. They found that the Gini coefficient of market income inequality is reduced by 4.8 points as a result of the effect of taxes and transfers, but this rises to 11.9 points when we include in-kind services, and to 13.9 if social security is included.[6] Higgins and Pereira (2013: 11) estimate that through all taxes and transfers, Brazil reduces inequality by 19 percent. This is similar to the United States but very modest by European standards, which is about one-third (Higgins et al. 2013; Immervoll 2006). This is not a trivial level of net redistribution considering that the pre-redistribution Gini is one of the world's highest, which makes redistribution via tax and spending very difficult.[7] As argued persuasively in Engel, Galetovic, and Raddatz (1999), this is crucially important: the higher the initial market income inequality, the harder it is to achieve redistribution via taxes and transfers.

Importantly, unlike other countries in the region, much of the reduction in inequality is not explained by growth and employment generation associated with the commodity boom nor by demographics but instead by reduction in the skill premium in labor earnings and by government transfers (Lustig, Lopez-Calva, and Ortiz-Juarez 2012). In the case of social security, the reduction resulted from the increase in the average transfer (which is pegged to the minimum salary). The poorest decile pays an unfair share of what it receives in transfers in the form of indirect taxation.[8] The poor pay 22 percent of their market income in indirect taxes compared to 16 percent in the United States. As a share of its disposable income, the figure is estimated to be significantly less but positive. The net beneficiaries are the second and third quintiles, particularly because

---

6 This is the difference in the market income Gini and the post-fiscal Gini (see Higgins and Pereira 2013).

7 Pre-pension market income Gini in Brazil is 0.600, compared to 0.506 and 0.509 in Argentina and Mexico, respectively: a whopping ten-point differential (Lustig, Lopez-Calva, and Ortiz-Juarez 2012: 24).

8 Higgins and Pereira (2013) show that when indirect taxes are considered, the reduction in extreme poverty is significantly tempered, while the reduction in extreme poverty nearly disappears, and moderate poverty actually increases when one compares market income with post-fiscal income.

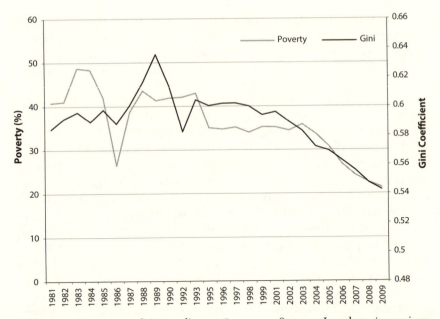

Figure 6.5. Poverty and inequality, 1981–2009. Source: Ipeadata (www.ipea .gov.br).

of the extensive coverage of social security for salaried workers (Higgins et al. 2013). These later groups are also those that benefit the most from the universal health system.

The pension system is equalizing in absolute but not relative terms. Following the changes introduced in the system by constitutional amendments under Cardoso and Lula, the present inequality in the system is to a large extent a problem of stock. Current pensioners disproportionally benefit from rules introduced in the Constitution of 1988, which the judiciary has deemed acquired rights. New contributors now pay into the system rates that are consistent with actuarial parameters.

The effects of fiscal policy on poverty have been important although less than impressive because of the effect of indirect taxation. Importantly, new measures have been introduced, in indirect taxation, which have been equalizing.[9] Ultra poverty (US$1.25 purchase power parity

9 In the wake of the street protests in mid-2013, the government issued *Medida Provisoria* 609, September 2013 eliminating federal taxes on a basket of food and services consumed by the poor. The only remaining obstacle for reducing the regressive impact of the poorest decile is the state IVA (value added tax), which accounts for roughly one-fifth of tax revenues.

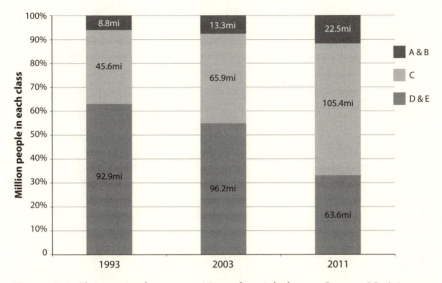

Figure 6.6. Changes in the composition of social classes. Source: Neri (2012: 47, 48) using data from PNAD/IBGE. Note: The definition of each class relates to people in a family with per capita monthly income equal to (in Reais of July 2011): Class E—0 to 1085; Class D—1085 to 1734; Class C—1734 to 7475; Class B—7475 to 9745; Class A—9745 and above.

[PPP] per day) is reduced by direct transfers (net of any direct taxes paid) by 55 percent, extreme poverty (US$2.5 PPP) by 28 percent, and moderate poverty (US$4 PPP) by 14 percent (Higgins and Pereira 2013: 12).

As a consequence of these changes, the size of the middle class (class C) has grown from 31 percent of the population in 1993 to 55 percent in 2011 (see figure 6.6, based on Neri 2012).[10] Over the same period, the richer classes (A and B) have also increased, doubling from 6 percent to 12 percent of the population. The growth of the three upper classes was achieved at the expense of the two lower classes (D and E), which nearly halved from 63 percent to 33 percent from 1993 to 2011. If it is true that a large middle class is important for economic growth (see Easterly 2000; and the discussion in Banerjee and Duflo 2008), then these recent changes in Brazil have the potential to be very consequential.

Figure 6.7 provides a less aggregated view of the fall in inequality in Brazil over time by separating the data into income deciles. The focus is on the evolution of household per capita income for each income decile from 1976 to 2009. From 1976 to 1985, there was a drop in per capita

10 See the note to figure 6.6 for the definitions of Classes A to E.

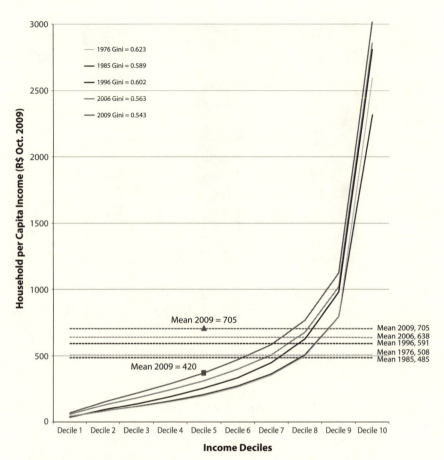

Figure 6.7. Household per capita income (deciles) in Brazil, 1976–2009. Source: Household income data in deciles from IPEA (www.ipeadata.gov.br). The values are in constant October 2009 Reais.

income for all deciles and especially the rich. In the following ten years, all deciles except for the extreme poor improved. Since then, there has been an increase in income for all deciles as the curves for 2006 and 2009 are everywhere above their previous curve. The figure also shows the value of the median and mean income for the selected years between 1976 and 1985. Recall that the distance between median and mean income has been used in the literature as a measure of the pressure for redistribution through the political process (Meltzer and Richard 1981). In Brazil, the ratio of median to mean income has gone up from 0.45 in 1976 to 0.59 in 2009. This data suggests that important changes have taken place in the political equilibrium. They also indicate that the fall in inequality in

Brazil over the past two decades is not a temporary fluctuation but rather the result of deep systematic changes in the country's social contract.

The data provided in this section shows that Brazil has clearly increased its level of redistribution and reduced the level of inequality since the return to democracy in 1985. This is the point in time where we identify a sharp change in beliefs toward what would become by the mid-1990s a belief in fiscally sound social inclusion. In short, Brazil has changed its social contract, moving from a low-redistribution/high-inequality equilibrium toward a higher-redistribution/lower-inequality equilibrium. We say "toward" because it is likely that a new equilibrium has not yet been reached and that the process of transition is still actively underway. Figure 6.8 plots federal social spending against inequality for 1980, 1985, 1990, and 1996–2009 (following from comparable data availability). The data shows a move from the southeast to the northwest, consistent with a change in the social contract. The changes appear modest given the scale of the graph, but keep in mind that the Gini coefficient has high inertia. Also, the near doubling of federal social spending from 1985 to 2009 certainly underestimates the level of redistribution, as a large part of the inclusive policies in Brazil are not through direct government redistribution but rather through regulation that increases access and participation. And importantly, as noted above, the direction of change in the past decade is indicative that the shift toward a more northwesterly equilibrium has not yet been concluded and that greater reductions in inequality and increases in redistribution are likely to materialize in the coming years.[11] As evidence that this is an ongoing process, as of the writing of this chapter (2014), two important policies with tremendous inclusive potential are being launched by the government. The first is an affirmative action policy that mandates all federal universities (which are typically the best universities in Brazil) to reserve 50 percent of their seats for students from the public school system (which are typically attended by the poor).[12] The other is the explicit extension of Brazil's extensive set of labor protection rules and regulations (paid overtime, paid holidays, maternity leave, unemployment benefits, etc.) to domestic servants who were traditionally excluded from such benefits. Although it is not clear whether these policies will in effect have the intended inclusionary impacts, nor is it clear what will be their impacts on growth and efficiency, it is symbolic that such policies have emerged at all, as they impose such tremendous costs on the

---

11 That the country would have taken this route is by no means obvious. M. Medeiros (2001: 6) analyzed the trajectory of the Brazilian Welfare State from the 1930s to the 1990s and concluded that "there is no evidence that the Brazilian Welfare State has undergone a change of trajectory in the 1990s towards more equalitarian models."

12 Here we are highlighting the inclusive potential of these policies. We will address the potential inefficiencies in a later section.

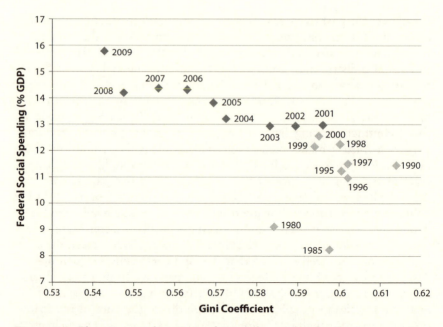

Figure 6.8. Changing combinations of inequality and redistribution over time. Sources: Federal social spending data for 1995–2009 from IPEA (2011). Data for 1980, 1985, and 1990 calculated using estimates of total (federal, state, and municipal social spending) and estimates of percent federal in IPEA (2009: 42–44). Using the estimates in IPEA (2009) to calculate the spending for 1995 and 2005 closely matches the data in IPEA (2011), so the numbers for 1980–1990 seem to be reasonably comparable. Gini data from Ipeadata (http://www.ipeadata.gov.br/).

nation's elites, whose children were traditionally entitled to most of the federal university slots and who hire most of the maids.

In the next two sections, we consider what is behind this paradox. The next section shows that in Brazil institutions do effectively limit governmental discretion, despite strong presidential powers. The subsequent section then questions whether "beliefs" is an appropriate explanation of why this structure of institutions has arisen and been so effective.

CHECKS AND BALANCES VS. STRONG PRESIDENTIAL POWERS

The data presented above leaves little room for doubt that there has been a profound transformation in Brazil in the past couple of decades. What may not be so uncontroversial is the interpretation of what the determinants of this transformation are. Why were the choices that led to these outcomes taken? It is quite unusual to see such aggressive inclusiveness so systematically pursued, going far beyond the usual rhetoric that all governments naturally proffer. By now, it is clear that our interpretation is that the fundamental determinant is the structure of beliefs that currently pervade Brazilian institutions and policies. However, we recognize that before turning to such an ambiguous concept as beliefs, it makes sense to consider other more standard explanations, such as standard political economy or simple electoral pressures. The government's systematic choice of policies that transfer resources and opportunities to the poorer strata of society may simply be a rational strategic response to the massive expansion of the franchised since 1985. Under this perspective, there is nothing surprising in the fact that the government should cater to the poor by providing inclusion and transfers.

Although electoral incentives are a central determinant of the policy-making process in Brazil, they alone cannot explain the government's behavior and the observed outcomes. We will first show that in addition to electoral incentives, the government also faces a binding series of checks and balances that limit its ability to pursue many different policies that at times it actually prefers. Instead of a scenario where the government uses its extensive set of presidential powers to transfer resources to the poor in order to assure its political survival, we show that what actually takes place is much more nuanced. Beliefs and institutions have erected a series of constraints, restrictions, and limitations, reinforced by a set of incentives (electoral, or following from globalized markets, etc.) that in a sense create bounds on what the government can and cannot do. Within these (admittedly spacious) bounds, the government has the freedom to set its policy choices and pursue its vision. However, when it hits against the bounds or crosses over, the checks, constraints, and limitations set into motion centripetal forces that rein that behavior back in. Both the Lula and the Dilma governments have systematically tested those bounds, as we show through examples below. In pursuance of their own policy preference and political vision, they tried to make changes that did not accord with the institutions derived from the belief in fiscally sound social inclusion. As we show, these events have raised all sorts of alarms from analysts, pundits, politicians, and academics who fear that such abuse of the strong presidential powers is evidence that the current model of development is being corrupted and overthrown, a harbinger of the demise of fiscal discipline and the return of inflation. Yet, what many of these analyses fail to consider is that these events are only the first part of the story; they are the crossing of the bounds by the government. That the transgression has taken place may be disturbing, but it is not sufficient evidence that the system has fallen apart or that the institutions in place no longer match the belief in fiscally sound social inclusion. To determine the actual impact of the events, it is necessary to consider the other part of the story, that is, the reaction by the centripetal forces that seek to block the defiance and rein behavior and policy back in.

We provide some examples below where the government sought to implement policies that directly clashed with the received institutions and was eventually barred from going all the way by the country's series of checks and balances. That the Lula government would test the boundaries in such a manner shows that the remarkable continuity that we have noted above was not so much a free choice but was in many ways institutionally imposed and sustained by shared beliefs. At any point in time in Brazil, there is a set of current issues that experts tend to recognize as potential evidence that the country is falling off the wagon. Recent examples (in the Dilma government) include spikes in government expenditure; slow GDP growth; use of the BNDES (federal development bank) to pick champions; creative accounting to assure primary surplus targets; myriad corruption scandals; political setting of gasoline prices with negative consequences for the financial standing of Petrobrás (the giant oil parastatal); supposed presidential pressure on the Central Bank not to raise interest rates despite inflationary pressures; diplomatic cozying up with unsavory dictators around the world; attempts to curtail the freedom of the media; and attempts to limit the power of public prosecutors to carry out investigations. This is an alarming list. But the list by itself cannot be an indictment that all is lost. If there are forces constraining and pulling presidential abuses back, these events may just be part and parcel of the Brazilian style of development given the current beliefs and institutions. This is a style we call dissipative inclusion, which will be explained below, where inclusion is pursued and achieved but not without distortions and inefficiencies.

If this depiction of how beliefs, institutions, and policy making interact in Brazil seems hard to believe, consider the following list of events in recent history when things seemed so desperately out of control and so hopelessly lost that at the time it seemed likely to lead to a marked shift in regime (new dominant network, beliefs, and institutions): the devaluation crisis of 1999; the electricity shortage of 2001; the electoral shock of 2002; the Mensalão scandal of 2005; and the world financial crisis of 2008. In each of these cases, uncertainty soared, and there were doubts about the government's ability and willingness to set things right. And yet in each of the cases, the country pulled through and in the end remained in the same regime of beliefs and institutions that it had been initiated in 1994. This was not due to luck or coincidence but rather to the centripetal forces generated by the country's beliefs and institutions. Clearly, this is not to say that some upcoming shock could not really knock Brazil off its current path, but rather the suggestion that the system is much more robust than is generally perceived.

The strength in institutions of checks and balances in Brazil has indeed been formidable. This strengthening was in large part fallout from the constitutional choices in 1988. Admittedly, existing measures of judicial independence are based on different conceptions of independence and do not provide consistent values across the countries; however, the existing measures suggest that Brazil is among the top performers (Melo and Pereira 2013). Brazil ranks first or second in six of them (Ríos-Figueroa and Staton 2008). In the widely cited Feld and Voigt de jure indicator, Uruguay, Chile, Brazil, and Costa Rica are the top performers in terms of judicial independence (IDB 2006).[13] The strength of the Brazilian National Audit Tribunal (TCU) is best captured in comparison to OECD countries. In an OECD ranking, Brazil is not only the best-positioned supreme audit institution in the Latin American region but also appears ahead of Spain and Italy and has a score roughly similar to France (IBP 2010; Melo and Pereira 2013). In addition to judicial and audit institutions, an independent media is also key to explaining good governance. Brazil, Chile, and Uruguay boast the most diversified and independent media in the region and have been consistently among the top four countries in the Reporters without Borders ranking (http://en.rsf.org).

Multiple parties also play a role in constraining the behavior of presidents, as a multiparty system creates incentives for presidents to extensively bargain with their coalition partners.[14] The Brazilian bureaucracy also represents an important constraint on presidential powers. According to an Inter-American Development Bank study, it ranks first in the Latin American context (see figure 6.9).[15] Professionalization has been extended to the legislature. The Brazilian legislature also exhibits a level of institutionalization unrivaled in Latin America. Whitehead and Santiso (2012: position 8587) argue that "one interesting and important exception in Latin America is Brazil, which successfully developed broad technical capacity within Congress in the 1990s on a level

13 The figure refers to the de jure judicial independence, that is, provisions aimed at insulating these institutions from the influence of the executive branch.

14 As discussed in detail in Melo and Pereira (2013), the downside is that its coalitional presidentialism reduces the identifiability of governments and weakens accountability. This is compounded when the coalitions are ideologically heterogeneous. It also generates some indecisiveness in governments, which is partially compensated for by delegation of powers to the president.

15 Two recent episodes in April 2014 point to the role of top officials in constraining executive's abuse. Through a massive media campaign, the National Association of Auditors successfully managed to prevent Dilma from appointing a senator charged with administrative impropriety to the board of the TCU. The second was when twenty senior staff from the Census Bureau resigned in protest against the government's actions instructing the agency not to publicize survey data containing negative findings.

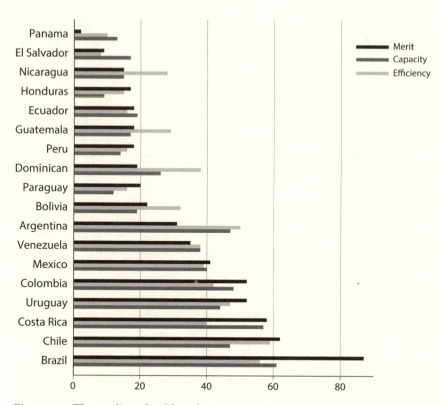

Figure 6.9. The quality of public administration in Latin America. Source: Data from Longo (2006: 582; x-axis shows synthetic scores created by Longo).

comparable to that of the older democracies of Britain, France, or the United States."[16]

Importantly, a parallel development has taken place in Brazil at the subnational level. Many states have strengthened significantly their institutions of checks and balances, which have affected profoundly developmental and fiscal outcomes (Melo and Pereira 2013: chap. 4). No other Latin American country has auditing, regulatory, and budgetary institutions comparable to those in Brazil. Robust federalism and political

[16] Congress has an advisory organ, the Legislative Consultancy, with 245 employees, recruited competitively, of which 190 are specialist consultants in diverse areas. In turn, a Research Office, consisting of about 35 full-time professionals, assists the budget committee of the lower house. It is a requirement that they should have a postgraduate qualification and prior executive experience or a record of work for the National Audit Offices. Similarly, in the Senate, there are 308 full-time consultants selected through a competitive public examination, 22 of whom are trained economists with PhDs (Whitehead and Santiso 2012).

competition at the subnational level allow for political checks on the executive branch.

In what follows, we give a couple of examples to illustrate in greater detail how the institutional safeguards and checks and balances work in Brazil, serving as a stabilizing force.

The attempts by the newly empowered Lula government in 2003 to change the regulatory system in Brazil provide a good example of clashes between executive preferences and institutional safeguards. In the opposition, the Workers' Party had been vehemently against the privatization of infrastructure industries by the Cardoso government. On coming to power, it could not realistically renationalize those companies, but it could change the regulatory system that had been erected as an integral part of those reforms. One of the defining characteristics of the regulatory system was the high level of autonomy of the regulatory agencies from interference by the central government. This characteristic had been purposefully crafted as a means to provide a credible commitment to investors against opportunistic behavior and administrative expropriation by the government (Mueller and Pereira 2002). The Lula government viewed this independence as a license for ill-intentioned (foreign) capital to exploit Brazilian society by monopolizing the markets and by offering shoddy and expensive services. Thus, from the onset, the administration exhibited great hostility toward the regulatory agencies and sought to change the rules so as to undermine their autonomy and gain greater control over those sectors. In what follows, we describe three attempts by the Lula government in its first two years in office to achieve these goals.[17] Each of these attempts raised grave concerns at the time that established rules were being violated. The fact that the newly vested government was so quick to subvert the received system, and to do so without regard for the proper channels and processes, instilled much concern that this would be the new government's overall approach to power. Many analysts at the time decried the end of the regulatory system and made dire predictions about the future of the infrastructure industries. Many others extended the concern to the economy as a whole.

All three attacks on the regulatory system by the Lula government that we describe were motivated by the government's (and the population's) perception that the regulatory agencies protected the regulated companies by granting them high tariffs. The Brazilian system, modeled on the British counterpart, is such that the rules for how public service tariffs are set is specified in the concession contracts signed between the private companies and the government. The role of the agencies is to follow the

17 For a more detailed description and analysis of these events, see Mueller and Oliveira (2009).

rules specified in those contracts to determine and enforce the tariffs and other standards. We interpret the motivation behind the government's attempts to reduce those tariffs as partly ideological—opposition to privatization, regulation, and foreign capital—and partly as means to benefit the poor while simultaneously restraining inflation.

The first attack was the attempt to change the price index used by the telecoms regulator to set the price for telecommunication services. The price-cap rule for most infrastructure network services involves a fixed tariff subject to yearly correction for inflation. The concession contracts specify the use of a specific index calculated by a private institution (the IGP-DI, elaborated by the Fundação Getúlio Vargas [Getúlio Vargas Foundation]). Most of the time, this index coincides quite closely with the government's own index, the IPCA. These indexes do differ, however, when there are abrupt exchange rate movements, given the different baskets of goods and services that they consider. The period in question was precisely one such instance, following from the turmoil of the Lula election. The upshot was that public service tariffs were readjusted at 30.5 percent while the official inflation figure was only 17 percent, sparking consumer complaints and motivating the new government to take action. The minister of communication first tried to negotiate tariff reductions with the companies and, when this failed, pressured ANATEL (the telecom regulator) to take unilateral action. When the agency refused, citing its mandate to uphold the concession contracts, the minister publicly incited the population and organized society to take their grievances to the courts. More than thirty cases were filed in state and federal courts across the country, including cases brought by consumer protection agencies and district attorneys. These cases were eventually unified into a single case that effectively won, forcing the agency to use the IGP-DI, thus breaking the contract and bringing down telecommunication tariffs. For observers and analysts of the Brazilian political system, this was a clear violation of the rule of law, raising the first red flag for the country's future in our analysis.

The second attack, related to the first, was the attempt by the government to undermine ANATEL by interfering in the five-member committee that heads the agency. In the face of noncompliance by ANATEL to the government's requests to alter the tariffs, the government sought means to increase its control over the agency's governing body. The extant rule was that each of the five members (appointed by the president and approved by the Senate) had a fixed four-year term, chosen in a staggered manner, such that each year one member got substituted. This meant that in 2003, Lula had appointed only one of the directors and would have appointed the median voter only in his third year in office. Unable to oust the current head of the committee (a liberal economist appointed by Cardoso) through legitimate means, the government proceeded to use extra-official pressure to make his permanence in office unbearable, leading to his resignation in early 2004. The second red flag went up.

The third attack involved an attempt by the Lula government to rewrite the entire set of rules for the regulatory system. Just three months into his mandate, the president established a work group charged with drafting a proposal to "perfect the institutional model of regulatory agencies" (Brasil, Presidência da República, Casa Civil 2003). By early 2004, two proposals had been drafted and were put up for public consultation. Whereas the proposals did retain the overall model of regulatory agencies, several details raised many concerns. The first proposal focused on the extent of the agencies' jurisdiction and the second on issues of organization, governance, and social control. Perhaps the most controversial proposed change was the transfer from the agencies to the ministries of the power of concession, that is, the granting of the right to explore public services. A second controversial change in the proposals was the creation of a management contract that would establish goals for the agencies, and punishment for when those goals were not met. The government presented this device as being a way to bring the agencies' policies into compliance with the government's programs, which in principle can be a legitimate concern. The fear, however, is that the contract can be used as an instrument to impose the government's will onto the agency as the punishments may conceivably involve things such as firing councilors and budget reductions. Clearly these proposals held the potential to significantly reduce the autonomy of regulatory agencies vis-à-vis the executive. The third red flag in little more than a year went up.

It is easy to understand that at the time, this behavior by government would be cause for alarm. Clearly these events can be construed as crossing the boundaries of accepted governmental behavior within the extant political institutions. It is natural, therefore, that many analysts would conclude that the old order was being undermined, leaving uncertainty as to what would emerge in its place. But we have argued above that these events are only the first part of the story: the violation of the accepted boundaries. In order to have the full story, it is necessary to consider the second part, that is, the centripetal forces whereby the checks and balances and other institutions attempt to rein in the deviant behavior. Before giving up on the system, it is only fair to let these forces respond to the attack.

What we see if we follow the sequence of each of the three stories is that the catastrophic interpretations were not realized. In each case, a series of institutions and safeguards came into play and put things back in order, so that today, a decade later, the Brazilian regulatory system is in essence on the same path as it was then (though naturally improved by ten years of learning and the assurance that comes from stability of the rules). In the case of the change of the price-caps index, the regulated companies appealed to the Supreme Court, which decided that the concession contracts should be upheld and thus the original index retained. It is true that the companies were not allowed to recoup the lost revenues for the period in which the lower index was used, nevertheless, this event was a clear indication that institutions worked, even when matched against a powerful and motivated executive. It provided an important learning experience to all parties involved of how the rules worked de facto, not only providing more security for future investors but also dissuading future executives from making similar mistakes.

In the case of the undue interference with the agency councilors, the system of appointments and autonomy has normalized and today works very much as planned (though it clearly still has much room for improvement). The government has realized that it is better off appointing new board members within the rules of the game, though it is also true that the governments of Lula and Dilma have never fully embraced the new regulatory framework and have often strategically taken a long time to make new appointments.

The learning process in this area was somewhat slower, with the government testing the boundaries in several other cases. But what was seen in each case was a reaction by various different parties, such as the media, political parties, district attorneys, civil society, NGOs, and other interest groups, that are encouraged and given entry points to participate in the process by the country's highly participatory institutions. This reaction is the expression of the centripetal forces reining in opportunistic behavior.

Finally, in the case of the new intrusive regulatory law proposal, it is currently lying dormant in Congress. When it was first introduced by the executive, it raised great controversies, which led it to be discussed and debated in a wide variety of forums, such as congressional committees, academia, the press, and sectoral entities. This process led to several rewrites of the proposal, which led to the removal of the most egregious material and watered down many of the most contentious issues. Since then, the proposal has submerged and resurfaced many times in Congress, but it does not seem likely to be passed anytime soon. In any case, looking back at the proposal's trajectory, rather than a case of executive opportunism, it paints a picture of well-functioning democratic debate subject to rule of law and checks and balances. In our assessment, these three events, and many others like them, are evidence that the system is remarkably robust to the natural tendency of strong executives to test the boundaries. The red flags have since come down.

A similar story can be told about fiscal policy. The public controversy over creative accounting in Brazil during the Dilma government provides a telling example. The national audit body has consistently denounced excessive fiscal creativity, prompting the government to provide extensive justifications for such practice, causing the government to incur reputational losses. The federal government's fudging of the fiscal target by omitting some infrastructure spending from the sums and bringing forward dividends from state-owned firms as a means to uphold its reputation for fiscal sobriety, made headlines worldwide in 2013 ("Brazil's Economy: Wrong Numbers," *Economist*, January 18, 2013, http://www.economist.com/news/americas/21569706-more-inflation-less-growth-wrong-numbers). The *Financial Times* also reported that in the first few days of 2013, the government announced a series of accounting transactions to meet its fiscal primary surplus target of 3.1 percent of GDP ("Brazil's Monetary *Jeitinho*," *Financial Times*, January 15, 2013, http://blogs.ft.com/beyond-brics/2013/01/15/brazils-monetary-jeitinho/). This move prompted the downgrading of two of Brazil's major public banks: BNDES and Caixa ("Brazil's BNDES and Caixa Hit by Downgrades," *Financial Times*, March 21, 2013, http://www.ft.com/intl/cms/s/0/0a07be4c-924f-11e2-851f-00144feabdco.html). In addition, in 2010, the volume of the federal government's "unpaid commitments"—a typical strategy of creative accounting—roughly equaled the total budgeted for investment in 2011 (Almeida 2011: 6). Despite the overall good health of the Brazilian economy, creative accounting has been a serious problem (Garcia 2010). These attempts at fiscal window dressing are consistent with our claim about beliefs in fiscal sustainability. Indeed, because there are reputational costs involved, governments have attempted to cover them up.

In April 2015, the fiscal watchdog, TCU, ruled that the Dilma administration had resorted to creative accounting and thereby breached the law. The TCU recommended indictments for the president, the finance minister, the secretary of the treasury, and other top officials. The opposition parties prepared a petition calling for the impeachment of the president on the basis of this decision. Even though this is unlikely to lead to impeachment, it is another example of checks and balances at work helping to keep the government in check.

A final example of the centripetal forces was the trial in 2012 resulting from the Mensalão scandal. This is the story of successful a posteriori accountability and a textbook demonstration of checks and balances and the separation of powers. The media, Congress, and audit institutions investigated; the Office of the Federal Public Prosecutor (Ministério Público Federal) prosecuted; and the Supreme Court handed down stiff sentences. The Mensalão trial accomplished something that is not commonly seen even in democracies—it guaranteed procedural justice and ex post enforcement, independent of partisan power dynamics. The case reflects not only striking adherence to the rule of law, but also institutional learning and policy coordination, and it is evidence of high levels of transparency.

When he first came to office in 2003, Lula managed to assemble a majority coalition consisting of a broad, ideologically heterogeneous base of support among twelve parties in Congress. This support, however, came with steep costs. Leading members of Lula's factionalized Workers' Party held firmly to power upon assuming office, occupying cabinet posts and positions that should have theoretically been apportioned among the large, heterogeneous coalition of allied parties. Lula over-rewarded his own party with cabinet and bureaucratic posts in order to entice hard-liners to vote for pension and tax reforms. The result was that Lula ran out of appointments and pork to reward coalition allies. The solution found to guarantee that bills survived the legislative process intact was to provide cash payments instead to members of the coalition—approximately US$15,000 per month. In other words, the Mensalão scandal resulted from a bad strategy of coalition management (Pereira, Power, and Raile 2011).

A congressional inquiry began one month after the initial revelations of the scandal in June 2005, with votes mustered from both opposition legislators and members of the government's majority base. Despite several governmental attempts to quash the investigation in Congress, and despite the inquiry committee, its president and rapporteur being part of the president's majority coalition, the investigation prospered with the support of both the Chamber of Deputies and the Senate. Numerous organizations assisted legislators in their investigations, including the Brazilian Audit Court, and multiple agencies whose highest authorities had been directly appointed by the president, such as the Federal Police, the Federal Public Prosecutor, the Internal Revenue Service, the Central Bank, and the Bank of Brazil. In April 2006, Congress officially handed over investigations to the Federal Public Prosecutor, which recommended indictment. Prosecutors worked hand in hand with the recently reformed Federal Police in order to organize evidence for trial, and even before Congress had formalized its final report, the Federal Public Prosecutor had brought its case before the Supreme Court in March 2006.

The Supreme Court began proceedings against forty defendants in August 2007. During the run-up to the most decisive part of the trial in early 2012, Lula paid visits to at least five of the eleven Supreme Court judges,[18] all of whom had been appointed during the president's two terms. Despite Lula's apparent efforts at suasion and popular expectations

18 "Ministro Luiz Fux Afirma Que Não Se Encontrou com Lula," *Folha De São Paulo*, May 31, 2012. Available at http://www1.folha.uol.com.br/poder/1098455-ministro-luiz-fux-afirma-que-nao-se-encontrou-com-lula.shtml.

of sham justice, investigations carried out in Congress and in the executive branch ultimately led to guilty verdicts for twenty-five of the original forty defendants, including President Lula's most trusted minister, José Dirceu, and former president of Workers' Party José Genoíno, as well as the former director of the state-controlled Bank of Brazil, three directors from Brazil's Rural Bank, thirteen legislators, and eight private intermediaries.

As Pereira and Michener (forthcoming) argue, "the Mensalão is no great leap forward. Rather, it is a giant step in the right direction for a country that began its democratic journey a relatively short time ago. . . . Above all, the Mensalão case shows the capacity of Brazil's legal system to remain independent in spite of political dynamics that overwhelmingly appeared to favor impunity."

The Mensalão scandal is not a special case. Rather its outcome appears to be consistent with Brazil's growing institutional maturity. It set an important precedent for a subsequent case, the Petrolão (the big oil scandal), which at the time of writing is still unfolding. The surprising outcome in the Mensalão case prompted key defendants to seek leniency to reduce future jail time. Critically, the scandal involves key members of Dilma's coalition, including the treasurer of her own party, for receiving kickbacks from the country's largest construction firms. The most remarkable aspect of the whole episode is that several of the wealthiest members of the Brazilian corporate world are among the fifty individuals who have been indicted by the prosecutors general, many of whom are currently in jail. An array of CEOs of large contractors and oil platform suppliers have been arrested and face charges of racketeering, cartel formation, and paying kickbacks to government officials. Prominent politicians, including the presidents of the Senate and of the Chamber of Deputies, as well as the treasurer of the PT, have also been indicted. As Dilma is a former chairwoman of Petrobrás and minister of energy, the scandal has had reputational costs for her, although no evidence of her direct involvement has yet emerged. The magnitude of the corruption—Petrobrás's own conservative estimate is $5 billion—underscores to the challenges involved. The outcomes have been similar to those of Mensalão with the rule of law prevailing. As the *Economist* concludes: "the unrelenting pursuit of executives and politicians responsible for the Petrobrás scandal (the Petrolão) shows that Brazil's judicial institutions are functioning as they should" ("Democracy to the Rescue," March 14, 2015, http://www.economist.com/news/americas/21646272-despite-epidemic-scandal-region-making-progress-against-plague-democracy).

The country has made progress in developing a priori (ex ante) accountability through audit institutions, a competitive media, intra- and interparty competition, and even new transparency measures. Yet, it is ex post accountability—bringing improbity to final resolution—where Brazil and other countries fall short.[19]

Checks and balances institutions in Brazil are part of the institutional deepening that took place in the last two decades. These institutions are endogenous to political competition and the formation of beliefs. A major threat to the judicial system and to autonomous institutions is noncompliance with their decisions.[20] The executive branch controls much of the means of enforcement and can therefore undermine the authority of these institutions. Power fragmentation may erode the conditions for successful direct attacks on these institutions, but widely shared beliefs, favoring the independence of the courts, is also crucial to counter noncompliance.[21] Undoubtedly, institutional design matters—and constitutional choices made at critical junctures (and the power balance underlying them) have long-lasting effects. However, the costs of reversing judicial decisions are a function of the effects of such interventions on public opinion, and ultimately on belief systems.

The New Economic Matrix and Dilma's Policy Switch

The dramatic policy reversal in Dilma's second administration provides a stark example of the underlying continuity in basic macroeconomic management and social inclusion. Dilma's announced departure from the New Economic Matrix had been anticipated in a series of measures such as interest rates hikes in 2013 and 2014 amid the deterioration of the fiscal situation and economic stagnation. Potential deviations from the path of fiscally sound social inclusion between 2003 and 2010 had been contained by the centripetal forces of beliefs and inflation aversion.

---

19 The principal issue is reconciling democracy with the rule of law. "Law" is about legal procedures, courts, and police; "democracy" is about electoral processes, representative institutions, and executive leadership. As Ferejohn and Pasquino (2007) have written, democratic institutions and the rule of law should, most of the time, work in unison. The political imperatives of governing may, however, put them at odds with each other.
20 Voters in unequal society face incentives to dismantle checks and balances (Acemoglu, Robinson, and Torvik 2011). In Brazil, they also had incentive to strengthen checks and balances on the basis of their previous experience with power abuse. Political competition and beliefs are ultimately the factors underpinning the strength of checks.
21 Our view of judicial independence, and the crucial role of public opinion and beliefs in underpinning it, is roughly similar to that of Staton (2010) and Vanberg (2005), who have proposed game-theoretic approaches to the issue of popular beliefs and court compliance (see also Vanberg 2008). In a detailed study of the German constitutional court, Vanberg (2005: 14) argues: "The principal inducement for governing majorities to comply with high court decisions is the threat of a loss of public support for elected officials who refuse to be bound by them. That is, governing majorities will be motivated to respect court decisions primarily when they are concerned about the electoral consequences of not doing so."

However, two shocks shattered this equilibrium: the discovery of the pre-salt oil and the international financial crisis. During the Lula years (2003–2010) the country benefitted greatly from the super commodity boom (2000–2009). An explosion in the demand for commodities from China boosted Brazilian exports, particularly in mining and agricultural goods, for which Brazil is one of the world's leading suppliers, and helped sustain GDP growth and employment expansion. In 2008 Lula famously boasted that by the time the "tsunami" unleashed by Lehman Brothers' collapse hit his country's shores it would dwindle to a "little ripple."

The economy's dynamism and the prospect of a decline in demand prompted an inflection in macroeconomic management. The international financial crisis thus represented a shock to the system and created strong incentives for the return of developmentalism. The spread globally of ideas related to fiscal stimuli legitimized the new approach. The administration justified the massive expansion of BNDES (Brazilian Development Bank) loans as a temporary anti-cyclical measure. Although there was no strong civil society demand for the return to the old ISI model, the PT's factions supporting the old ISI policy tools gained the upper hand. There was some internal support for state intervention from industrialists, but social movements, unions, and voters remained averse to inflation.

The Lula government used the BNDES as its main tool in the new macroeconomic strategy. It consisted primarily of measures to expand credit (in the form of mortgages, consumer credit, and loans to private and public companies) via state-owned banks—such as BNDES, Bank of Brazil, and Caixa Econômica—as well as fiscal spending and tax exemptions to counteract the fall in demand resulting from the crisis. From 2004 to 2010, bank credit to the private sector more than doubled as a percentage of GDP, while BNDES expanded its leading position in the long-term market as a result of its much increased counter-cyclical financing (Torres, Macahyba, and Zeidan 2014). The BNDES lending grew by an annual rate of 25 percent and Caixa Econômica by almost double this rate. Treasury loans, which imply a heavy subsidy, were BNDES's main source of funds and by extension is a source of fiscal pressure (Musacchio and Lazzarini 2014).

Fiscally sound social inclusion was also threatened by the government's virtual abandonment of one of the pillars of the macroeconomic tripod, the generation of fiscal surpluses. The Program of Growth Acceleration (PAC) launched in 2007 envisaged investments of US$ 0.6 trillion, mostly for infrastructure. Initially planned to involve private public partnerships, the program ended up as primarily a public initiative financed by the BNDES (whose share in total funding exceeded 80 percent), and depended mostly on Petrobrás investments.[22] A vast program of concessions in infrastructure failed to attract private investors because of excessive and cumbersome regulations (Pinheiro and Frischtak 2014).

In 2010, Dilma came to power in an election in which she benefitted greatly from the short-term gains that followed the interventionist turn in the economy producing a short burst in higher growth and lower unemployment. The government's response to the international crisis had created incentives for a developmental coalition led by the government to grant permanent status to some of the emergency measures taken, which included a massive expansion of credit, public subsidies, and extensive public works. This coalition included large contractors, public sector bureaucracies, and elected officials. These groups benefitted from the national champions policy inaugurated under Lula and strengthened by Dilma, which involved targeted subsidized BNDES loans to domestic individual firms, involving some element of cronyism. They also disproportionally benefitted construction firms and large contractors in the oil and gas sector, including service firms and shipbuilders. These sectors thrived under the strict local content rules introduced since 2008, which required up to 85 percent of domestic participation in the new oil and gas operations (Mendes 2015). The new dominant network that underpinned the new developmentalism involved primarily domestic actors, such as state-owned enterprises, construction companies, favored private companies, and some unions. The short-term growth that developmentalism fostered also affected sectors not included in the national champions policy. The strong currency harmed manufacturing firms. The private banking sector benefitted from the expansion of credit. The resulting fiscal imbalances and inflationary pressures engendered general discontent.

Although unemployment reached a record low of 4.6 percent, interventionism led to severe macroeconomic imbalances, which ultimately resulted in a stagnant economy. In 2010, the Brazilian economy growth rate climbed to 7.5 percent, but this turned into a fall of 1 percent in 2012 and a drop to 0.4 percent in 2014. More importantly (at this writing), a recession is predicted to occur in 2015 and 2016. The government began extensive "creative accounting" to mask the increasing fiscal deterioration that ensued from the concession of heavy subsidies to energy, oil, and transportation and the extensive use of public banks (mainly the Caixa Econômica and the Banco do Brasil) to expand dramatically subsidized credit. The nominal budget deficit reached 7 percent in early 2015, and the primary fiscal surplus declined from 3.4 percent in 2008, to 1.9

---

22 In 2012, 62 percent of total investments in infrastructure had public funds as its primary source. For transportation, the share reached 75 percent (Frischtak and Davies 2014).

percent in 2013, and –0.7 percent in 2014. The interventionist turn also affected regulatory policy and decisions on infrastructure concessions.

The impact on foreign direct investment was critical because the government's increasing interventionist stance has led to a confidence crisis. Foreign direct investment declined 2.4 percent in 2014 and has no longer been sufficient to cover the current account deficit of the balance of payments that reached 4.2 percent in 2014.[23]

In the oil sector, representing 13 percent of the Brazilian economy, political interference is at the center of the interventionist turn. The discovery of the *pré sal* (ultra-deep oil reserves) in 2007 was also tantamount to an external shock to the Brazilian economy. When Brazil started pumping oil from the pre-salt fields in 2010, the country was predicted to be in the top five largest oil producers by 2020 ("Filling Up the Future," *Economist*, November 5, 2011, http://www.economist.com/node/21536570). Because of its strategic and geopolitical role, the government was able to overcome resistance to the reversal of existing rules for oil production (introduced under Cardoso, which required concessions to be sold at auctions in which any company, Brazilian or foreign, could bid equally). They were replaced by domestic content rules and by a sharing regime (in which Petrobrás, the oil giant, is required to be a partner in all pre-salt operations). The massive capital requirements for the pre-salt operations led Petrobrás to embark on the largest market capitalization in world history (US$70 billion). The politicization and explosive expansion of Petrobrás under the administrations of Lula and Dilma led to the multibillion-dollar corruption scandal (Petrolão), which dominated the final stages of the electoral campaign in 2014. Importantly, the unfolding of this scandal is the single most important variable affecting Dilma's second administration.

The country's deteriorating macroeconomic situation, the increasing critical fiscal position, the rise in inflation and stagnant economy, and corruption adversely affected Dilma's reelection bid but did not prevent her from winning, although by a slim margin. In the most competitive race of the previous seven presidential elections since the return to democracy, Dilma was elected with 51.6 percent of the vote. In a classic pattern of pocketbook vote, voters responded retrospectively to gains in their welfare associated with previous (yet declining) growth; relatively low (but rising) inflation, high (but unsustainable) social spending, and low unemployment.

Dilma's campaign rhetoric rested on developmentalist language and anti-neoliberalism. She also insisted on the PT's record in social inclusion

23 Brazilian Central Bank, *Nota a Imprensa*, 2015. Available at http://www.bcb.gov.br /?ECOIMPEXT.

under Lula's and her administrations. Dilma used strong language regarding her opponent's future monetary and fiscal policy only to announce, once elected, her opponent's future agenda as her own. In one of the most remarkable cases of policy switch in Latin America, Dilma disclosed in the wake of her inauguration a set of measures targeted at eliminating subsidies and implementing harsh monetary policies to reduce inflation. She signaled her commitment to restoring government credibility by appointing as finance minister Joaquim Levy, a Chicago-trained economist and CEO of Brazil's largest asset management firm—Bradesco Asset Management. Levy suspended Treasury loans to BNDES, cancelled tax expenditures, and cut spending, aiming at a primary surplus of 1.2 percent at the end of 2015. In turn, the Central Bank raised the basic interest rate six times in the months after the election: it reached 12.65 percent in April, up from 11.15 percent in October 2014.

Dilma's policy reversal points to the demise of the new developmentalism. Beliefs in fiscally sound social inclusion have not changed significantly during all these years despite the short-term legitimacy enjoyed by large-scale government intervention. The Dilma government has imposed a host of institutional changes that challenged the boundaries of fiscally sound social inclusion. The government has incurred massive reputational costs owing to its reneging on previous commitments. But changing course attests to the strength of the centripetal forces as main drivers of governance in contemporary Brazil.

BELIEFS? REALLY? . . . REALLY!

In the previous section, we made the case that Brazilian society is undergoing a dramatic process of change that has in effect transformed the social contract. Institutions have a central role in determining the direction and nature of that change. But why were those institutions chosen? If institutions are the key to development, then why doesn't every country choose institutions that are the most conducive to those objectives? Remember from our framework in chapter 2 that the dominant network's understanding of how institutions map into outcomes is shaped (in an interactive manner) by beliefs. In this section, we explore this interactive pattern incorporating beliefs explicitly into the empirical analysis.

But why resort to a concept as ambiguous and malleable as beliefs when other, more standard explanations are available? Why complicate the analysis with beliefs when it is more parsimonious to look for simpler and more usual treatments that might have induced the observed changes? These other treatments are easier to measure, test, and explain than the slippery notion of beliefs and should thus be preferred if they can account for the facts. In particular, before turning to beliefs, it would make sense to consider the following explanations that have often been invoked: (1) commodity prices, (2) a Lula effect, (3) macro policies, (4) ideology, and (5) interest groups, that is, a standard political economy explanation. If any of these individually, or in combination, can provide a coherent explanation for the Brazilian transformation of the past three decades, then even if our perception that there reigns in Brazil a belief in fiscally sound social inclusion is correct, Occam's razor would recommend sticking with the simpler explanation. Therefore, it is incumbent on us to show that some of these hypotheses simply do not fit the facts while others do play a role but can be fully understood and become a much stronger explanation only within the context of a framework in which beliefs are central. That is, we need to show the value added from bringing beliefs into the picture.

Let us consider initially whether commodity prices can account for the changes in Brazilian society. The logic behind this hypothesis is that because Brazil is a large exporter of commodities, such as soybeans, sugar, coffee, iron ore, and so on, the distinct increase in the prices of these products starting in 2003 has produced a windfall of revenues, foreign exchange, and economic activity that has raised all boats. In such good times, there are naturally more jobs and opportunities, and it is much easier for the government to provide public services and make concessions to a broader set of interest groups. In this explanation, the observed betterment and inclusion comes directly from the improved state of the economy, and even if there is some role for beliefs, ideology, or preferences, it is enabled and subservient to the fact that the country faces a very favorable outlook in the market for internationally traded commodities.

The problem with this explanation is that the timing does not really fit. While the period of quickly expanding commodity prices started in 2003, we have shown in the previous chapters that the process of inclusion in Brazil began as early as the mid-1980s. We have highlighted and described events prior to 2003 that were unmistakable moves toward social inclusion. In fact, we have even argued that there is evidence of early precursors to the belief in social inclusion as far back as the 1930s, when highly pro-labor regulation was instituted in the Vargas era. Some evidence corroborates that the emergence of this belief arises even before redemocratization proper, for example, the *Diretas Já* movement for direct elections and the 1985 passage of the law that initiated the move of public prosecutors to become a highly independent and combative check on governmental power (the Public Civil Action Law N.7347/85). During the first ten years under the new regime, the sharp turn of institutions and policies toward social inclusion is undeniable, with the 1988 Constitution, the priority given to land reform, and the extension of the franchise to the illiterate as three examples among many. And in the Cardoso years, and thus still prior to 2003, the pattern of social inclusion continued despite the new constraint that it now be fiscally sustainable. As figure 6.2 shows, between 1990 and 2006, Brazil had the highest per capita social spending in Latin America, which was only surpassed by Uruguay and Argentina by 2009. In this period, for example, Cardoso had already introduced the conditional cash transfers that the Lula government would transform into *Bolsa Família* and achieved almost universal enrollment in Brazilian schools. Note also that the sustained reduction in the Gini coefficient of inequality to the present day began in 1993 and thus a decade before the treatment effect from commodity prices. The notion that social inclusion began in earnest only since 2003 is thus simply not supported by the facts.

The same arguments that debunk the notion that commodity prices are the main determinant of the Brazilian transformation also undermine the hypothesis that it is due to the coming to power of President Lula and the Workers' Party. This hypothesis has some intuitive appeal given that the ideological stance of Lula and the PT is more rhetorically pro-social inclusion than that of previous administrations. However, the PT era started in 2003, the same year when the rising trend in commodity prices began, so for the same reasons noted above, the timing of events simply does not support this hypothesis.

The notion that the improvements in Brazil are simply a consequence of better economic policy is somewhat more convincing. Once fiscal and economic policy are put into order in the mid-1990s and inflation is reined in after ten years of hyperinflation and a longer history of recurring cyclical inflationary bouts, everything starts to fall into place, allowing the mass of necessary ancillary policies and reforms to be instituted, with the result being the transformation of the country into a more inclusive and orderly state. This explanation has much appeal, for it is quite evidently the case that better policy is in place and it is intuitive that these policies are responsible for whatever changes have taken place. But the policies and reforms are only the proximate causes of the outcomes, and the question naturally arises why the policies were chosen in the first place. The obvious answer is that they were chosen because they work. But then why weren't they chosen earlier? Our framework provides an explanation for why the policies and institutions that led to those policies arose when they did. This explanation involves the concepts of beliefs and leadership. Because the exercise here is to see if some other more standard and direct explanation can account for the facts, let us continue considering the candidate hypotheses listed above to see whether they can provide a satisfactory rationale for why policy suddenly became functional in Brazil since the mid-1990s.

The first of the two remaining hypotheses is that there was a change in the objectives and perceptions of those in power and in charge of making policy, but that rather than calling these "beliefs," it would be simpler to consider them "ideology." Interpreting ideology as the political views of a group or individual, the political history in Brazil provides a natural experiment that refutes the notion that ideology may be the main determinant of the observed changes. The election of President Lula and the Workers' Party in 2003 is certainly the biggest ideological shift of the ruling group ever experienced in Brazilian history. Never before had an explicitly left-wing party been elected and remained in power in Brazil. If ever there were circumstances where ideology would have had an impact on policy, this would be the time. But, as we have argued, despite the changes in personal style, in terms of the essence of the policies and reforms during the Lula and Dilma administrations, what has been observed has been a staying of the course and a deepening of the received institutions. Conversely, the actual shift toward sustainable macroeconomic policy in the mid-1990s did not come as a result of a dramatic shift in the political ideology of those in power. Though the Cardoso administration was certainly different than the previous administrations, in terms of location in the ideological spectrum, the shift was not particularly noteworthy. The pursuit of an agenda of privatizations, for example, which is among the most highly charged political issues in Brazil, began before the Cardoso administration and continued after. Summarizing, the small change of ideology in 1994 brought great change in outcomes while the great change in ideology in 2003 brought little change in outcomes. Ideology seems to lack explanatory power.

Importantly, the failed developmentalist experiment under Dilma's administration reflected a change not in ideology or policy preference, but rather in the incentive structure when the fiscal constraints appeared to have softened because of the pre-salt discovery amid a commodity boom. The institutions supporting fiscal responsibility were not dismantled, nor did they become ineffective. The same applies to beliefs: rising inflation and the deteriorating fiscal condition almost cost Dilma her reelection. And more important, Dilma's dramatic policy switch suggests that there are costs to deviating from the equilibrium path.

The final candidate explanation for the transformation of Brazilian society is that the observed changes are the result of the political equilibrium through which different groups with differing levels of influence vie to shape policies so as to redistribute resources in their own favor while imposing costs on other groups. Under this hypothesis, the observed pattern of outcomes, that is, high levels of social inclusion and monetary stability, is simply what arises as politicians and policy makers consider the support and opposition that each policy decision elicits from the myriad groups in society, taking into consideration their size, level of organization, and capacity to reward and punish, in the context of the information asymmetries, constraints, and incentives determined by the formal and informal political institutions. We do not disagree that political economy is a crucial determinant of all observed changes. The analysis in our book relies heavily on exactly this type of thinking. The issue is not whether the movement toward fiscally sound social inclusion is affected fundamentally by the competition among interest groups. It clearly is. The issue is, rather, whether taking into account our notion of beliefs, together with the political economy logic, improves our understanding of the remarkable changes in Brazilian society.

We argue that it does in at least two important ways, which if not considered would leave the analysis incomplete. The first is that beliefs put some issues and policies on the agenda that might not otherwise have arisen from the standard interest groups competition. The second is that once any issue is on the agenda, beliefs can significantly bias the playing field on which the game is played as different interests try to shape the final policy. The standard political economy story is that different groups seek redistribution in their favor by actively pursuing policies that they see as beneficial to themselves. The political issue emerges endogenously by the actions of the groups and is disputed in the usual political markets. This certainly does take place in Brazil. Nevertheless, some issues also arise without there being a group directly working to shape policy so as to redistribute to themselves. This does not mean that there are no clear winners from the policy but rather that those beneficiaries are not responsible for initiating or effectively assuring the issue gets on the political agenda. In most cases, this is because the beneficiaries are too unorganized, heterogeneous, and diffuse to pursue their own interests. In the standard political economy analysis, this would lead to the expectation that the resulting policy would not significantly benefit these groups.[24]

But there are often cases when a policy emerges onto the political agenda without it having originated from the efforts of an interest group seeking redistribution or from political entrepreneurs seeking to garner support from those groups or voters in general. Of course, once an issue is put into public debate, there will always be potential winners, so it is always possible to say that those politicians and policy makers who

---

24 Median voter and probabilistic voting models are consistent with our expectation that policies are not a result of interest group mobilization but of incumbents actively targeting groups (the median voter or core/swing votes). These models are incomplete to the extent that actors' shared mental models about how the world works play an important role in the process. The nature of the beliefs affects the ability of different interest groups to organize, pressure, and get what they want. Similarly, the beliefs of the incumbents are also crucial for understanding which groups will be targeted and why.

introduced the issue have made the political calculations of the effects this will have on their net political support, so that the standard political economy calculus is still the driving force. But we will show some examples for Brazil where issues emerged into the political debate and were transformed into policy where it is not so obvious that the simple calculation of net support following an incidence analysis of the probable winners and losers and their relative strengths can adequately explain the facts. At the very least, these examples suggest that besides the usual interest group dynamics and the standard electoral game, there may be other forces that influence which issues and policies are put on the agenda. We hold that beliefs are one such force.

The second way in which beliefs can add to and/or alter the standard interest group competition is by creating a biased playing field that allows some interests to be represented beyond what their size, level of organization, and capability to provide support or opposition would warrant. This can be done, for example, by creating institutionalized entry points into the policy-making process for such groups and their representatives. In chapter 4, we described not only how the 1988 Constitution contained such entry points in the process through which it was written, allowing for mass participation in the constitution-drafting procedure, but also that the final document created myriad such entry points, such as committees for all sorts of policy areas (education, environment, health, water basins, etc.) that assured the means for voice and participation to a wide array of interests in society thereafter. Similarly, the nature of several institutions, such as the courts, public prosecutors, and regulatory agencies, have evolved or were designed so as to have a corrective bias toward groups that left to their own devices would not go too far in the competition for redistribution. This does not mean that groups such as the poor, workers, or consumers always win in the struggle against better organized groups; far from it; but it does mean that the outcomes that emerge are very different than that which would be predicted by a standard political economy analysis that does not factor in the biases brought in by the beliefs.

Two examples should help illustrate this impact of beliefs on standard interest group competition. The first is the high priority that has been given to land reform since 1985. During the early military period (1960s), land reform was pursued because it was believed that this would help make the country's backward agriculture more productive. But by 1985, the modernization of Brazilian agriculture through large agribusiness obviated the need for land reform for this purpose. Instead, the motivation for having land reform as the flagship program of the new civilian government after 1985 was the concern for social justice (Alston, Libecap, and Mueller 1999: chap. 2). The initial fallout of this program was what one would expect from a standard interest group analysis. The landowners were a richer, smaller, more organized, and more homogeneous group that managed to offer intense political opposition, while the landless peasants who were the beneficiaries were unorganized and diffuse. The program was effectively abandoned, having reached less than 5 percent of its targets. But nevertheless, the issue kept coming back, even though the beneficiaries remained unorganized and incapable of pursuing their own interest. The Landless Peasant Movement (known as the MST), which would eventually become extremely successful at promoting the interest of the landless, though created in 1985, really started to become effective only after 1993, when provisions were introduced in the 1988 Constitution and set in practice by complementary laws that created the biases and the unleveled playing field that would allow the landless peasants to have a chance in the interest group struggle. Alston, Libecap, and Mueller (2010) show that the subsequent success of the MST in pressuring for the transfer of land to the peasants through land reform was not achieved primarily because of the lobbying ability of this group, but rather because the voters sympathized with the cause and pressured the government for land reform. Looking only at the end result, one may conclude that what was decisive was voter preferences and interest group competition. But one can really understand why the situation arose where these forces could play out as they did only by realizing that something kept insisting on pushing for land reform, the quintessential inclusive policy, despite all odds. Everything falls into place only if one considers that this something is the belief in social inclusion.

The second example is more recent but has many of the same elements as the land reform example and, we argue, many other cases in Brazil. In March of 2013, legislation was introduced in Congress to regulate the labor legislation for maids and other domestic servants. Although other professions have long been tightly regulated concerning rights and benefits, such as paid holidays, extra time, rest breaks, maternity leave, special funds redeemable in case of dismissal, and so on, domestic labor has always been in a regulatory limbo. In part, this is due to the special characteristics of this kind of work, but also it has always been a privilege for the Brazilian middle and upper classes who employ these workers in their homes to have laxer regulatory standards. The fact that this legislation has arisen now is not because the group of domestic servants has begun to organize to fight for their rights or because they have managed to be represented by some political entrepreneur who expects to gain from spearheading this initiative (though now that it has been introduced, many sides are trying to claim the credits). On the contrary, these groups remain unorganized and largely unrepresented. Instead, the initiative has come from the top down, in a sense being proposed and accepted by the very elite that will bear the costs that it will necessarily impose. Clearly, once the issue has been put on the agenda, the standard interest group competition has been set into motion, and this will contribute to shape the legislation that will finally take hold. One may try to tell a standard interest group story explaining these events as the attempts by political groups to cater to a group in exchange for future electoral support. Any such story would be incomplete and unconvincing if it does not consider the role of a belief in fiscally sound social inclusion. In fact, once those beliefs are taken into account, the whole event all of a sudden does not seem that surprising, but rather even quite expected.

THE MESSY PROCESS OF DISSIPATIVE INCLUSION

If we accept that Brazil has changed its social contract to a more inclusive yet sustainable status quo, the question automatically arises: what has been the impact of this change on social welfare and economic performance?[25] Social contracts are not Pareto rankable, as by definition there are distributional consequences. One cannot, for example, state unambiguously whether a US-style social contract is better than a European-style one. Therefore, in principle, we cannot judge if the new equilibrium in Brazil is superior to that prior to 1985.

If we look narrowly at economic growth instead of social welfare, the picture remains inconclusive. Until the mid-1970s, Brazil's economic growth was predominantly above the world average and often higher than the top twentieth percentile. Thereafter, economic growth has been overwhelmingly below the world average, including most years after 2000. This pattern of high growth under inequality/low redistribution and low growth under less inequality/higher redistribution would seem to suggest that Brazil is moving from a stereotypical US social contract to a European social contract. However, the growth implications of different social contracts are more nuanced than this dichotomy implies, depending instead on the relative magnitudes of the tax distortions associated with redistribution and the presence of credit constraints that hinder investments in human capital and entrepreneurship.[26] More specifically, when tax distortions are high and credit constraints are low, redistribution is expensive and does relatively little to improve the allocation of investment expenditures. In this situation, a more redistributive social contract leads to lower income growth. On the other hand, when tax

25 This section is taken from Alston et al. (2013).
26 See Banerjee (2009) for a discussion on the channels through which credit constraints impede those without wealth but with the talent and drive to invest from doing so.

distortions are relatively small and credit constraints are high, there are net gains to redistribution, and a more redistributive social contract induces higher economic growth.

> Are the potential growth-enhancing effects of redistributive policies in the presence of credit constraints significant, or trivial compared to the standard deadweight losses? While the answer must ultimately come from empirical studies of specific policy programs or experiments, recent quantitative models suggest very important long-run effects, ranging from several percentage points of steady-state GDP to several percentage points of long-run growth, depending on the presence of accumulated factors, such as physical capital or knowledge spillovers, that complement individual human capital. (Bénabou 2005: 1606)

What have been the growth implications for Brazil from these two forces? How does the extent of the deadweight losses involved in the increased redistribution of the past decades compare to the potential for improved investment allocation as redistribution compensates for ill-functioning asset markets? It is not straightforward how each of these constraints can be measured and compared. Given that growth has been below par for the past two decades, also during which redistribution has been effectively reducing inequality, one might presume that the tax distortion effect had a greater impact than the credit constraint effect. But such a conclusion may be premature. Although the growth in incomes as measured by GDP per capita has certainly been low relative to the world average, or even the Latin American average, it is nevertheless also the case that parallel to the reduction in inequality the Brazilian economy has been undergoing dramatic changes in other economic variables besides GDP, such as the drop in poverty, attainment of investment grade status in 2008, record levels of foreign reserves and foreign direct investment, and a dramatic modernization and growth of agriculture (see Alston and Mueller 2011). It may be that the increased redistribution in Brazil has been compensating for credit constraints and that many of those who have the talent and opportunity, but did not have the wealth, have been investing more and better, but that the impacts on economic growth are simply slow to materialize and have not yet been captured by measures of GDP. This is quite plausible as many of the gains to be had from redistribution work through investment in human capital, entrepreneurship, and innovations (or new ways of doing things), all of which typically pay off only in the long run.

What can we say about the relative impacts of tax distortions and credit constraints in Brazil? There are good reasons to expect both to be quite large. A highly unequal country with myriad untapped productive opportunities like Brazil is likely to have huge gains from getting around constraints to better investment allocation. As for tax distortions, Brazil has a highly developed tax system but one that is nevertheless full of inefficiencies and distortions. Furthermore, the relevant distortions are those not only in the formal tax system but in all kinds of redistributive policies, such as labor regulation, judicial bias, and social security rules that provide work disincentives and impede contracting.

If both tax distortions and credit constraints are high in Brazil, which prevails? We propose to answer this question by looking at how Brazil transitioned from one social contract to the other. This process of transition is more nuanced than would be suggested by most theoretical models. When beliefs and other determinants of the social contract change, the country does not automatically jump from one equilibrium to the next. The process through which beliefs change is not immediate and consolidates only slowly as outcomes match expectations over time. There is a long and messy transition during which it is far from obvious what transformations are taking place. New institutions emerge, creating new constraints and new incentives with many distributional consequences. Those harmed by the changes resist, distorting the intended outcomes of the new policies and capturing part of the gains intended for others. Those who benefit often do not immediately recognize the gains and are often reluctant to back up the changes. Old habits die hard, and a clear understanding of how things work under the new institutions takes time to emerge.

Tax distortions and credit constraints crucially affect the ultimate outcomes on growth and inequality. But, we interpret tax distortions more broadly than mere deadweight losses to include all the rent dissipation that arises as people react to the new institutions and policies (e.g., lobbying, rent seeking, striking, political squabbling, gridlock, and corruption). In the extreme, this dissipation can wash out all the gains that the redistribution creates. In turn, we also interpret the gains from redistribution more broadly than simply the removal of credit constraints for investment in human capital and entrepreneurship. The redistribution enables access by formerly excluded sections of society both to economic and political organizations and to markets. Much current research on economic development stresses "access" as playing a central role to a sustained process of economic and political performance. North, Wallis, and Weingast (2009) have open access, rule of law for all, and impersonal administration of the law as the defining characteristics of a developed society. Similarly, Acemoglu and Robinson (2006, 2012) argue that the lack of inclusive political and economic institutions is the main reason why nations fail.

The shift from low to high redistribution social contracts prompts both dissipation and inclusion. The relative impact of each and the net impact on economic growth and performance depend on the context of each country. In Brazil, the transition to a new social contract embodies both considerable dissipation and inclusion. We classify this transition as a process of "dissipative inclusion."

The starting point of dissipative inclusion is the belief in fiscally sound social inclusion. Social inclusion without the fiscal discipline is self-defeating, as it was from 1985 to 1994 in Brazil when it led to hyperinflations. The inclusion gets written into the laws and policies and gradually becomes a part of the way of doing things. In many cases, these goals may initially seem like folly or wishful thinking and are often ignored or badly enforced, generating perverse incentives and other distortions. But over time, formal laws and informal norms embody the inclusion, prompting organizations and individuals to accept the changes.

Some examples of dissipative inclusion help describe the process. These examples highlight both the dissipation involved and the inclusion that takes place. A prominent example is land reform, which was a central policy of the first civilian government in 1985 and has featured high in the programs of all governments since. The goal has been to redistribute land from unproductive *latifundia* to the masses of landless peasants. The unintended consequence of these policies has been more than eighteen thousand rural conflicts and more than twelve hundred deaths from 1985 to 2010 (Comissão Pastoral da Terra 2010). The land reform programs have clearly entailed significant dissipation. But at the same time there has also been significant inclusion. By 2010, more than 900,000 families received land through the land reform programs, in what amounts to a transfer of approximately 87 million hectares, an area larger than many countries. Even though a large proportion of these have not managed to become independent producers and many have eventually sold their land, large-scale redistribution of resources has nevertheless taken place (Alston, Libecap, and Mueller 2010).

A second example has been the rise of participatory institutions, allowing the common citizen and representing organizations to take part directly in the process of policy making. The Constitution of 1988 explicitly included the "participatory ideal" to foster empowerment and make the democratic process more open and transparent. The size and scope of the participatory experiment in Brazil has made it a reference point in any analysis of civic engagement (Avritzer 2009). The participation includes councils, budget procedures, and municipal master plans. Initially, most initiatives were local, but soon federal policy making adopted many similar characteristics. Participatory institutions can be found in a wide array of policy areas: education, health, environment, housing, water basins, urban policy, sports, culture, and racial equality. What has been the impact of this experience in Brazil? It is very hard to tell. An edited volume dedicated to the analysis of how to evaluate the impacts of participatory institutions in Brazil finds both elements of dissipative inclusion (Pires 2011). On the one hand, there is evidence that the participatory arrangements fail to provide participation or to affect outcomes, leading to higher costs, delays, capture, gridlock, and bad policy. On the other hand, there is increasingly more evidence of cases where participation has provided access, transparency, and accountability, sometimes directly and other times simply by improving the debate. Pires (2011) recognizes the difficulty in reaching a conclusion regarding the net impact of participatory institutions in Brazil and calls for further research to try to answer whether the inclusion achieved is greater than the accompanying dissipation.

Other examples of dissipative inclusion in Brazil are: expansion of the social security net (J. Castro and Ribeiro 2009), judicial activism toward social goals (Brinks and Gauri 2012), pro-worker labor laws (Barros and Corseuil 2004; Almeida and Carneiro 2009), quotas in public universities, extension of labor legislation to domestic servants, inter alia.

The net effect of dissipative inclusion in Brazil is hard to determine not only because is it difficult to quantify both the dissipation and the inclusion, but also because the process is still ongoing and the outcomes on either side do not necessarily materialize at the same time. In many cases, the dissipation is quicker to emerge and tends to be much more conspicuous than the inclusion. It may also be, as suggested by P. Lindert (2003), that over time, social spending tends to become less distortive, whereas learning and adaptation tend to make inclusion more effective. For these reasons, it is common for the process of dissipative inclusion to be confused with purely dysfunctional policy making that has no compensating benefits. In the end, only time will tell whether the net effect on growth and welfare will be positive or negative. Yet, the belief of fiscally sound social inclusion has certainly produced an incredible amount of institutional strengthening in Brazil in the past decades. As a result, we cannot discount the powerful transformative impact that inclusion is silently achieving amid the fury of the accompanying distortions and inefficiencies.

CONCLUSION

Anybody who follows Brazil closely knows that development is a rough ride. Given the nature of dissipative inclusion, there are myriad distortions, inefficiencies, and glaring mistakes being committed. The daily paper asserts that things are going terribly awry: the most recent corruption scandal; the sorry position of Brazil in the latest Doing Business ranking; or the most recent absurdity in the area of government expenditure. Similarly, the tendency for governments to repeatedly cross the bounds of policy compatible with the current beliefs is highly unnerving. There is often the suspicion that, this time, Brazil has crossed the point of no return, and the centripetal forces that emanate from beliefs and institutions will not manage to rein things back. This often turbulent state of affairs leads to a flurry of criticism by a large cadre of observers, journalists, bloggers, politicians, and experts of every sort, despairing that the recent evidence shows that the country is once again about to lose (or has lost) its way. Much of this opinion is highly educated and well informed. In fact, this speaking out is an important part of the centripetal forces that pull deviations back in line.

Our point is not that these events are nothing to worry about. On the contrary, it is not impossible that a big enough shock will knock Brazil off the current path and into a much less desirable cycle with more perverse beliefs, institutions, and outcomes. By stressing the existence of the centripetal forces, however, we are suggesting that the system is more robust than seems to be the general perception. To see this, cast your mind back to the series of incredibly disruptive shocks that the country did manage to overcome in its recent trajectory: the devaluation crisis of 1999; the Lula shock of 2002; the Mensalão scandal of 2005; the financial crisis of 2008–2009; the pre-salt oil discoveries; the Petrolão scandal; and the fiscal crisis in 2014–2015. These events were not mere bumps in the road; they were major shocks that held the potential to knock the country off course. Yet, in each case, the course was held, the hardships endured, and actions taken such that Brazil remained within the same cycle of beliefs and institutions. This does not mean that this will always be the case, but rather that one should recognize the robustness of the system and not be so quick to despair when confronting the most recent dismal piece of evidence.

Finally, our analysis is in no way intended as an endorsement or otherwise of whatever party or president is, or may come to be, in power. Similarly, we do not endorse or criticize any specific current policy or program, as our interpretation of Brazilian development is not based on analysis at this level. Instead, in our framework, the main determinants of outcomes are institutions, which in turn are sustained in an interactive fashion by beliefs. Although we are very explicit about which beliefs and institutions are responsible for the fundamental changes in Brazil, we understand that there are an infinite number of specific policies, programs, and other manifestations through which these beliefs and institutions can lead to change. We have no way of telling whether the specific set of government efforts that have materialized are the best path to economic growth. In fact, given the messy nature of politics and the complexity of the task, it is quite likely that the observed policies are probably not the best that can be done and may often be counterproductive. What we do expect, however, is that the beliefs and institutions are such that there will be forces that push for those policies and programs to be eventually revised as they prove to be mistaken. Whereas in many countries institutions are such that inefficiencies may be there by design, as they suit the ruling dominant network, we see Brazilian institutions as providing the incentives and the means for the inefficiencies to be continually, though imperfectly, transacted away in political markets. Like co-integrated variables that may stray apart but are always eventually pulled back together, our view does not require that government policy be always efficient and in line with the beliefs in fiscally sound inclusion. We do expect, however, that there will be forces to pull them back toward those beliefs.

PART III

A General Inductive Framework for
Understanding Critical Transitions

CHAPTER 7

A Conceptual Framework for Understanding Critical Transitions

ECONOMIC AND POLITICAL DEVELOPMENT IS CONTEXTUAL.[1] THE NASCENT transition of Brazil differs from transitions in other countries, but there are general lessons that we learn from the past fifty years of Brazilian history. For most years that we studied, persistence or incremental changes were more common than "constitutional moments." As noted in the introduction, it is a puzzle that a greater number of middle-income countries have not embarked toward (or embarked toward and failed to achieve) a critical transition, given that there are role models they could emulate.[2] By emulate, we do not mean that institutions can be directly imported but only that the leaders of countries have a good idea of some of the key ingredients that today's developed societies possess: for example, rule of law; clear, secure, and impersonally enforced property rights; competent and honest bureaucracies; and open and competitive economic and political systems.[3] As sketched in chapter 2, our framework consists of several interconnected key concepts that we first define in a static context and then utilize to show how they produce a dynamic of

1 By contextual, we mean that there are many multiple paths to sustainable development, though ultimately the extant success stories entail economic and political openness. We do not believe that it is best to first open up economically and then politically or vice versa. History has examples of either path as well as a relative balanced path between economic and political openness. Our book provides a detailed case study of Brazil from 1964 to 2014, which allows us to establish the importance of context and the heavy hand of historical institutional dependence. Our book complements and augments the recent literature on development and institutions by proposing a framework for understanding Brazilian development along with a detailed case study. In this regard, we are following in the footsteps of many: Acemoglu and Robinson (2006, 2012); Eggertsson (2005); Greif (2006, 2012); Mokyr (2009); North, Wallis, and Weingast (2009); North et al. (2012); and Schofield (2006). There are also scores of articles on institutions and development. We differ from much of the literature, which relies on historical examples of today's developed countries.
2 We return to the issue of role models when we discuss leadership. Greif (2006: 195–96) recognizes the importance of role models: "Such comprehensive changes are more likely to be attempted if there is a role model, a known alternative institution with better outcomes."
3 We are not arguing that there is recipe for development. There is not; the institutions of open societies emerged out of a process of changing beliefs over time, and each country transitioned in a different way depending on their historical antecedents and political and economic endowments at the time.

institutional change or persistence.[4] The key concepts include: windows of opportunity, beliefs, and leadership. Our major contribution is wedding the concepts of windows of opportunity, beliefs, and leadership to the dominant network, institutions, and economic and political outcomes to form a dynamic.

UNDERSTANDING CRITICAL TRANSITIONS

Today the primary role of institutions as defining countries that are on a sustainable trajectory of economic and political openness is now widely accepted in the literature (North, Wallis, and Weingast 2009; Acemoglu and Robinson 2012; inter alia). By sustainable development, we mean that economic growth is seldom negative and there is relatively little fluctuation in growth rates; this coupled with political development of real competition in elections in which ex ante the outcome is not known, the process is transparent, and ex post society accepts the outcome without violence.[5] But, though we know the differences in institutions between the most developed and the rest, we do not have a recipe for countries on how to make the critical transition from less open to more open economic and political institutions. We have analytical narratives on how the pioneer countries like France, the United Kingdom, and the United States made their transitions.[6] But, the developmental paths of these countries differed even though they ended up with more or less the same set of institutions. In short, transitional paths are contextual, and institutional change is embedded in different belief structures that define and limit the feasible set of institutions that any country can implement at a certain time. But, if beliefs define and limit institutional changes, what changes beliefs in ways that allow a country to embark on a new trajectory? In our framework, when economic and political outcomes differ from expectations, it creates a window of opportunity for changing institutions. Beliefs about the relationship between institutions and outcomes held by some organizations in the dominant network become malleable.

---

4 Eggertsson (2005) analyzes the factors that can account for "imperfect institutions," by which he means that actors are aware of alternative institutions that would produce more economic growth. He lays the major blame on social models. We will return to this in our section on beliefs. Eggertsson (2005: 151), Greif (2006), and Schofield (2006) are closest to us in arguing that experience and shocks shape beliefs/mental models.

5 Of course, other attributes are also important and are captured in the term "open access" as used by North, Wallis, and Weingast (2009).

6 North et al. (2012) present an analysis of the developmental paths of countries that have not yet transitioned (with the possible exceptions of Chile and South Korea). The paths taken by all countries vary enormously.

Moreover, this malleability creates an opportunity for leadership to co-ordinate institutional change. Why? Because beliefs about how the world works change when outcomes deviate from expectations. In such situations, coordination among the dominant organizations in society is critical for moving to a new trajectory because the dominant organizations may differ in their beliefs on how to change or maintain institutions to get desired outcomes. The dominant network may become fragile and porous, and leadership during such windows of opportunities could be decisive for whether a country embarks on a new path and, moreover, whether it can stay on the path.[7] It is one thing to "give it a go" and quite another to stick to it.

Our framework enables us to understand the fundamental transition that has been underway in Brazil from a closed, corrupt, clientelistic society to one that is driven by a belief in fiscally sound social inclusion, which has significantly decreased inequality and promoted democratic stability. Generally, social inclusion ends up in populism with too few restraints on government spending. This was Brazil from 1985 to 1994. On the other hand, fiscally sound policies alone, for example, the "Washington Consensus," are not politically sustainable in a democracy that has not yet transitioned to developed country status. Brazil embarked on its transition toward a more sustainable developmental path by wedding social inclusion with orthodox monetary and fiscal policies. The hallmarks of making the transition include: (1) the organizations in society agree to play by the rules, (2) politics are open and competitive, (3) macroeconomic stability as well as social inclusion dominate decision making, and (4) the state should play a significant role in ensuring the playing field becomes more level. This set of beliefs has driven institutional change in Brazil since 1994.

How Does Our Framework Fit in the Literature?

Our goal is to explain why and how Brazil embarked on a critical transition. The framework developed more fully in this chapter aids our understanding of developmental outcomes in general and with its most obvious applicability to other countries in Latin America. Our framework relies on windows of opportunity as a crucial part of its dynamics. Although endogenous incremental change is an important part of the dynamics, so too are relatively abrupt endogenous or exogenous shocks. Equally

---

7 Our use of the terms "organization" and particularly "dominant network" builds on the work of Wallis (2014), whose purpose differs from our analysis. Wallis is interested in explaining the existence of government(s) and the role of impersonal rules.

important, continual supporting institutional changes must follow in the wake of the window of opportunity in order to buttress the new beliefs and maintain the society on the road to sustainable development.[8]

Compared to the pioneer countries that have transitioned to open societies, there is a greater comprehension today of what is going on and a wider offering of tried and tested institutional alternatives. To stress this difference, we use the term "window of opportunity" rather than "critical junctures" to refer to the shocks that initiate a process of change.[9] Although the difference may appear subtle, "window of opportunity" implies that there is a role for leaders to purposefully react to the new circumstances to change institutions by coordinating other organizations in the dominant network to a focal core belief, which forms an umbrella over institutions.[10] In addition, most decision makers in the past acted to solve current problems without seeing that solving a particular problem (e.g., corruption in banking in the nineteenth-century United States) could have downstream positive (or negative) effects. In our framework, leaders are both backward looking (in the sense of solving a current problem) and forward looking—they can foresee (never perfectly) downstream consequences.[11] We view the inability to foresee downstream events not as probabilistic but in terms of uncertainty in the way that Frank Knight viewed uncertainty; that is, the downstream consequences are unknowable (Knight 1921).

A critical juncture, on the other hand, conveys the notion of a shock in the more distant past to which rulers and citizens reacted with less understanding of all that was involved and a weaker notion of what could possibly be done. This does not mean that windows of opportunity will always be seized or that they will lead to sustained development, as leadership may be absent or the dominant network is such that growth-enhancing change is blocked. Also, whereas it is relatively easy to look back at history and recognize a critical juncture, it is not straightforward to sort out which of the myriad events in a country's current life are

8 Our focus on the importance of repeated supporting institutional changes has much in common with the formal model of Bidner and François (2013), who stress the role of repeated virtuous actions by leaders in order to transition to a democracy. We come back to this point in our sections on beliefs and leadership.

9 Acemoglu and Robinson (2012) use the term "critical juncture" to describe a discrete change in a country's trajectory.

10 On core beliefs, see Greif (2006) and Schofield (2006).

11 Eggertsson (2005), Greif (2006), and North, Wallis, and Weingast (2009) are closest to our concept of window of opportunity in that the process is not a "big bang" and must be sustained over a period of time sufficiently long to affect beliefs in the general population about how the "new" world works. We differ in our stress on the forward-looking ability of today's decision makers because of the role models played by the pioneer countries.

consequential and may turn out to be realized windows of opportunity, and which are just full of sound and fury but will signify nothing tomorrow. The difference is the combination of a decisive action taken at time *t* when the window is recognized and the necessary downstream supporting institutional changes taken to affect outcomes and in turn beliefs. All societies face numerous windows of opportunity, some big and some small, and most are not seized. As social scientists, we can look back and identify missed windows of opportunity. In the empirical sections of the book, we highlighted examples of missed windows of opportunity for Brazil.

Given that windows of opportunity are a chance that can be seized, who will do the seizing? In many instances, realizing the opportunity requires leadership to perceive the situation, propose what must be done, coordinate the effort, and persuade the dominant network to take the leap of faith. Many windows of opportunity go by undetected or unrealized because of a lack of leadership (which might be an individual or a group) to provide the necessary elements of change. The role of leaders is typically absent in the literature on institutions and political science but is often overplayed by historians and business/public administration scholars.[12] We see a circumscribed, yet often crucial, role for leaders as the catalysts during windows of opportunity.

The final distinguishing characteristic of our framework is the central role played by beliefs in the dynamics between institutions and outcomes. A central question in the literature on institutions has always been why all countries don't put in place good institutions given that they are widely recognized as the key to long-term growth. The standard answer is: new institutions have redistributive consequences that cannot be renegotiated owing to transaction costs and commitment problems, such that those in the dominant network prefer to block change and retain a larger expected share of a smaller pie. Such social conflict issues are essential

---

12 Peele (2005) argues that there is a big, but not insuperable, hiatus separating leadership studies from political science; whereas the former explicitly attempts to identify personal qualities that individuals possess and how they deploy those skills in a particular context and situation, the latter mostly derives explanatory power from the analysis of political structures and institutions, thus marginally exploring the difference made by key political actors. Peele (2005: 188) states, "For those who study leadership—whether it is political leadership or leadership in some other organizational or societal environment such as a school, a company or a gang—the specific way the leaders interact with their followers is what needs to be isolated. The exploitation and strategic use of authority in a range of different settings by individuals or elites is a necessary building block to understanding. But it is not the whole story; and approaches to leadership like approaches to politics reflect the intellectual and social environment of their times." We differ from Peele in that our leaders do not so much have "followers," but instead coordinate the dominant network to a new core belief. More on this below.

for understanding the process of development. However, this explanation requires that all economic agents calculate the impact of each set of new institutions and rationally pick the ones that maximize the discounted present value of the inherent rental streams. In the absence of such unrealistic powers of rationality, beliefs arise out of the need to interpret the way the world works. When assessing whether to pursue or block changes in institutions, those in power have to have a map in their heads of how each set of institutions leads to different outcomes. Beliefs are those maps or instructions, though they lack the specifics of a technical manual. They provide an interpretation of cause and effect between how different institutions translate into economic and political outcomes. If the world were such that those maps varied little across different groups and circumstances, and that beliefs had a natural tendency to reflect reality very closely (when there even is a "true" relationship between institutions and outcomes), then beliefs would not be very consequential. However, the diversity of human experience shows that interpretation of how the world works has varied dramatically across societies, so that understanding why particular institutions have emerged and persisted in specific countries requires careful and explicit attempts at understanding the country-specific core beliefs of those who are in power. In many societies, there is not a widely held consensus across all organizations on core beliefs. But what matters for the establishment of formal institutions are the core beliefs of those in power. Whether these become a consensus depends in large part on the outcomes that the institutions produce; for example, in democracies, if the institutions produce outcomes that benefit more organizations, they will gravitate toward the belief of those in power. Even in autocratic societies, many organizations may not like the outcomes, but those in power have the ability to maintain the formal institutions and dominant organizations in society so that other marginalized organizations and citizens at large realize that "this is how their world works."

THE BUILDING BLOCKS OF OUR CONCEPTUAL FRAMEWORK

Windows of Opportunity

Windows of opportunity are historical occasions when there is a chance to change the trajectory of a country's economic and political outcomes by changing beliefs and institutions. We stress that windows of opportunity are not just decisive moments, but rather a series beginning with an opportunity and ending with a change in the dominant core belief held by the dominant network and most citizens. Windows of opportunity begin when (1) the rental streams fall short, or exceed the expectations of members of the dominant network; (2) a new member or organization enters the configuration of power because of an unanticipated economic or political shock; and (3) the beliefs of some members in the dominant network change either because of the change in the economic and political outcomes or because of an exogenous event.[13] All crises are windows of opportunity, but windows of opportunity do not require a crisis.[14] There are undoubtedly many windows of opportunity, but it is the interaction among windows of opportunity, beliefs, and leadership that matters. Windows of opportunity are not only "windows" for changing institutions; they are windows through which leaders can initiate a transition toward a society that is more or less open, economically or politically.[15]

Dominant Network

In our framework, political power means the ability to change formal institutions (e.g., the laws of a society), and during windows of opportunity, the potential to influence changes in beliefs. In figure 7.1, we show how the nature of the dominant network becomes more complex as development progresses. Panel A depicts an early stage of development, when there are few organizations (X, Y, and Z) headed by elites (superscript E) and their clients (superscript C).[16] The elites in each organization possess some form of violence potential that they use to control their clients

13 For example, the financial crisis of 2008 and its aftermath has affected the beliefs of many actors in the sanctity of the existing relative prices of securities or housing to reflect long-run values. In short, many (but not all) economists now believe that bubbles can and do happen. This is no surprise to economic historians, several of whom have stressed financial bubbles (see, in particular, Kindleberger and Aliber 2011; Neal 1993).

14 The window of opportunity may be open for some time and awaiting a leader to seize the moment. This was the case of hyperinflation in Brazil, which we discussed in chapter 5. This also appears to have been the case in the dramatic changes in institutions put in place by President Rafael Correa in Ecuador. Bidner and François (2013) similarly do not rely on a crisis for a transition to democracy to begin. See Higgs (1987) for a convincing discussion of the important role of crises in the United States prompting and sustaining the growth of government.

15 The emphasis here is on a transition path toward sustainable development. This concept of a window of opportunity is consistent with Eggertsson (2005: 151): "opportunities for reform are created by real factors that upset the political balance, by real shocks and exogenous impulses that induce actors to revise their models."

16 Panel A is an adaptation and extension of figure 1 in Wallis (2011). We also borrow some terms, such as "violence specialists" and "adherent and contractual organizations," from Wallis (2011). We borrow the term "dominant network" from Wallis (2014). Network, rather than coalition, stresses the multitude of relationships among those in the network. Not all the members of the network are directly connected, but they have a stake in sustaining the network to sustain their rents.

a.

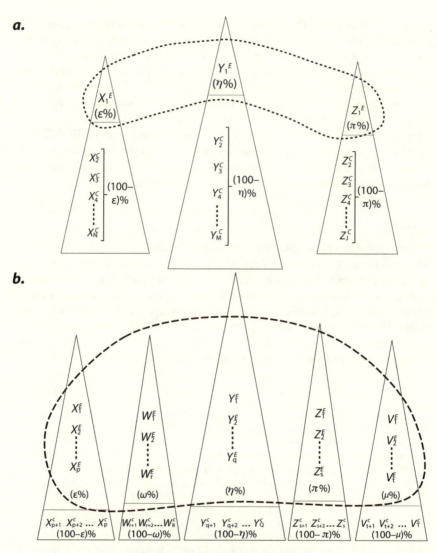

b.

Figure 7.1. Dominant network

and possibly to appropriate wealth from other organizations. A group of kingdoms is an example of this scenario.

The potential for increased productivity and economic gain from peace might prompt the organizations to establish a pact where each refrains from violence. The dotted line demarcates the dominant network formed by the elites across organizations. By refraining from violence, each is able to reap greater rents than would accrue when violence was endemic. The dominant network is an adherent organization that will function only as long as the rents make compliance incentive compatible. Each individual organization, on the other hand, is a contractual organization that benefits from the third-party enforcement provided by the dominant network, making it easier for each organization to control its own clients. The third-party enforcement also allows for anonymous exchange among members of different organizations. The gains in specialization and productivity that can be achieved are limited, however, by the fact that the creation of rents, which keeps the dominant network together, requires entry into economic and political markets to be restricted. The barriers to creation of new organizations restrict investment and innovation with deleterious consequences for long-term economic growth. Furthermore, periods of peace and cooperation are often precarious, as shocks that change the violence potential of any of the organizations may cause peace to break down until a new network can be formed through a new configuration of rents. Many countries remain endlessly stuck in cycles of this nature.

While some countries have been able to achieve considerable progress under limited access, historical experience suggests that there is a limit to how much growth can be achieved under such arrangements. A few countries, however, are able to develop an increasingly complex social organization that expands access into a dominant network, allowing for even further specialization and trade. This situation is represented in panel B of figure 7.1. Note that not only have new (economic, political, religious, and educational) organizations emerged, including a central government, but access to the rents in each organization has become more widespread.

While in panel A the proportion of the population that is in the elite (parameters ε, η, and π) is extremely small, in panel B greater numbers have been granted access to rents and to the creation of new organizations. This incorporation can take place as a strategic decision by the current dominant network during times of upheaval as a means to preempt unrest and revolution (as in Acemoglu and Robinson 2000, 2006). Alternatively, greater access may take place when the creation of new organizations increases productivity and growth in ways that expand the rents that the current dominant network appropriates (as in North, Wallis, and Weingast 2009). In this process, the rule of law and impersonal exchange may emerge within the elite network, creating a society where rents and privilege, while still present, are increasingly dissipated by economic and political competition among this extended dominant network.[17]

---

17 Brazil is at this stage in the development process. By granting open access to the creation of new organizations to increasing proportions of its population, Brazil has created circumstances for the Schumpeterian process of creative destruction that underlie the growth trajectory of most developed nations.

As development proceeds, the plethora of organizations "at the table" increases, which in turn expands the dominant network. Organizations in the dominant network may include political, economic, social, or religious organizations. We are not concerned with the factors determining what is in an organization's "interest" but simply that some organizations have power and others do not; power is a matter of the access to influence or shape institutions.[18]

In functioning democracies, citizens also matter because they vote. Politicians listen to public opinion because disregarding it could mean being voted out of office. All these forces combine to produce a de jure and de facto configuration of political power. It is this set of organizations and their relative power that defines and enforces the formal institutions in a society. The institutions in a society are shaped by those in the dominant network (and their beliefs, which we come to shortly) and their preferences, that is, the outcomes that they would like to see; but there is uncertainty about the precise impact of laws on outcomes. The organizations differ in their beliefs about the cause-and-effect relationships between institutions and economic and political outcomes. It is the beliefs of the organizations in the dominant network, rather than their preferences, that ultimately constrain and shape the institutions of societies.

Beliefs

By beliefs, we follow North (2005), who defines them as the subjective views of actors about the way the world works. Beliefs are very different from preferences, which are views about what organizations would like to see transpire, whereas beliefs are about perceived outcomes from institutional change or maintenance, though, because the world is nonergodic, there will also be some degree of unintended consequences. In equilibrium, institutions are consistent with beliefs. But, we are interested in beliefs during windows of opportunity.[19] Most of the time, societies operate on a "core" set of beliefs, but during "constitutional quandaries," core beliefs become fragile (Schofield 2006). It is the fragile moments that enable societies to change their trajectories.

Ultimately, beliefs about how the world works will shape the institutions that those leaders/organizations implement to achieve a desired expected

18 Wallis (2011) argues cogently that preferences, the range of choices, relative prices, and beliefs determine "interests."
19 Greif (2006) has analyzed the role of beliefs and institutions in detail in a deductive game-theoretic fashion.

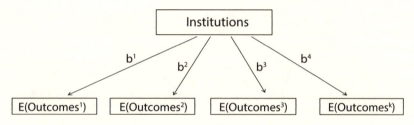

Figure 7.2. Expected outcomes given a set of formal institutions

set of political and economic outcomes.[20] But it is not obvious which institutions will lead to the outcomes they want, given the constraint of beliefs about how others will act. This is important in the transition from one set of core beliefs to another. If there were some comprehensive manual mapping institutions to outcomes, those in the dominant network could look it up and see exactly which institutions they need to put in place to get the outcomes they want. But there is no manual; there is uncertainty about how things work and about the causal mechanisms between institutions and outcomes. As shown in figure 7.2, a given set of institutions can lead to many different expected political and economic outcomes. The outcomes, which are expected to emerge from a given set of institutions, will depend on the beliefs of how institutions affect outcomes.

For the leader(s)/organizations in power, formal institutions are a choice variable during windows of opportunities, although the choice process is quite complex. In addition, during some windows of opportunity, beliefs can also be somewhat endogenous to those in power. It depends on the size of the window of opportunity and the fragility of the ex ante beliefs. Figure 7.3 shows the full set of expected outcomes that can emerge from the full set of conceivable institutions.

There are $j=1, \ldots J$ possible set of institutions, $k=1, \ldots K$ different sets of beliefs, and expected outcomes x^k_j for each combination of institutions and beliefs. If it were clear how the world worked, then it would be easy to choose the institutions that lead to the best outcomes. But given the uncertainty, it is not clear which branch b^k society is on. So, those in power need some way to map—even though always imperfectly—from institutions to outcomes. Institutions shape choices that people make because they influence incentives. But, formal institutions are not the only influence on the choices that people make that determine outcomes. In

20 This is consistent with Greif's definition of "internalized beliefs." He argues that internalized beliefs of those with power can motivate them to change institutions consistent with their beliefs.

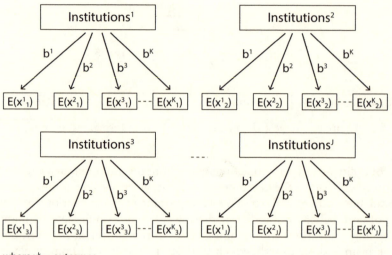

where x^k_j = outcomes

Figure 7.3. Expected outcomes from all possible formal institutions

addition to the unintended consequences from changing formal institutions, there are unintended consequences from informal institutions; and internal and external shocks, which all play a role in the ultimate outcomes.

Beliefs emerge from history, experience, interaction, and serendipity, though those in power have a greater scope to act on their beliefs.[21] Once beliefs emerge, the choice in institutions becomes tractable. Given belief b^k emerges, the group in power will choose *Institutions^j*, where j is the set of institutions that leads to the best expected outcome for them. If, for example, given beliefs b^3, $E(outcomes^3_j) > E(outcomes^3_i)$ for every $i \neq 3$, then the leader/organization in power would choose institutions that best fit their preferences.

In figure 7.4, beliefs b^3 have arisen, and the choice of institutions is then a matter of picking those institutions that maximize the *expected* outcomes for the group in power. We stress that institutions never map directly into outcomes, but rather those in power can choose the institutions that they believe will give the best expected outcomes.

21 When outcomes are very different from expectations, beliefs change, at least for those in power, and a window of opportunity emerges for leadership. Schofield (2006) argues that Benjamin Franklin, acting on news that the French would support the colonies in their independence struggle with Great Britain, convinced the elite in the colonies to draft and sign the Declaration of Independence.

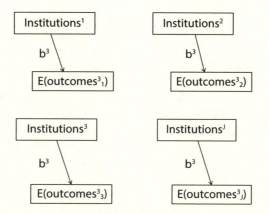

Figure 7.4. Choice of formal institutions given beliefs

Once those leaders/organizations with power choose and implement institutions, the outcomes that emerge have to match their expectations at least approximately; otherwise the divergent outcomes will change the organizations in the dominant network, or the beliefs of those in the dominant network, or both. The degree to which new formal institutions change outcomes depends on the extent to which they are compatible with the beliefs and norms of the economic and political organizations in society. If the beliefs of a sufficient number of organizations are firmly held and are inconsistent with the new incentives, the expected outcome for those in power will not materialize. Greif (2006) argues that the incompatibility of possible new institutions with the extant beliefs held by actors at large is a significant part of the explanation for institutional persistence. This is persuasive; however, if beliefs are malleable during windows of opportunity, institutions will have a bigger impact on outcomes because behavioral beliefs by organizations outside the dominant network may also change with repeated behavior and institutional deepening.[22]

When expected outcomes do not materialize, there will eventually be a revision of the beliefs of those in the dominant network, or the dissatisfaction with the outcomes might, given a window of opportunity, lead to a punctuated change in the dominant network, beliefs, and institutions. We argue that experiences (political and economic outcomes) are

---

[22] Repeated play by the dominant network is what drives changes in beliefs by citizens about the actions (and motives) of those in power. Repeat play is at the heart of the model in Bidner and François (2013).

the main factor shaping and changing beliefs of leaders/organizations in the dominant network as well as shaking the beliefs of citizens at large.[23]

We are not proposing a full theory of the determinants of beliefs. Our goal is more modest. Like North, Wallis, and Weingast (2009: 262), we argue that "the cultural environment—the political, economic, social context—fundamentally influences beliefs." It is the beliefs of those in the dominant network that matter because those in power face windows of opportunity and make the laws. Nevertheless, the beliefs of citizens do matter in many countries. Indeed, the beliefs held by the citizens are a constraint on those in power. Those in power have preferences over outcomes, but it is their beliefs that determine their actions. Our view on the role of beliefs matches Mokyr's view of the role of enlightenment in enabling the British Industrial Revolution:

> To sum up: Britain became the leader of the Industrial Revolution . . . thanks to the great synergy of the Enlightenment: the combination of the Baconian program in useful knowledge and the recognition that better institutions created better incentives. (Mokyr 2009: 122)

According to Mokyr (2009: 40), "Enlightenment beliefs followed in the footsteps of Bacon's idea of understanding nature in order to control her." It was a belief that with the application of useful knowledge, a country could progress over the status quo. The application of knowledge in turn needed institutions that promoted "progress." At the time, this was a new belief as well as a belief not shared by all powerful actors. It is the very nature of subjectivity of beliefs that gives rise to different views about the impact of institutions on outcomes. For a modern example, following the financial crisis of 2008, there is a lively debate among economists, politicians, and other interest groups about the impact of a stimulus plan versus an austerity plan for promoting recovery.[24] The actions that get taken result from the relative power of the organizations in the dominant network and beliefs of those with the power, as well as the role of leadership.

An even more forceful account of the centrality of beliefs for promoting prosperity comes from Deidre McCloskey in her two volumes: *Bourgeois Virtues* (2006) and *Bourgeois Dignity* (2010).[25] McCloskey views "ideas"

---

23 Our view is very similar to Eggertsson's (2005: 26) definition of a policy model: "Policy models are the operational models that guide decision makers, whether in the private or public sphere. Policy models define for the actor his or her choice set, rank the elements in the choice set, and describe relationships between means and ends (instruments and targets)."

24 This is written in 2014 in the shadow of the "euro crisis" and persistent high unemployment in the United States and across many countries in Europe.

25 Obviously, the locus classicus for the notion that ideas matter is Max Weber's work. Hall (1989) provides a more recent treatment of the role of ideas in economic policy making.

and not institutions, geography, natural resources, or other determinants as the catalyst of modern economic growth starting in Europe in the mid-eighteenth century. In particular, the idea that started the "Great Enrichment" was the change in the belief about the dignity of commercial pursuits. Once commercial and mercantile activities stopped being viewed with contempt and dishonor—as opposed to the pursuits of warriors, noblemen, and the clergy—trade, commerce, exchange, and innovation flourished, unleashing the unprecedented explosion of prosperity.[26]

In today's modern world, political and economic actors can have a more forward-looking view of beliefs because there are role models. Whereas the pioneer countries were trying to solve problems in light of their past experiences, today's countries can draw on the experiences of the already-developed world for some of their beliefs. Not only can those in power draw from these experiences, but in some instances they do so inappropriately for a particular country. This was the problem with blindly relying on the "Washington Consensus."[27] The failure of the consensus to work in certain countries was a result of the incompatibility of the rules/incentives with the beliefs held by citizens. We stress that learning from other countries does not mean that the implementation will have the same effect, but nevertheless, it can affect not only their "belief" but the depth of their belief, which determines how long those in the dominant network hold on to the cause-and-effect relationship. For example, if those in power want to control inflation, there is a consensus among many analysts that this is easier to accomplish if the central bank has independence from political pressure. So far, we have simply posited that beliefs shape actions; but if beliefs shape institutions, it is paramount to posit how beliefs change, at least on the margin. We will do so later in this chapter when we discuss the dynamics of the framework. For now, we posit that belief deepening depends on outcomes and the actions taken by others, including the support of citizens.[28] Belief deepening is

26 Although we share McCloskey's position on the centrality of ideas/beliefs in economic growth and development, we do not go as far as she does in downplaying the role of institutions. In our framework, beliefs are important because they affect which institutions get put in place, and, by affecting outcomes, institutions feed back into beliefs. For this reason, it makes little sense to argue whether institutions or beliefs matter the most: they are both crucial parts of the dynamics.

27 On the incentive compatibility problem of policy advice, see Acemoglu and Robinson (2013).

28 For examples of how belief deepening depends on the outcomes being consistent with the prediction of those in power, who first held the belief, see Bates, de Figueiredo, and Weingast (1998), who examine Zambia and the former Yugoslavia; Eggertsson (2005), who analyzes the persistence and eventual change in beliefs in Iceland; Rakove, Rutten, and Weingast (2004), who examine beliefs in the colonies leading to the Revolutionary War between the North American colonies (United States) and Great Britain; and Greif (2006), who examines beliefs in the context of medieval trade.

also iterative between the institutions established by those in power and the perception of the outcomes by organizations and citizens.[29]

Leadership

Leadership is a relatively absent concept in most frameworks of institutional change, though its importance has seen resurgence.[30] By leadership, we mean that certain individuals at certain moments in a country's history make a difference because of their actions. The counterfactual situation is that if someone else or another group of people were in the same position of power with the same beliefs, the forthcoming institutions could have been different. Our view is akin to the "structural theories" of leadership and most similar to leadership as espoused by Schofield (2006). Ahlquist and Levi cogently describe Schofield's concept of leadership:

> For Schofield, pivotal moments in history—what he calls "constitutional quandaries"—occur when core beliefs no longer conform to reality or, slightly more formally, when there is extreme variation in individual assessments of the appropriate action relative to the common, shared understanding. When these moments occur, small shifts in the beliefs of a few may trigger a cascade that results in an entirely different configuration of beliefs.

29 On the importance of the dynamics for belief deepening, we are consistent with Bidner and François (2013).

30 We thank Avner Greif, Patrick François, and Barry Weingast for discussions on the roles of leadership and beliefs. For an excellent analytical survey of recent contributions to the literature on leadership, see Ahlquist and Levi (2011). As examples of the resurgent importance of leadership in frameworks of institutional change, see Bidner and François (2013), who model the interaction of leaders and citizens in transitioning to democracy; Greif (2006: 201–2), who discusses the importance of "institutional entrepreneurs"; Jones and Olken (2005), who use deaths of leaders as an exogenous change in leadership and find that leaders matter for economic growth; and Schofield (2006), who argues that during "constitutional quandaries" leaders can influence the shift to a new core belief. Schofield posits that Benjamin Franklin, James Madison, Thomas Jefferson, Abraham Lincoln, and Lyndon Johnson were "architects of change" (leaders). Earlier scholars recognizing the importance of leadership include Harberger (1998), who strongly argues that leadership mattered enormously for the economic reforms in Latin America; and Higgs (1987) and North (1981), who discuss "ideological entrepreneurs" (for Higgs in times of crisis). Leadership has been recognized by the "Austrian" school as entrepreneurship but for the most part has been applied to business organizations, not political organizations. See Wagner (1966) and Frohlich, Oppenheimer, and Young (1971) for a role for political entrepreneurship. Political scientists have elaborated on leadership, but mostly in the context of principal/agent models. See Fiorina and Shepsle (1989) for a discussion of formal theories of leadership in which they discuss the strengths and weaknesses of principal/agent models. For an earlier discussion of the coordinative role of leadership, see Neustadt (1990) and Riker (1983, 1996). We draw most heavily on Ahlquist and Levi (2011), Greif (2006), Riker (1996), and Schofield (2006).

A leader is the agent most likely to trigger such a cascade. According to Schofield, "architects of change" must do two things: (*a*) communicate a model of the world in which there are specific outcomes associated with differing courses of action and (*b*) convincingly advocate a specific outcome. (Ahlquist and Levi 2011: 8)

We differ from Schofield in that we do not believe that beliefs change in a "cascade" but rather deepen, depending on outcomes consistent with the beliefs initially held by a "few." We agree that leaders start the process because they hold beliefs about institutional changes that can set the country on a new trajectory. This change in trajectory is just a start and must be reinforced over time. We are not arguing that leaders simply impose beliefs from the top down but rather leaders sense and articulate what is likely a latent belief held by many.[31]

As noted in chapter 2, the fact that history is replete with the mention of individuals lends considerable anecdotal weight and circumstantial evidence to the argument that certain individuals *did* make a difference. Leadership comprises several concepts that are not mutually exclusive: (1) cognition, (2) heresthetics or coordination, and (3) moral authority.[32] Before one can be a leader, he or she has to cognitively be aware that a window of opportunity exists. In addition, that person must know how to take advantage of the window of opportunity. In short, cognition entails being able to address two questions: What is the problem or opportunity that we face? How can we solve the problem or take advantage of the situation? This should not be construed that leaders perfectly foresee all downstream consequences, but only that they see the problem and have a provisional "game plan" on how to both correct the problem at time t and understand that they will have to react to downstream consequences in unforeseen ways to sustain the solution to the problem at time $t + n$.[33] Indeed, without downstream institutional deepening, the initial "big bang" would not produce long-run benefits. It is the combination of the initial institutional change that, if successful, affects beliefs in a way that will enable later institutional deepening. Leaders also never act alone; it is the orchestration of other powerful organizations in the dominant network that allows the initial change and subsequent institutional deepening to take place. Another way of putting it is: if the initial institutional changes produce outcomes that benefit extant organizations or create new organizations that win, the

---

31 This view is consistent with Bidner and François (2013).

32 See Greif (2012, esp. chap. 3) for the leadership roles of cognition, moral authority, and coordination.

33 Knowing ex ante that there will be unforeseen consequences that need to be met is consistent with what North (1990) called "adaptive efficiency."

beneficiary organizations now have a stake in sustaining and deepening the new institutions.

Political entrepreneurship to overcome the collective-action problem is another way to portray leadership (Wagner 1966).[34] We refer to political entrepreneurship, following William Riker (1996: 9), as heresthetics, which Riker defined as: "the art of setting up situations—composing the alternatives among which political actors must choose—in such a way that even those who do not wish to do so are compelled by the structure of the situation to support the heresthetician's purpose." Heresthetics involves strategy, especially dynamically in the course of decision making.[35] There are two aspects of "dynamic": (1) the art of compromise in the interest of getting most of what you want and (2) staying the course temporally in order to solidify beliefs. Heresthetics is the "art" of policy making and is not justified by ex post rational choice and could certainly not be designed ex ante by a mechanism design approach. Successful leadership entails cognitive ability of knowing what to do along with the coordinative ability of getting others in power to go along.

Leadership can be in leaders' and their supporters' narrowly construed self-interest, but leaders at times take reputation or "moral" rents into account (Greif 2008). Some leaders try to do "the right thing" for their country by "playing for the history books." Harberger (1998) maintains that several Latin American leaders from the 1960s to the 1990s took courageous steps to help their economies with unselfish motives driving them. In addition to seeking "moral" rents, some leaders have moral authority either because of their past or because they earned it. Moral authority does not necessarily make heads of state "leaders" but it gives them legitimacy, which in turn can induce a public to trust their motives, which may lead more readily to accepting new beliefs during windows of opportunity.[36]

Leadership can change the trajectory of a society for better or worse. Leadership is an important concept only when there are windows of opportunity. For much of the time, countries are on "autopilot," such that the rental streams are within a tolerable band to those in power so that there is no reason to rock the boat by changing institutions in a big way. It is not the case that all you need for development are "great" leaders but rather that individuals and certain organizations at times make a

---

34 Indeed, as we argue in chapter 4, President Collor recognized the problem of inflation but did not possess the coordinative ability to quell inflation.

35 Riker (1983, 1996) applied heresthetics to the establishment of the electoral college and the ratification of the US Constitution.

36 Nelson Mandela in South Africa or Václav Havel in the Czech Republic commanded moral authority because of their time spent in prison. On the use of parliament for legitimacy of kings in England, see Greif and Ruben (2014).

difference. For example, if this were not the case, there would be no need to discuss France without Napoleon; the United States without George Washington; Great Britain absent Churchill; China after Mao and with Deng; Argentina after Perón or, in our case, Brazil after Cardoso. We believe that these individuals, along with their allies, made a difference. Similarly, today there are discussions about Cuba after Castro; Venezuela after Chavez; Korea after Kim Jong I; and Egypt after Mubarak. If individuals did not matter, then these discussions would be pointless.[37]

Institutions

We follow in the now standard tradition of North (1990) by defining institutions as the formal and informal "rules of the game," along with enforcement for noncompliance, that shape behavior. Formal institutions include the laws of society and how they are enforced. In Brazil, laws are passed by Congress and approved or vetoed by the president. Informal institutions include the norms of behavior within a society. A critical difference between formal rules/laws and norms is enforcement. Formal rules mean that there are recognized formal sanctions, even if only in a probabilistic sense. Norms do not have a specified enforcer but are typically enforced through some form of societal sanction, ostracism being such a form. The sanctions emanate from the shared belief by most members of society in the norm.[38] In legitimate democracies with checks and balances, laws are passed under the shadow of the Supreme Court.[39] Together, formal rules/laws and informal norms provide the incentive structure for economic, political, and social actions. By the incentive structure, we mean the perceived reward structure faced by all individuals in political activity, in market activities, and within firms and other internal organizations. The perceived rewards vary enormously across individuals in political and economic activities. The perceived rewards and the actions undertaken produce economic and political outcomes, some of which may be consistent with the underlying beliefs of cause and effect as expected by those in power and others inconsistent with the beliefs of

---

37 We recognize that the exit of certain individuals may simply be a tipping point and that many other underlying economic and political organizations may have already changed. This appears to be the case for Cuba, which has now embarked on reforms. As of this writing, the exit of Mubarak has not produced significant changes in the powerful economic or political organizations controlling Egypt.

38 We draw on Alston, Mueller, and Nonnenmacher (forthcoming, esp. chap. 2).

39 The size of the shadow of the court varies from country to country. For example, in Argentina, from 1946 to 2010, every administration but one (de la Rúa) has either impeached Supreme Court justices, forced resignations, or added justices (Alston and Gallo 2010). This has led to little if no constraints on the executive and legislative branches.

the designers of the formal institutions. Deep-seated behavioral and in-ternalized (core) beliefs (as defined by Greif 2006) may often be the cause for why the outcomes deviate from the belief of policy makers. In short, the set of beliefs held by those in power about how a new institutional change will affect expected outcomes deviates from the actual outcome because the actors in society hold onto their set of behavioral beliefs, which differs from those in power who can change the rules.

The laws that countries pass will frequently entail political or eco-nomic side payments. When the side payments are transparent, we call the process lobbying or "pork." When the process is not transparent, we label the process as "corrupt." Whether it is pork or bribes, many policy mak-ers condemn these practices, but, as North, Wallis, and Weingast (2009) point out, they are the glue that prevents the entire system from unravel-ing into violence in less mature societies. For advanced societies, the pork may enable welfare-enhancing measures, and eliminating pork may make policy change impossible (Alston and Mueller 2006) or dysfunctional (Pereira and Mejía Acosta 2010). In the process of institutional change in Brazil, we need to recognize the important developmental role of pork.

Economic and Political Outcomes

Institutions generate incentives for economic and political activity that in turn produce economic and political outcomes. Again, we recognize that it is not simply formal institutions that determine the full set of incen-tives; norms also matter, as well as the differing relative prices or costs of taking certain actions—which in turn depend on institutions—and the perception of actors of the outcomes from choices. It matters for those in power if the outcomes are consistent with their beliefs because they enact institutions to change incentives, which in turn will produce outcomes that they perceived as beneficial for their goals. Political outcomes include both narrow outcomes (e.g., politicians want to get reelected) and broad outcomes (e.g., the degree of personal freedoms in a society). Economic outcomes, as well, are narrow (e.g., Did import protection increase the profits of a particular industry?) or broad (e.g., How did policies impact unemployment levels, economic growth per capita, or income inequal-ity?). The economic and political outcomes can have two effects. If they are sufficiently different from expectations or repeatedly different from the expectations, they can affect the beliefs of those in power.[40] In addi-tion to affecting beliefs, the political and economic returns can change the relative power of the economic and political organizations in the

---

40 This is consistent with Eggertsson's (2005) argument that experiences affect social/policy models.

dominant network. It is the change in beliefs or the change in power that generates the *dynamics* in our framework, producing either incremental institutional changes or more discrete large institutional changes when a window of opportunity opens along with the necessary leadership.

Dynamics

Now that we have the elements, we can discuss in broad terms the dynamics of the framework that we summarize in figure 7.5. This is essentially the same as figure 2.1 shown in chapter 2, with time shown more explicitly moving from left to right. At time *t*, a society is at the left side of the figure in "autopilot" mode. This is the situation in societies in most periods. There is a set of core beliefs held by the dominant network as well as other organizations and citizens. The core beliefs shape laws and their enforcement, and we see only incremental changes because the economic and political outcomes match the expectations of the dominant network. In this state of the world, there is no role for leadership as we defined it. The world that the players face is never static, so they always take some actions to change some institutions on the margin, though others they leave as fixed.

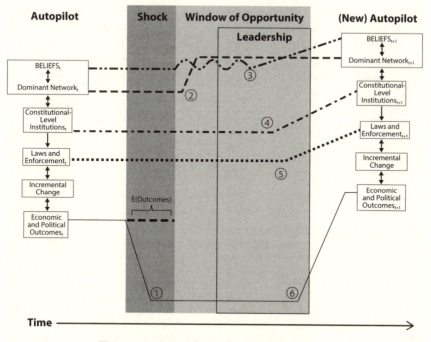

Figure 7.5. Autopilot and critical transitions

Most institutions remain fixed because the incentives that the institutions generate lead to outcomes that produce a sufficient rental stream to the organizations such that they see no reason to "rock the boat."[41] For other institutions, the dominant network tinkers on the margin. They make decisions, for example, pass laws, issue decrees, and render judicial decisions, inter alia. All these institutional modifications change incentives on the margin but do not fundamentally affect beliefs. We are in a world in which Greif (2006) argues that the institutions are consistent with the beliefs of economic and political organizations.

Beliefs about the impact that the institutional changes will have on incentives and in turn outcomes determine the institutions that are put in place, though the institutions also produce some unintended consequences, sometimes small and sometimes large.[42] To the extent that the overall outcomes produce adequate rents to the players in the configuration of power, we will not see "big" institutional changes, and societies may cruise along in this "autopilot" mode for decades.[43] Societies function and operate under a belief system of "this is the way our world works." The system is meeting the expectations of those in power as well as citizens; it is like a tide that washes over society. The belief system is predictable and is sustained by the social fabric of society, that is, familial, religious, social, and cultural relationships. In such a world, outcomes are consistent with expectations, so there is no organization sufficiently powerful (or with the incentive) to push for big changes.

But, at some historical moment, the cumulative effect of small changes reaches a tipping point, or there is an exogenous shock, either internal or external to a country, that shocks the system. This is shown as the shaded area moving to the right in figure 7.5. The lines from each element in the "autopilot" part of the figure indicate whether that element (that is, beliefs, dominant network, institutions, and so on) stays the same—horizontal line—or changes over time—slopes up or down. At this level of generality, we are not interested if the change was positive or negative, but simply whether something "big" has changed or not.

---

41 Eggertsson (2005) argues that for centuries, Iceland held onto "imperfect institutions" because they benefited the agricultural elite. He argues that they held a misguided partial equilibrium social model. The landed elite feared that fostering fishing would drive agricultural wages up. They neglected to see that "a rising tide raises all boats," that is, that reaping the benefits from fisheries would foster economic growth sufficiently to increase the rent for landowners as well.

42 Unintended outcomes result from a myriad of forces: formal institutions alone do not feed directly into outcomes; norms matter as well as the relative prices of choices faced by organizations (see Wallis 2011).

43 This is analogous to how most of us live our lives. Most of us operate according to certain routines, and it takes something out of the ordinary, for example, a heart attack, to cause us to fundamentally change our way of life, though again we tinker on the margin.

When a shock takes place, the only thing that changes in a first moment are the outcomes, which now no longer match expectations; see (1) in figure 7.5. If this effect is large enough, it may create pressure for change, leading to a window of opportunity. As shown in figure 7.5, during a window of opportunity there is the potential for leadership to initiate a critical transition. If leadership does not emerge, most societies will cycle back to the ex ante shock world with changes initiated to patch up the repercussions from the shock.[44] But, if the shock is sufficiently large to shake the beliefs of many in the dominant network and someone (or some organization) takes on a leadership role, "constitutional-level" changes are possible that can set a country on the path to a critical transition. The wavy lines after point (2) in the figure indicate that the old beliefs have been lost and have not yet been substituted by new beliefs.

The way these changes take place depends on the country and the situation, and there are infinite possibilities. As drawn in figure 7.5, at point (3) leadership steps in to catalyze new beliefs of those in the dominant network, or some organizations with differing beliefs gain or lose power within the dominant network. Change does not happen simultaneously. It takes time for leadership to coordinate organizations within the network to "make a leap of faith," and sometimes, if the shock is sufficient, the rents to the dominant network have fallen sufficiently that they have little to lose.[45]

In the period leading to constitutional-level changes, leadership can emerge from either within or outside the current dominant network of power. For Brazil, the leadership of Cardoso took place while he was in the dominant network, but as discussed below, Perón in Argentina emerged outside the dominant network.[46] To solidify the "constitutional moment" will take years of institutional deepening where the new beliefs shape new laws that have the expected outcome that in turn feed back to organizations and citizens within and outside the dominant network.

Leadership over time is instrumental for institutional deepening because the dominant network needs to be coordinated and rents need to

44 The fallout from the Arab Spring could be considered a potential window of opportunity, but no leader took charge, most likely because it was not in the interest of the dominant network whose belief did not change.

45 This was the case for Brazil during the hyperinflationary period just prior to the *Plano Real*. Tipping points seem most likely in the case of mass movements, for example, the demise of the Soviet Union, as successfully negotiated transitions to an extremely different dominant network are not common. We do not discuss this possibility, but it is compatible with our framework. On tipping points, see Kuran (1995).

46 As exposited in chapter 6, Lula being from the opposition party sustained the transition to the new set of beliefs set in motion by Cardoso. Bidner and François (2013) stress that changes in beliefs require a change in leadership to affirm that governments are now different.

flow to its members under the new belief system. In rare cases, the new beliefs simply emerge as a result of the shock, but in others, leaders can purposefully influence them.[47] Not everyone changes their set of beliefs simultaneously, and some organizations in power may never change their beliefs. But if leaders can exercise cognitive and coordinative roles, a big institutional change affecting the trajectory of a country is possible. Schofield (2006) argues that Madison and Hamilton played this role in the ratification of the US Constitution in writing the majority of the Federalist Papers, which swayed voters in their belief for a larger role for the federal government at the expense of the power of states. The critical transition happens ultimately because beliefs about the way the world works have changed.

The change in beliefs leads to new formal institutions, that is, both the constitutional-level institutions and the laws/enforcement (points 4 and 5 in figure 7.5). These changes in turn affect the incentives faced by individuals and organizations, affecting in turn their choices. This leads to a new trajectory toward new outcomes (initiating at point 6 in figure 7.5). If outcomes now once again match expectations, this society reaches a new autopilot, on the right-hand side of the figure. For a fortunate few societies, this leads to a critical transition to a more open economic and political society. However, the outcomes in the new autopilot might be better or worse than before. Yet, they are stable in the sense that they accord with what is expected. The outcomes will naturally vary over time as they are affected by small internal and external shocks, leading to incremental changes in beliefs and organizations in power. Occasionally, large shocks or endogenous tipping points lead to new windows of opportunity, and the process may repeat, though within a different context and with different details. Note, however, that there is no reason to expect that with each new cycle the country will move ever closer to a critical transition to being more developed. On the contrary, the historical experience suggests that such trajectories are rare, and countries are more likely to shift from one underperforming state to another or to cycle forward and back without much overall long-term improvement.

The key element in the dynamic is the change in beliefs. When beliefs become uncertain, some leaders can sway which beliefs get acted on in terms of the institutions that get established. This can come about through the "art of policy making." If the new institutions produce incentives that in turn generate outcomes that are viewed as "good" or consistent with the subjective view of the way the world works, as expounded

---

47 In some situations, the shock may be sufficiently large that no matter who is in power, the actions taken will be similar. As an example, after 9/11, every conceivable president in the United States would have vowed to "hunt down" Bin Laden.

by the organizations that implemented the institutional change, then beliefs about the causal role of institutions on incentives and on outcomes deepen. For example, Rakove, Rutten, and Weingast (2004) argue that prior to the Revolutionary War between Britain and her North American colonies, only a minority of those in power in the New England colonies "believed" that Britain would take away the liberties of the colonists. Actions taken by the British, including the quartering of troops in New England and the disbandment of the Massachusetts legislature, gave credence to the beliefs of the New Englanders, and over time this belief that "the British will take away our freedoms" propelled the colonists to take up arms against the British.

In the empirical chapters we showed that, in Brazil, during their initial "miracle" years, there was a belief from the mid-1960s until the late 1970s held by the dominant network that "developmentalism" increased the size of the economic pie for Brazil. Increasing the size of the pie was more important than the distribution of the pie; concerns over distribution would come later. Consistent with this belief was the central planning role of the military along with some degree of authoritarianism and censorship. Of course, not all organizations held this belief, but those that did not were outside the dominant network; for example, the intellectual left and the unions did not adhere to many aspects of this belief, but these organizations did not have sufficient power to change the prevailing de facto belief in the face of a system that produced double-digit economic growth. Only when growth slowed down in the late 1970s did some key organizations within the dominant network, mostly business organizations, begin to question their belief in "developmentalism." This change in beliefs by the business organizations proved crucial for bringing down the military, and bringing in its wake a belief in social inclusion, that is, a more open and participatory political system.[48]

The beliefs in the benefits from change do not happen in a vacuum: those in the dominant network (and at times, citizens at large) view the expected impact of new institutions (and their resulting incentive structure) based partially on institutions around the globe, for example, an independent judiciary, or secure property rights. In addition, many in the dominant network may have acquired part of their education in wealthy countries, which shaped their beliefs and their perceived benefits of importing institutions, though with modifications to suit

---

[48] It was not just business organizations that prospered in the early years of developmentalism but also many middle-class workers, though they did not have a voice. Similarly, the middle class also saw eroding standards of living during the periods that business profits declined.

their needs.[49] This is true for many in the dominant network in South America as well as in Asia today. Knowledge of institutions from the outside world also allows leaders more conviction "to stay the course" when there are up-front costs for downstream benefits from institutional change.

During a window of opportunity, it is the competing and incompatible beliefs among organizations within the dominant network, either the new organizations or old organizations with new beliefs, that bring about the potential for new institutions that change incentives and (at times beliefs) and move a society toward a critical transition.[50] In such a situation, competing powerful organizations are constrained by the beliefs of each other and their relative power. A new set of institutions emerges through leadership (which could be a consensual group of organizations) in the Riker sense of coordinative activity that enables a new belief system to take hold among a winning network of organizations. In the case of Brazil, the winning network following the military government consisted of business organizations that were disappointed in the slow rate of growth, some centrist politicians at the state and local level, and the "social reformers," consisting of the union leadership and "intellectuals" (academics, artists, the Catholic Church, and others who opposed the censorship of the military).

Leadership entails orchestrating powerful groups to react to the perception of a problem and that the perceived solution to the problem is shaped by the beliefs of leaders about the likely consequences of the new incentives emerging from the new institutions. In this sense, our actors are both forward and backward looking.[51] Here is where today's threshold countries, like Brazil analyzed here as well as many other countries, can learn from the experiences of countries that have already made the

49 The recurrent problem with transplants, however, is the incongruence between institutions and beliefs.

50 Competition over beliefs brings about only the "potential" for moving to a more open society. The result depends on the beliefs of those who win the competition for power. Our concept of "windows of opportunity" is similar to that of Acemoglu et al. (2008), who argue that economic growth does not necessarily lead to democracy and whether it does they label a critical juncture. They reach this conclusion after an econometric exercise that convincingly demonstrates that country-specific effects make the difference. As discussed earlier in this chapter, the difference between a critical juncture and a window of opportunity is that in a window of opportunity, the actors realize the potential and are forward looking as well as solving current problems.

51 This differs from the North, Wallis, and Weingast (2009) view, where the actors are primarily solving extant problems and not as forward looking as today's leaders/organizations can be. But, we agree with North, Wallis, and Weingast that actors are solving current problems; the difference is that today's leaders can be more forward looking because of the experiences of other countries.

critical transition. Of course, those in power can't perfectly foresee the outcomes of their actions, but they can make an educated prediction.[52] In addition, today's leaders recognize that a "big bang" (e.g., the dissolution of the former Soviet Union) is not sufficient for development, though it may be necessary. As we stressed earlier, the "big bang" must be sustained with complementary changes in beliefs along with further downstream institutional deepening. All that leaders can foresee is that putting in place certain incentives—through institutional change—will have some likely foreseen outcomes and some unforeseen outcomes. Leaders must be responsive to unanticipated downstream consequences. North (1990) referred to this process as "adaptive efficiency."[53] Of course, knowing what to do differs from having the incentive to change. In many countries, it is in the economic and political interests of the dominant network in power not to initiate changes to a critical transition. Not everyone wins during a critical transition. Today, it is less likely a cognitive issue than 150 years ago when the pioneer countries began their critical transitions.

A critical transition is problematic because the future has uncertainty. Some groups will lose, for example, the military elite in Brazil in the mid-1980s.[54] Moreover, generally opening up the economy entails considerable up-front costs; for example, stabilization policies typically have short-run costs with long-run benefits. This means giving up political and economic rents in the short run for some unknowable but perceived ex ante increase in rents in the future for society as a whole, though with unforeseen distributional consequences. Part of the solution to development is recognition that a winning political network of organizations foresees more advantages from promoting openness than the extant status quo. This is why windows of opportunity are so important. As we saw, the *Plano Real* succeeded in part because after a series of hyperinflationary periods and failed stabilization plans, those in the dominant network in Brazil believed that taming inflation was the number one priority for Brazil in the early 1990s. Enacting political and economic institutional changes requires some risks to those in power, and this is where the leadership of Cardoso and his economic team mattered. Opportunities

---

52 Of course, this does not dismiss the role for unintended consequences of which history redounds.

53 In this sense, our actors are forward looking, similar to the Acemoglu, Johnson, and Robinson (2005) versions of England and Spain responding differentially to oceanic trade. In other versions of Acemoglu and Robinson (2006, 2012), the elites are forced by citizens to give up rents. We believe that today, citizens have a greater role to play in the developmental process in proportion to the extent that the rule of law pertains to a greater percentage of citizens.

54 Often, as in Brazil in the early 1980s, members of the military insulate themselves from later prosecution.

present themselves, but not all potential leaders take advantage of the opportunity, either because they lack the perception to see the opportunity, they perceive an opportunity but lack the knowledge of what to do, or they lack the art of policy making in the dynamic sense expounded by Riker (1984, 1996).

Recognizing a role for leadership is a departure from the standard economic and political rational-choice models consisting of "representative agents." We recognize that this leads to a certain degree of arbitrariness, which is why our Brazilian case study entailed thick description in the same way that courtrooms need to rely on circumstantial evidence when there is not a "smoking gun."[55] Windows of opportunity allow leaders to affect institutional changes that can lead to incentives that produce less or more political or economic openness than the previous order. Windows of opportunity are not unidirectional in proceeding from less to more openness; the reverse is equally likely.

At times, leaders enact "big" institutional changes that lead to incentives producing outcomes consistent with expectations and also lead to a critical transition because a greater number of organizations in the dominant network see a higher expected gain from the new institutions. This requires a complementary change in the way the world now works. For example, in the political arena, if the electorate rewards politicians for increasing political and economic openness within a framework of rule of law, there is a tendency for the dynamic to become virtuous with institutional deepening; that is, successive smaller institutional changes buttress the initial "big" institutional change. Belief deepening must accompany institutional deepening (Greif 2006; Bidner and François 2013). Institutional deepening is necessary for countries to reach a critical transition— the big institutional change is neither sufficient nor sustainable without a belief deepening. Moreover, many seemingly "big" institutional changes are never sustained because they are not buttressed with other supporting smaller institutional changes and are not accompanied by changing beliefs among the dominant network in society. Whether institutional changes are really "big" can be judged only ex post.

In the empirical chapters of this book, we demonstrated that the *Plano Real* led to taming inflation, but it was the subsequent smaller but important institutional changes from 1994 through today that produced a very different Brazil from the one in 1994, or 1985, the end of the military regime. Politicians found it in their interest over time to provide public goods to secure votes, and citizens in a competitive political system

---

55 On the role of circumstantial evidence in history, see Fogel (1982). See also Collier (2011) for the distinctions between "smoking gun" and other types of explanations in political science.

tolerate less corruption in society. Increasingly, the rule of law evolved and applies to political rulers in the sense that they are not above the law; impeachments are a sign that leaders are not above the law.[56] In the economic system, regulation and loans can be used preferentially or in patron-client fashion, but politicians came to realize that such treatment no longer delivers the same political support nor generates economic growth for consumers. In Brazil, the movement to a critical transition produced a more impersonal and open society.

From the lenses of history, we know that reaching a critical transition is not an easy task and is not inevitable. Indeed, those countries that have made the critical transition are the exception rather than the rule (North, Wallis, and Weingast 2009; Acemoglu and Robinson 2012). The answer appears to be so highly country-specific that generalizations can take the form of only very broad frameworks such as the one we present here based on the Brazilian experience. Whether the inductive framework developed here will be helpful in understanding development in general will come from its successful application to other case-study countries. In the next section, we present an illustrative overview of how our framework can be applied to Argentina, a country that in the early twentieth century was seen as on a trajectory to sustainable development.

ARGENTINA: AN ILLUSTRATIVE USE OF THE FRAMEWORK

From 1890 until 1950, Argentina ranked between 7th and 30th in its GDP per capita (Alston and Gallo 2010: 180).[57] In 2013, it ranked 55th, clearly a fall from grace. What happened? At the dawn of the twentieth century, Argentina had a relatively good endowment of natural resources coupled with little or no ethnic tensions or indigenous issues. The country had fertile land in the Pampas especially suited for wheat and cattle. It was an attractive destination for immigrants. Using our framework, we

---

56 As discussed in chapter 4 on the early years of democratization, Collor, the first elected president in Brazil, was impeached for corruption, and yet the transition of the vice president to the presidency was peaceful, and the process evolved according to the formal institutions put in place in the constitution. There was never a hint that the military would take over the government.

57 We stress that this section is illustrative and we can certainly not capture the nuances of Argentine development over the period discussed. Our hope is that the illustration will motivate scholars of Argentina to more fully develop a case study using the framework that in turn will inductively help make our framework more generalizable. This material draws extensively on Gallo and Alston (2008), and Alston and Gallo (2010). We single out Alan Dye, along with an anonymous reviewer, for giving us detailed comments on this section.

will discuss the development of Argentina in three periods: (1) 1912–1930, (2) 1930–1946, and (3) 1946–present.[58] We will devote most of our attention to the period 1930–1946, which was the crucial period for understanding the condition of Argentina today.

The Camelot Years: 1912–1930

From the late nineteenth century until 1914, the dominant network consisted of the rural agricultural landowners and the educated elites of Buenos Aires. The dominant network stayed in power through their control of the electoral process, which conforms to being on an autopilot dynamic. The lack of political voice sparked three failed armed revolts in 1890, 1893, and 1905, consisting of some factions of the military and the rising class of laborers in Buenos Aires and the countryside. The rising discontent also led to the formation of political parties to champion the voice of laborers. But, this was for naught until the election of Sáenz Peña in 1910. Sáenz Peña saw the protests and the increasing power in the streets held by the Radical Civil Union Party as a window of opportunity for change. Though part of the ruling elite, Sáenz Peña believed that to be a modern nation required open elections. He made his intentions known of moving to open elections in his speech before Congress in 1910. By 1912, his leadership had convinced a majority to support his law calling for a secret ballot. The law giving universal suffrage to males, enforcing compulsory voting, and, most importantly, instituting the secret ballot passed in 1912 and bears his name, the Sáenz Peña Law. The Sáenz Peña Law called for stricter monitoring for electoral fraud and also promoted naturalization of immigrants and the granting of citizenship to the children of immigrants. The Sáenz Peña Law changed the trajectory of Argentina because it initiated a change in the beliefs toward a democracy that believed in checks and balances.

Prior to the secret ballot, the Conservatives, dominated by the agricultural producers in the Pampas, controlled the legislative and executive branches and appointed relatively conservative Supreme Court justices. Hipólito Yrigoyen, a leader in the Radical Party, won the first presidential election in 1916 following the introduction of the secret ballot. The Radical Party controlled the presidency and the House of Deputies, with the Conservatives having a majority in the Senate. Divided governance held throughout the 1920s. Alston and Gallo (2010) refer to this as the

---

58 We are taking some liberties in classifying 1946–present as one period, but its oscillations between populism and conservative military regimes until the military budget was stripped in 1983 are a form of autopilot.

Camelot period for Argentina, one in which the players (for the most part) respected the nascent system of checks and balances.[59]

Argentina in many ways considered itself "different" from the rest of South America. The increased openness in the political arena represented a belief in democracy and a prominent role for checks and balances. The belief in checks and balances was a budding belief from below and fragile within the dominant network, though firmly held by the Radical Party. During this period, the dominant network was relatively large with several constituencies having a voice—urban and rural workers who tended to vote for the Radical Party, and the urban and rural elite who tended to vote for the Conservative Party. One measure of transparency was the dramatic increase in the number of roll call votes following 1916 and continuing through the 1920s. In addition, the number of voters went up dramatically, and even more importantly, the Supreme Court exercised a degree of independence overturning laws favored by the legislature and the president. The losers respected the judgment of the court. Much of the legislation during the period dealt with issues of concern to the working class, for example, rent control for tenants and rural workers. Overall, the period brought high growth with GDP/P averaging 4.2 percent over the period. Both the elite and the workers benefitted during this robust period of growth. But, as we noted earlier, "development" is about more than economic growth. Its hallmarks are transparency, rule of law, and economic and political competition, inter alia. For these reasons, this period in Argentine history represented true "development." Unfortunately, this fourteen-year run on the path to a "critical transition" came to a hiatus with a military coup in 1930 that ousted the Radical president Yrigoyen.

Electoral Fraud and the Rise of Perón: 1930–1946

The Great Depression shocked the economic system. The Conservatives, particularly those aligned with agriculture, felt that the government must "do something." Precisely what action to take was not clear. Being a major exporter of wheat and beef, Argentina was hit hard by the plunge in commodity prices; from December 1929 to December 1930, wheat prices (in Liverpool) fell from $1.41/bushel to $0.74, and Argentine beef fell from $5.92/100 lb to $3.67/100 lb (US Department of Agriculture 1936: 21; 216). Both parties believed that the crisis warranted action. Legislative bills languished at the executive level, where neglect was the norm. The aging President Yrigoyen either was incapable of sensing the

---

59 We note that Yrigoyen resorted to executive interventions relatively frequently during his two terms in office in order to circumvent legislation proposed by the Conservatives. We thank Sebastian Saeigh for this insight.

depth of the recession or simply did not know what to do. Either way, the Great Depression coupled with the passive Yrigoyen prompted the military to oust Yrigoyen at the behest of the Conservatives and with the countenance of the Radical Party. The Radical Party did not mount a protest because many in their party were also frustrated with Yrigoyen in not grasping the seriousness of the downturn. Though the coup was an affront to the electoral process and the constitution (as well as the first in Argentine history), most parties anticipated a quick transition back to legitimate elections. This was not to be.

The military installed the Conservatives in power (de facto) and looked for legitimacy. During this early period, the military and the Conservatives were closely aligned. The Supreme Court labeled the coup a "triumphant revolution" (Alston and Gallo 2010: 182). Only one Supreme Court justice resigned in protest. The military planned to transition back to elections and the path to solidifying the critical transition. The Conservatives thought that citizens would recognize that the Conservative elite should run the government during an international economic crisis. The military and Conservatives misread the public. The first free election was in the province of Buenos Aires in April 1931. To the surprise of the Conservatives, the Radicals won the election, and the military annulled the results. The military called for a national election in 1932 but did not allow any candidates from the Radical Party who had been in office during Yrigoyen's final term. The Radicals protested by refusing to recognize and participate in the election. As a result, the Conservatives returned to power in 1932 with the military in the wings if needed. The dominant network consisted of agricultural producers and others associated with exports; the Conservative Party; and the military. The combined actions of annulling an election and preventing the Radicals from having candidates marked the beginning of the departure away from sustainable political and economic development.

The prevailing belief held by the Conservatives and their military allies—the de facto dominant network—was that the emergency of the Great Depression necessitated rule by the Conservatives. Ironically, the Conservatives received high marks for their macroeconomic policy during the 1930s (Della Paolera and Taylor 1998, 1999, 2001). But, to stay in power, the Conservatives resorted to electoral fraud (known by its advocates as "Patriotic Fraud") throughout the 1930s.[60] The economic out-

---

60 For an in-depth account of fraud in the 1930s, see Alston and Gallo (2010) and sources cited therein. A slight majority of the total reports of fraud come from three provinces in the Pampas: Buenos Aires, Entre Rios, and Santa Fe. The Province of Cordoba (in the Pampas) never engaged in fraud and consistently elected Radicals to the House of Deputies.

comes desired by the dominant network met their expectations, but they trampled on the political rights of the Radicals and their allies. The Radicals protested but to no avail. The Supreme Court stood on the sidelines on the grounds that the fraud was a political, not a constitutional, issue.

The persistent fraud throughout the 1930s led to an erosion among the electorate in the belief that a system of checks and balances could ever be legitimately implemented in Argentina:

> The Conservative regimes of the 1930s, in spite of their flirtations with fascist reformism, brought to a halt the modest momentum for political and social reform started by the Radical governments. Their failure to buttress the relative healthy economic structure with social and political arrangements allowing for growing security and political participation for rural and urban masses contributed to the creation of revolutionary possibilities. In short, the Conservatives appeared to have won the battle by fraud but lost the war by abandoning the rule of law. (Díaz Alejandro 1970: 107–8)

In 1940, President Ortiz promised to return to nonfraudulent elections in 1942. Ortiz signaled an intention to return to the path that had been interrupted by the Great Depression and the nonlegitimate rule of the Conservatives. This marked a potential window of opportunity created by the leadership of Ortiz. Whether transparent elections were possible under the rule of Conservatives is a counterfactual that we will never know because Ortiz fell ill early in his term and died on June 27, 1942, several months before the general elections. His successor, President Castillo, resorted to fraud to sustain the Conservatives in power in the elections of 1942.

Castillo's reign was short-lived. A faction of the military defected from the former dominant network of Conservatives and some generals, and it ousted Castillo in June 1943. Many thought (or hoped) that the new military government would return quickly to democracy. This might have happened, but a nationalistic faction within the military relatively quickly took control. Juan Perón was an important player within the nationalistic faction and held several powerful posts. He quickly demonstrated his support for labor and opposition to the Conservatives and the rule of law.

To the surprise of many, the military government called for free elections in 1946 with Perón as their candidate. Perón campaigned through skillful oratory as well as on his record for supporting labor. He openly showed his populist streak and contempt for the conservative court, which had countenanced the electoral fraud in the 1930s. The election was clean. Perón won the election with a majority of 52 percent (Ciria and Astiz 1978). In the absence of fraud in the 1930s, Perón may well have not won the election in 1946 (Alston and Gallo 2010).[61] Perón's support was strongest in the provinces where fraud had been the greatest. Additional support for the view that electoral fraud in the 1930s drove the support for Perón comes from the electoral results in Cordoba. Cordoba did not engage in fraud in the 1930s, and Perón did not receive a majority of votes in Cordoba in 1946.

We view the election of Perón a "shock" to the system, and a new window of opportunity under the leadership of Perón that set Argentina on a new trajectory with a different set of beliefs from those held by the dominant network of Conservatives in the 1930s. A majority of citizens had lost faith in the system of checks and balances because of the electoral fraud. Perón played to the choir by expressing his support for the "will of the people." The new dominant network under the leadership of Perón consisted of factions of the military, labor, and most of the rural provinces. In addition to being able to count on the working classes because of his policy positions, Perón exhibited leadership by coordinating the dominant network through the use of subsidies to rural provinces outside of the Pampas. The transfers to rural provinces made governors more powerful, and in return they supported Perón. Perón took advantage of the window of opportunity and, with the support of the new dominant network, initiated institutional changes consistent with a belief in populism. Perón saw the Supreme Court as an obstacle to his agenda, and impeaching most of the court was his first order of business. This would turn out to have long-run consequences.

Instability Is the Rule: Oscillations between Populism and Military Rule: 1946–Present

We treat this sixty-eight-year period as one episode, not because it remained constant but rather because the entire period has been marked by incredible policy instability that until the mid-1980s led to oscillations between populist governments siding with labor, and conservative/military governments siding with the conservative agricultural sector in the Pampas.[62] Oscillations between the military and Perónists became a de facto autopilot until President Alfonsin slashed the budgets of the military in 1984. Menem recognized a window of opportunity in the

---

61 Alston and Gallo (2010) report regression results that show that if there had been no fraud in the 1930s, then Perón would not have won the election. Of course, without fraud, there may never have been a military coup, but the purpose of the exercise is to show the rise in the belief of populism promoted by Juan Perón.

62 For a more detailed discussion of the subperiods, especially related to policy instability, see Spiller and Tommasi (2009). Gallo and Alston (2008) show the instability in banking, fiscal policy, foreign trade, and constitutional politics.

mid-1990s to change the trajectory of Argentina, but he failed to exercise sufficient leadership to accomplish his goal of fiscal and monetary orthodoxy.

After being elected president, Perón acted quickly to solidify his populist agenda.[63] He displayed the leadership characteristics of cognition of the issues that he wished to address, an extraordinary ability to coordinate interests in his dominant network, and some moral authority based on his time in prison as well as his great oratory skills. Many of his actions most likely would have been considered unconstitutional by the conservative Supreme Court that Perón inherited. Perón set his sights early on impeaching all but one of the Supreme Court justices. Perón clearly expressed his contempt of the court:

> In my opinion, I put the spirit of justice above the Judicial Power, as this is the principal requirement for the future of the Nation. But I understand that justice, besides from being independent has to be effective, and it cannot be effective if its ideas and concepts are not with the public sentiment. Many praise the conservative sentiment of the Justices, believing that they defend traditional beliefs. I consider that a dangerous mistake, because it can put justice in opposition with the popular feeling, and because in the long run it produces a rusted organism. Justice, in its doctrines, has to be dynamic instead of static. Otherwise respectable popular yearnings are frustrated and the social development is delayed, producing severe damage to the working classes when these classes, which are naturally the less conservative, in the usual sense of the word, see the justice procedures closed they have no other choice than to put their faith in violence. (Diario de Sesiones del Honorable Senado de la Nacion Constitutido en tribunal, T. VI, December 5, 1946: 89; quoted in Alston and Gallo 2010: 192)

With this statement, Perón clearly aligned himself with working classes and felt the executive power should reign supreme. The Perónists in the House of Deputies went to great lengths to tie the impeachment of the court not just to their obstruction to the new Perón policies but also to their countenance of the electoral fraud of the 1930s. Perón and his allies won, and all the accused justices were impeached. With new appointments to the court by Perón, there was no opposition to the new Perónist agenda. A new belief system was in place with a new dominant network consisting of the working class (urban and rural), nationalists, and allies

---

63 By populism, Perón (and we) meant ruling by the will of the people with little respect for the minority rights of the agricultural elite in the Pampas. Perón saw as his primary constituencies the urban and rural working classes. To bring the outlying provinces into his network, he relied on transfers.

from the outlying provinces that Perón brought into the network through the strategic use of directed transfers. The Perónist agenda consisted of, to a large extent, taxing landowners in the agricultural Pampas and redistributing it to members of the dominant coalition. He did this by establishing a national price for cattle and wheat that the government paid and then exported at a higher price. He used the surplus to subsidize outlying provinces. To promote his agenda, he nationalized several public utilities (e.g., railroads, telephone, and water). As populist measures appeasing his major constituencies, rent controls and the thirteenth-month wage payment stand out.

Perón increased expenditures faster than revenues increased. His sources of revenues included export taxes (particularly beef and cattle), revenue from state enterprises (many nationalized utilities), and seigniorage from increasing the monetary base and monetizing debts of provincial banks. To rely on seigniorage required taking away the independence of the Central Bank. At first, outcomes matched expectations, but over time, deficits mounted to an unsustainable level such that toward the end of Perón's reign, Argentina could no longer borrow on the international market (Díaz Alejandro 1970). The taxing of the Pampas also led to less domestic and, most notably, foreign investment in the Pampas. Inflation during Perón's time in office was nearly 20 percent but increased even more rapidly in the years following Perón's first two terms. Most notable was the decline in foreign investment.

The steadily eroding fiscal situation in Argentina slowly but surely opened a window of opportunity for Conservatives to retake control of the dominant network. A military coup in 1955, with a faction opposed to Perónists, set in motion the oscillations in policy that dominated Argentina's slide from one of the wealthiest countries in the world. The new military-led dominant network in 1955 consisted of Catholic nationalists and a liberal/conservative coalition. The new regime tried to undo some of the confiscatory and redistributive policies of Perón, especially the control of beef and cattle prices and the elimination of price controls. But, given the extant power of unions and the large number employed in the public sector, the military regime ultimately resorted to inflation to stay afloat. Of course, this was not sustainable. Policy oscillated because the military favored the Pampas. Like Perón, the military regime wrote a new constitution and forced the resignation of all five members of the Supreme Court. The military regime allowed limited elections in 1958 (the Perónist Party was formally banned).

We view the oscillations of policies and regimes as an ex post form of autopilot. We see the populists and the Conservatives as competing for control of the dominant network, but neither side having sufficient power once Perón was initially ousted from power in 1955. With a return to limited democracy (1958–1962), policies again oscillated, continuing to hurt foreign and direct investments. The administration reinstated price controls and nationalized the oil industry. The court also increased to seven justices. The democracy proved short-lived and was followed by another coup in 1962, which too was short-lived. Argentina continued to oscillate back and forth from military to democratic regimes from Perón's first two terms up until Perón's return to Argentina and reelection in 1973. Each government (except de la Rúa's short term) forced resignations, impeached justices, or added justices. As a result, the judiciary was never a constraint on the executive, and the legislature was either pliable because of its reliance on transfers from the national government or nonexistent during the military periods. Argentina eventually tied the hands of the military during the term of Alfonsín (1983–1989) and has remained populist since 1983, except for an attempt during Menem's ten-year term (1989–1999) to stabilize the economy.

Like in Brazil, the hyperinflation in Argentina in 1989 (12,000 percent/year) gave Menem a window of opportunity to fundamentally change Argentina. He tried with the convertibility plan in 1991, pegging the peso to the dollar with open convertibility. It was a bold move signaling to the world that the provincial overspending in Argentina must be reined in. Regrettably, Menem lacked the leadership skills to change the fiscal game in Argentina, and the convertibility plan began to unravel in 2000. The Convertibility Law was officially repealed in January 2002, and Argentina went back to its populist ways with the election of Néstor Kirchner in 2003, followed by the current president, Christina Fernandez (the wife of the deceased Kirchner). Except for a brief period in the late 1990s, foreign direct investment has remained low, frequent bouts with hyperinflation (triple-digit inflation from 1976 to 1990), and federal deficits swinging wildly. Since 2001, Argentina and its creditors have been waging legal battles over whether Argentina reneged on its contractual obligations. In 2012, a New York District Court ruled that Argentina was in default of its obligations, and in 2014 the same court ruled them in contempt of court for not meeting its judicial decision. At the time of this writing, Argentina's credit rating is one of the worst in the world. The inability to secure global financing may open a window of opportunity with a chance for Argentina to change its course.

CONCLUDING REMARKS

We reiterate: economic and political development is contextual. But, there are lessons for development from understanding the process, which has some general features. We developed a framework for understanding development in Brazil over the past fifty years and, developed in such a way, our framework is inductive from the Brazilian experience. To illustrate its wider applicability, we applied the framework very generally to understand the critical transitions in Argentina from the early twentieth century to 2014. The key elements in our framework are beliefs and leadership, which interact synergistically and vary across countries. Because beliefs and leadership cannot be measured rigorously and classified, the use of the framework necessarily involves subjectivity and interpretation. With more case studies applying our framework, we can construct more general lessons on the dynamics among beliefs, power, leadership, institutions, policies, and outcomes that form stasis or development.

CHAPTER 8

Conclusion

ON JUNE 15, 2013, BRAZIL PLAYED JAPAN IN THE INAUGURAL MATCH OF the 2013 Confederations Cup, a warm-up tournament one year prior to the World Cup. Sixty-seven thousand fans packed the newly rebuilt Mané Garrincha stadium in Brasília. Brasília has no major soccer teams and, until recently, no major sport venue, so the chance to watch such an important match filled the fans with excitement. President Dilma Rousseff held the privilege of declaring the cup open. As Dilma started her speech, spectators booed from all corners of the stadium, drowning out the words of the president. The world witnessed the embarrassing spectacle of Dilma on television. No one saw the outburst coming. In the previous months, there had been several small and localized protests throughout the country as well as criticism in the press, but this was democracy as usual. Ironically, one month earlier, the president's popularity had reached the highest level since she took office in January 2011 (CNI-Ibope 2013). Outside the stadium, about 500 people protested public expenditure for the World Cup in Brazil in 2014, but this unlikely prompted the booing inside. Whatever the cause of the outburst in the stadium, massive street protests erupted two days later on June 17: 100,000 people in Rio de Janeiro; 65,000 in São Paulo; and proportionally for most other large cities. Waves of protests continued in the following days. On June 20, more than 1.4 million people participated in street protests throughout the country.[1] The protests were mostly pacific, though there were isolated cases of violence and vandalism, and at least two deaths. The protests continued sporadically until early July and thereafter popped up unexpectedly and unpredictably throughout the country.

What caused the extraordinary outbursts? Unlike some of its neighbors, such as Argentina and Venezuela where the streets are a regular locus of policy making, Brazil does not have a tradition of massive street protests (Stein et al. 2008). The previous instances of large demonstrations include the 1992 Impeachment Now protest that helped oust President Collor (750,000 protesters in São Paulo; 60,000 in Brasília; and similar numbers elsewhere), and the Direct Elections Now protests in 1984 that pressured for presidential suffrage (1.5 million protesters in

---

[1] Estimate by G1.Globo.com using data from the military police, Datafolha, COPPE-UFRJ, and other sources.

São Paulo; 1 million in Rio de Janeiro; and proportionally throughout the country). Each of the two previous instances coincided approximately with two windows of opportunity that we recognized in earlier chapters.[2] Will the protests in 2013–2014 usher in a new change of beliefs taking Brazil off its current trajectory of a critical transition?

The protests surprised everyone. Hypotheses abounded to explain the protests. Perhaps the poor in the *favelas* found the time ripe to descend from the hills to the asphalt and assert their greater numbers. Yet, protests by the poor were incongruous with the massive reduction in poverty and inequality in the preceding decade. Furthermore, the protests had a distinctly middle-class flavor with much communication over social media, similar to the Arab Spring and Occupy Wall Street movements. The coordinative capacity of social media played a role, and some analysts predicted that a new form of social participation had emerged in Brazil. Like the Arab Spring and Occupy Wall Street, the participation lacked leadership or a focal point of protest. Many participated because their friends participated. Established organizations such as labor unions and NGOs felt usurped but quickly joined the bandwagon and claimed the protests for their own causes.

Federal and state governments scrambled to address many of the demands. Several cities reduced their bus and train fares. President Dilma met with all governors and the mayors of major cities and subsequently proposed a five-point national pact that included a plebiscite calling for a new constitution. Dilma committed to improve transportation, health, and education and reaffirmed a commitment to fiscal responsibility, economic stability, and control of inflation. The mix of realized and forgotten promises seemingly appeased the protests. Subsequently, many groups attempted protests, but none percolated to the extent of the June 2013 protests. Nevertheless, because of the unanticipated nature of the 2013 protests, there remains a nagging feeling that the right circumstances might align and prompt a new and bigger round of protests bringing down the government and with it the set of beliefs built up since 1994.

Better and Worse at the Same Time

Whether a protest emerges depends on the decentralized choices of numerous locally interconnected heterogeneous agents linked in networks following simple rules, such as "participate if x percent of the right people

---

2 The protest for the impeachment of Collor was during the hyperinflationary period that we label "the window of opportunity" that Cardoso seized as finance minister, and after which, during Cardoso's presidency, institutions deepened.

I know also participate."[3] Protests have nonlinear dynamics that often produce tipping points. The grain of sand that starts an avalanche can seem to be the cause—for instance the self-immolation of an unemployed fruit seller in Tunisia at the beginning of the Arab Spring riots—but the real issue is how the system reaches the state where a small push can initiate a cascade.

The discontent over bus fares, though a legitimate grievance, was a trigger and not the fundamental cause of the 2013 protests in Brazil. But, what were the fundamental underlying causes? Answering the question is extremely difficult because of confirmation bias and ex post rationalization.[4] Even with the benefit of hindsight, it is hard to determine which candidate's causes and circumstances were consequential and which were cursory. An analyst predisposed to seeing the protests as arising out of deep dissatisfaction with government policies can list multiple causes: shoddy public services including transport, housing, health, and education; the hardships of urban life in Brazilian cities; corrupt politicians; rising and wasteful public expenditures; police brutality; and income inequality. Similarly, analysts predisposed to dismiss the protests as inconsequential have a countervailing list of improvements: tremendous strides in the reduction of poverty and inequality, record low unemployment, unprecedented growth of the middle class and domestic consumption of durable goods, high presidential popularity prior to the protest, and massive social inclusion and voice in public affairs. Given our bullish forecast for the trajectory of Brazil, how do we reconcile the mixed evidence?

To interpret the protests and yet retain our optimism, we rely on the institutional possibility frontiers (IPF) put forth by Djankov et al. (2003) (see figure 8.1). Figure 8.1 illustrates the trade-offs existing in any country between disorder and dictatorship (authoritarianism) and shows that "a state that has more powers to control disorder also has more for dictatorial abuse" (Djankov et al. 2003: 598–99).[5] Greater state intervention reduces disorder (e.g., violence, monopoly, or inequality), but it increases the risk of public abuse of the private sector. Similarly, a less interventionist state raises the risk of expropriation of the public good by private

---

3 See Miller and Page (2007) for models that have been proposed to explain this type of phenomena, in particular: standing ovation models, percolation models, tipping point models, self-organized criticality, and complex adaptive systems in general.

4 In commemoration of the twenty-fifth anniversary of the fall of the Berlin Wall, a new wave of debate emerged among scholars and journalists over the causes of the collapse (Sarotte 2014).

5 Weingast (1995: 1) posited a similar analogous view: "A government strong enough to protect property rights and enforce contracts is also strong enough to confiscate the wealth of its citizens."

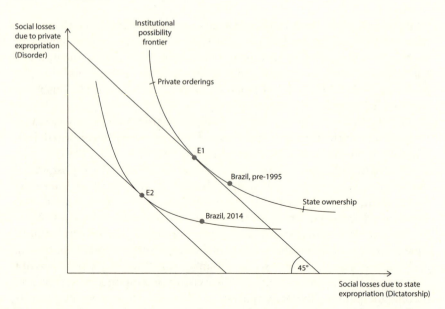

Figure 8.1. Better institutions with more discontent. Source: Adapted from Djankov et al. (2003: 599).

organizations (e.g., monopoly power or excessive risk by banks at public expense). The IPF in figure 8.1 shows the opportunity cost of trade-offs. Every country has its own shape and location of the frontier. The point of tangency with the 45-degree line represents the best institutions for a country (importantly ignoring political transaction costs of attaining the point). The point of tangency represents the mix of policies that minimizes the sum of losses from disorder and dictatorship. In the northeast curve, we labeled different mixes of private orderings and state ownership. If the country has a relatively high mix of private orderings, there will be few losses from existing state interventions but high losses from private expropriation. Note that this point is not the best (in theory) that could be done as E_1 yields a lower sum of losses. Similarly, if the country is a relatively high interventionist state, moving to more private ordering would bring gains.

We portray Brazil's IPF circa 1995 in figure 8.1 as relatively far from the origin, which means that even the best possible institutional arrangements (E_1) would involve high levels of both types of social losses. We portray Brazil in 1995 closer to the state intervention side of the curve, still early in the Cardoso administration. Note: the point is not close to E_1, but given the shape of the curve, the additional benefits of moving northwest are not huge. The high levels of social losses result from the location of the curve far from the origin.

The second curve, closer to the origin, portrays Brazil's position in 2014 after two decades of growing belief in fiscally sound social inclusion. The movement toward the origin denotes the marked process of institutional strengthening during twenty years. The move to the southwest of curve two illustrates the great reduction in total social losses. But, we place Brazil relatively distant from the best that the country could do at point $E2$ (again given zero political transaction costs). By reducing state intervention in the economy, Brazil could reduce social losses. President Dilma's greater use of state-led policies exacerbated the losses, especially as perceived by the private business community and international investors. The social losses manifest themselves in Dilma's policies of picking national champions, discretionary subsidies, greater public expenditure in the face of lower revenues, creative accounting in public finances, tinkering with public tariffs for political gain, and importing doctors from Cuba. Directly and indirectly, Dilma's actions led to the perception that the state could do better by moving in the northwest of the figure. The perceived extant social losses led to the protests in 2013 and the close electoral results of November 2014. While Brazil is vastly better in its mix of policies compared to 1994, protesters still perceive social losses relative to theoretical optimum mix at $E2$.

Significant improvement fused with distortions is the essence of dissipative inclusion that accompanies development. You are never at a theoretical optimal mix of policies in any country; it is the nature of politics. In Brazil, participatory institutions in public decision making provided voice but at the same time led to gridlock. Similarly, subsidized access to the courts for the poor, and judges who put social objectives before the law, leveled the playing field but created excessive court loads, along with defensive measures by those potentially harmed (e.g., employers not hiring for fear of oppressive labor costs and court suits). Clearly, it would be better to have the inclusion without dissipation, but for Brazil's development today, dissipative inclusion is the only way forward. But, the electoral results of 2014 suggest that Brazil may be able to implement a better mix of policies.

Will dissipative inclusion prevent Brazil from making the critical transition to sustainable development? It depends on the benefits from inclusion increasing more than the costs of dissipation. While benefits from inclusion are silent, inconspicuous, and long term, dissipation is on the front page every morning. This explains in part the paradox of protests amid long-term improvements in outcomes and institutions. Protestors saw dissipation as a good reason to take to the streets.

ASSESSING THE FRAMEWORK

In April 2006, the BRIC foreign ministers met in New York for a series of high-level meetings to discuss a new world order in which emerging economies would play a much weightier role. Eight years later and well into a drawn-out global economic depression, Brazil became associated with the Fragile Five—together with Turkey, India, Indonesia, and South Africa—a less prestigious grouping deemed most vulnerable to shocks. The fall from BRIC to Fragile Five led many analysts to question Brazil's current development path. In this prism, the protests reflect another Brazilian failed burst of development.

What do the protests and the accompanying negative naysayers portend for our analysis and claims? At first blush, given the rosy picture we portray, Brazil's fall from grace seems damning. Development is complex and not linear. Even a successful developmental path—for example, the United States or most of Europe—is rife with bad policies, policy reversals, inefficiencies, and corruption. A transitional path is nuanced and much of the evidence circumstantial. In Brazil, dissipative inclusion brings a mixture of better and worse with our bullish view: two steps forward, one step back.

Our analysis contains two contributions and one expectation. Our analytical framework is our first contribution, the wedding of beliefs, dominant network, leadership, institutions, outcomes, and windows of opportunity to form an iterative dynamic. A new understanding of fifty years of Brazilian history through the lenses of our framework represents our second contribution. Most importantly, under the leadership of President Cardoso, Brazil promoted institutional development under the belief of fiscally sound social inclusion. Twenty years under the umbrella of fiscally sound social inclusion enabled Brazil to embark on its critical transition. Finally, and more controversially, the expectation in the book is that Brazil will continue on its virtuous trajectory though with bumps along the road.

Our first and most general contribution is our analytical framework expounded at length in chapter 7. If Brazil reverses its course and does not complete the critical transition, does this lessen the analytical lenses of our framework for understanding development in Brazil, and elsewhere? The answer depends not on the outcome but whether Brazil's future trajectory fits the dynamic of our framework. The current troubles may lead to systematic large deviations in actual outcomes from expectations, creating a window of opportunity for a leader to coordinate a change in beliefs and institutions and new trajectory. This would validate rather than refute the usefulness of our framework as an analytical instrument for understanding development.

What evidence would be incompatible with our framework? The key concept is beliefs emanating from a dominant network of powerful organizations. If a set of beliefs and its influence on institutions cannot be discerned, then the framework does not fit reality. If beliefs seem to be changing erratically and without connection to expected outcomes or windows of opportunity, then the usefulness of the framework is doubtful at best. Similarly, if a set of beliefs is replaced during a window of opportunity and yet institutions remain fixed, our framework misses its mark. Finally, we put considerable emphasis on leadership in catalyzing changes in beliefs. Whether leaders matter—and if so, how they exert impact—is controversial. If we lack evidence from other country case studies, then the role of leadership in our framework may be a sufficient but not necessary condition for changing beliefs.

A test drive of the framework against Brazil's trajectory since the 1960s is our second contribution. We identified three windows of opportunity and the associated beliefs that first deepened and then faded over time: 1964 (developmentalism), 1985 (social inclusion), and 1994 (fiscally sound social inclusion). Strong disconnects between expected and actual outcomes ushered in each cycle: political chaos and economic fluctuations before 1964; lack of freedom, oppression, and economic weakness prior to 1985; and hyperinflation in the decade before 1994. For the first two periods, beliefs emerged diffusely, and without leadership. In cycle three, President Cardoso played a leadership role by first coordinating the dominant network to embrace the *Real Plan* and following up with institutional deepening that in turn solidified the belief in fiscally sound social inclusion. With Brazil operating under the belief in fiscally sound social inclusion for twenty years with alternations in party leadership poverty fell; income inequality lessened; economic growth was modest but always positive; adherence to rule of law expanded; and ex ante uncertain elections were accepted ex post; inter alia.

Brazil straying from its developmental path to a new set of beliefs would not negate our interpretation of the past fifty years. One can question our interpretation of the roles of beliefs, dominant network, leadership, institutions, and outcomes in Brazil from 1964 to 2014, but the future would not negate the past interpretation. Development is a complex journey with few countries completing the critical transition.[6]

6 See our discussion of Argentina in chapter 7.

Brazil and the Critical Transition

Finally, because of the past twenty years of belief and institutional deepening, we expect Brazil to make the critical transition to a society more akin to the current developed countries in the world. We use the word "expectation" instead of the more hubristic "prediction."[7] We base our expectation not on simple extrapolation of the past to the future but on the vast literature on the fundamental causes of development. In the past decade, the subset of the explanations for sustained development emphasizing inclusion and open access as the key determinant has gained significant traction:

> This mechanism, through which the extent of inequality affects the way institutions evolve, not only helps to explain the long-term persistence of differences in inequality among the respective societies, but it may also play a role in accounting for the differences in the growth rates of per capita income over the last two centuries. (Engerman and Sokoloff 2012: 35–36)

> Political and economic institutions, which are ultimately the choice of society, can be inclusive and encourage economic growth. Or they can be extractive and become impediments to economic growth. (Acemoglu and Robinson 2012: 83)

> Institutions Rule: The Primacy of Institutions over Geography and Integration in Economic Development. (Rodrik, Subramanian, and Trebbi 2004)[8]

North, Wallis, and Weingast show that all countries that made the transition

> developed new economic and political institutions that secured open access for economic organizations through a general incorporation procedure; secured open access for political organizations through the development of articulated and competitive party organizations and

---

7 Acemoglu and Robinson (2012) use the failed Arab Spring in Egypt as an example of "Why Nations Fail" in the preface of their book. But more than 450 pages later, in which they provide dozens of rich examples of failed development, the authors end on a bullish account of Brazil: "The rise of Brazil since the 1970s was not engineered by economists of international institutions instructing Brazilian policymakers on how to design better policies or avoid market failures. It was not achieved with injections of foreign aid. It was not the natural outcome of modernization. Rather, it was the consequence of diverse groups of people courageously building inclusive institutions. Eventually these led to more inclusive economic institutions" (457).

8 Title of the article.

broadening of suffrage; and secured open access to legal enforcement of rights through changes in their legal systems. (2009: 27)

A middle class consensus distinguishes development successes from failures. (Easterly 2000: abstract)

A just society requires the good economy; the good economy requires high dynamism and wide inclusion; and these qualities require a well-chosen mix of economic policies: some aimed at dynamism, some at inclusion. If further goals of economic policy are valuable, as productivity might be, either they derive value from what their achievement would add to dynamism or inclusion *or* their pursuit does not get in the way of dynamism or inclusion. (Phelps 2008: 1; emphasis in original)

The growing consensus that inclusion, open access, and a large middle class are crucial for development is intuitive, and the historical record is clear, with all countries thus far transitioning doing so by adopting (ultimately) inclusive policies, leading to open access and a significant middle class (North, Wallis, and Weingast 2009; Acemoglu and Robinson 2012). Although looking back, we clearly see the link between inclusion and development, real-time observations bring much noise.

Banerjee and Duflo (2008) provided an example of the disconnect (or long lag) between standard historical reasons given for the centrality of a large middle class for investment or innovation. They examined survey data from individuals in thirteen developing countries. Instead of finding the middle class a hotbed for entrepreneurial spirit, saving, and innovation, they found that the middle class mostly desires a well-paying job, often in the bureaucracy. Although this initially goes against the received wisdom of the importance of the middle class for growth and progress, it does not mean that the middle class is unimportant. On the contrary, the authors find other, perhaps less glamorous, mechanisms through which a large middle class impacts development: "if good jobs mean that children grow up in an environment where they are able to make the most of their talents, one might start to think that it may all be worth it" (Banerjee and Duflo 2008: 26). Similarly, when we reflect on the raw realities of inclusion in Brazil, there is little sign of hidden talent being uncovered, new breakthrough ideas being given the time of day, and entrepreneurial spirit being unleashed from its constraints. Instead, *Bolsa Família* beneficiaries just get along; affirmative action beneficiaries in the federal universities struggle not to drop out; and participatory budgets appear to do little to solve the problems of poor-quality public services. But, this is the nature of dissipative inclusion that is at the heart of development in Brazil.[9] Dissipative inclusion also accompanied the development process in the pioneer countries (e.g., boss politics in the late nineteenth century to mid-twentieth centuries in the United States). Nevertheless, the evidence from the pioneer countries clearly indicates that inclusion and openness in the long run leads to prosperity. Brazil is still in the early phases of inclusion where dissipation is apparent, especially because it makes headlines.

The achievements in Brazil in the past twenty years are truly extraordinary for a middle-income country.[10] For Brazil, where the concentration of wealth had been among the highest in the world for five hundred years, to suddenly reduce inequality for fifteen years straight in a global context of structurally increasing inequality is quite remarkable. Most of the decline in inequality has come through a rising middle class.

One of the hallmarks of the developed countries is that they are more resilient to shocks.[11] Resilience manifests itself in fewer booms and busts as well as more stable prices. In table 8.1, we show annual growth rates in GDP per capita and inflation rates along with their variation in Brazil in the periods 1964–1994 and 1995–2013.

Although average growth rates have decreased, they have also become considerably less volatile. Also, inflation has fallen dramatically and become much more stable over time. Whereas most of the developed countries suffered periods of negative growth rates after 2008, Brazil's growth rates remained positive—clear indication of resilience.

Brazil has also become more politically open and increasingly transparent. In 1985, Brazil gave the franchise to illiterates, dramatically expanding who had a voice. In its 1988 Constitution, it added considerable checks to the power of government through creation of state and federal ministérios públicos (public attorneys) whose mandate is to act in the public interest. The Ministério Público takes corporations to court as well as the government. This is a unique Brazilian check on power. Unlike much of the world, Brazil has consolidated democracy. Since redemocratization, Brazil has experienced seven presidential elections. Lula came to the presidency with a fourth-grade education. Dilma, Brazil's first female president, followed Lula. In all presidential electoral races, there was outcome uncertainty ex ante and acceptance ex post. Competition in elections was the norm, and there were no allegations of fraud at the ballot boxes. Moreover, a lack of violence and cooperation marked presidential

---

9 By dissipative inclusion, we mean that inclusion is not costless. It creates winners and losers. Losers attempt to lessen the blow in efforts to thwart well-intentioned policies. A good example is land reform (Alston, Libecap, and Mueller 1999).

10 Brazil is not alone. See the cases of Chile and South Korea in North et al. (2012).

11 North (1990) referred to this more than two decades ago as "adaptive efficiency."

TABLE 8.1. GDP Growth and Inflation

	1964–1994	1995–2013
GDP per capita		
Mean	5.17	3.01
Standard dev.	4.68	2.18
Inflation		
Mean	379.5	8.96
Standard dev.	644.4	6.49

Sources: GDP per capita real annual growth (IBGE/SCN 2000 Anual—Brazilian Institute of Geography and Statistics/System of National Accounts, http://www.ipeadata.gov.br/ BaseFontes.aspx); Inflation—IGP-DI—(% per year)—Fundação Getulio Vargas, Conjuntura Econômica.

Note: The differences in the means and variances are statistically significant at the 99 percent confidence interval.

transitions, most importantly for the Cardoso to Lula transition. In addition, Brazil boasts a very lively, competitive, and investigative web of accountability institutions including a very independent and respected judiciary, an honest and competent bureaucracy (by Latin American standards), audit institutions, and an independent media.

Will Brazil complete the transition? Any country can regress—remember Argentina and the past empires of the ancient world. Development is not a stock of attributes but rather a process of adapting to natural, social, political, and economic shocks. The journey is never without bumps in the road, but if Brazil continues its virtuous reinforcing trajectory, then history will vindicate our positive prognosis.

AFTERWORD

WE COMPLETED OUR MANUSCRIPT IN SPRING 2015. IN THE PAST SIX months, Brazil has been pounded by events akin to a "perfect storm." This afterword gives us the opportunity to check recent events in Brazil against our framework and analysis. This is similar to testing the estimates from an econometric model against out-of-sample data that was not used in the original estimation process. And what new data it is, with a barrage of seemingly bad news resembling huge waves without respite. None of these events are completely surprising or unexpected, as there were prior manifestations and early warning signs. In chapters 6 and 8, we had already taken note of the attempt by Dilma Rousseff's government to flexibilize—a common euphemism in Brazil for bending without breaking the rules—the understanding of the belief in fiscally sound social inclusion through greater expenditures, undue interference in several markets (e.g., gasoline and electricity prices), creative accounting, and negligence in managing its coalition in Congress, among others. But what astounded us was the magnitude and concurrency with which these forces hit the country. We described earlier how prior to 2015, these actions by the government had set in motion what we called centripetal forces that pulled the government back in line with the prevailing beliefs, not the least of which were widespread popular protests and then the slim margin with which the president was reelected in 2014. Since we finished our manuscript, events have continued to unfold, but the overall scenario has amplified dramatically. The amplified events are a stress test for the belief in fiscally sound social inclusion.

History never stops, but a book must have an end. We will not give a detailed account of the events but instead will paint a broad picture. What was the reaction of the government, society, markets, and other players to these same events? It is a situation in which outcomes are not in consonance with expectations, given the belief in fiscally sound social inclusion. The disappointing outcomes fueled frustration, anger, and dissatisfaction. The protests since 2013 have been a manifestation of these feelings, though the reelection in 2014 suggested that up to that point the sentiment was not overwhelming. In a window of opportunity, the extant beliefs become malleable. There is no doubt that 2015 has been a window of opportunity for Brazil. We do not venture to predict whether this window of opportunity will be seized and, if so, what new beliefs and institutions will be ushered in, nor the potential outcomes. Nevertheless, in light of our framework and the past fifty years of history, we can pose some possible scenarios.

Before discussing these scenarios, what were the waves of events since the reelection of Dilma Rousseff in November 2014? During the first ten months of 2015, the economic situation deteriorated dramatically. Inflation, which closed in 2014 at 6.4 percent (still within the top of the target range of 6.5 percent), rose to nearly 10 percent in the first nine months of 2015. Growth of GDP, which was 0.1 percent in 2014, is expected to drop to –3.0 percent in 2015. Unemployment was at 4.8 percent at the end of 2014, the lowest level since the current measurement methodology was adopted in 2003. By mid-October 2015, unemployment stood at nearly 9 percent and was still on the rise. The value of the Real fell from 2.69 R$/US$ at the close of 2014 to a record low of 4.19 R$/US$ in September 2015. And the official interest rate, which closed in 2013 at 9.9 percent and in 2014 at 11.7 percent, reached 14.2 percent by September 2015. These statistics are worse than even the most pessimistic forecasts. It is now the worst recession in Brazil since the Great Depression. The gravity of the current situation prompted Standard and Poor's to downgrade the government bond rating to speculative. Other rating agencies will likely follow suit, which will lead to the loss of investment-grade status.

This dismal economic situation required that the government react with leadership, vision, and policies to address the crisis. But, just when executive strength was most needed, the Dilma administration proved weak and indecisive. Since her reelection, Dilma has lost control of her coalition in Congress, and there is disunity within her own party. This is striking because in Brazil, the president has strong powers to shape congressional behavior. A sign of Dilma's weakness is that the speakers of the Deputy and Senate Chambers are not from Dilma's PT party. In October 2015, Dilma's approval rating stood at 8 percent, the lowest since polls began. (To put it in perspective, at the time of the impeachment of Collor, his approval stood at 9 percent).

The pitiful popularity indexes are not due solely to the deteriorating economy; a number of corruption scandals have continued to rage, implicating several high-level government officials and members of the Workers' Party. Moreover, the allegations are now tainting the president. Even ex-president Lula, on whom no allegation or denunciation has ever seemed to stick, has been implicated and might be officially investigated. Whereas he had seemed a shoo-in for the 2018 election, that is no longer a sure thing or even likely.

The biggest corruption scandal, involving kickbacks in Petrobrás (the giant government-controlled oil company), had already broken out in early 2014, but it has grown impressively. Petrobrás already admits losses of R$6 billion, and the federal police estimates more than R$19 billion.

These estimates do not include the impacts on the rest of the economy. The oil and gas sector is an important area of the economy, with Petrobrás alone accounting for almost 13 percent of the country's investment. Many CEOs have been sentenced to prison, and the energy sector is in complete disarray. There have been suggestions, as yet unsubstantiated, that other public organizations may eventually reveal similar corruption scandals. In particular, an alleged scandal involving BNDES (the official development bank) could surpass that of Petrobrás.

To make matters worse for Dilma, the National Audit Tribunal (TCU) rejected the government's accounts for 2014 because of "creative" accounting. The vote was unanimous from a tribunal composed of appointees from the executive and legislative branches. The role of the TCU was always seen as a yearly bureaucratic routine that happened in the background and never stirred much attention. But in 2015, the tribunal proved extremely diligent and independent in pointing out improper maneuvers to mask the real state of the government's public accounts. The decision of TCU may provide legal standing and evidence to directly or indirectly initiate impeachment procedures.

The Dilma administration being cornered and under attack in a quickly deteriorating economy, and with low popularity, few friends, and waning power, what has been its reaction? And more importantly, what has been the reaction of other groups and organizations? Is the magnitude of the shocks briefly described above sufficient to change beliefs and prompt new institutions?

The government's most credible move to stabilize markets and signal a return to fiscally sound social inclusion has been the appointment of Joaquim Levy—an experienced, no-nonsense fiscal conservative economist trained at the University of Chicago—as finance minister. Levy initiated fiscal adjustment procedures, implementing cuts and other inescapable painful policies. Naturally, this type of adjustment has led to widespread criticism and resistance from the public and Congress, as well as the president's party. Levy is a significant anchor holding government policy together, so far, and bringing it back to fiscally sound social inclusion. No matter how much the president, her party, or their coalition in Congress dislike the idea of having to undergo the painful fiscal adjustment, the belief that this is the only way to go has thus far prevailed.

From the public, there have been protests of all different types, in the streets and in the media. Most importantly, the manifestations of dissatisfaction have all taken place fully within institutional and constitutional rules. There has been much talk of impeachment: in the media, in the streets, in Congress, in the Supreme Court, and in other accountability institutions. The discussion of impeachment has been framed within the proper constitutional procedures. The press, opinion makers, and the man in the street vigorously reject suggestions of coups, military take-overs, or violence as a solution. It is clear that democracy is the only game in town, even under the current dire circumstances.

The actions in response to the crisis by the accountability institutions such as the judiciary, public attorneys, the TCU, and federal police are most noteworthy. These organizations have truly stepped up to the plate by investigating, prosecuting, condemning, fining, and even imprisoning those parties involved in corruption scandals and misuse of power. The zeal, which had been seen in the Mensalão scandal in the mid-2000s, has now been taken to new heights. Not only have investigations uprooted entrenched corruption schemes involving a large number of important political appointees and high-level officials in some of the country's larg-est companies, but this has also been done swiftly (which has always been a key weakness of the Brazilian judiciary) and with great transparency. The efforts and accomplishments have been recognized by the press and the population, which have expressed explicit and unconditional support for accountability. Individual judges, who naturally come under all sorts of pressure to drop the cases and turn a blind eye, are sentencing promi-nent individuals. The old dictum in Brazil that such investigations and prosecutions "end in pizza" (never reach a conclusion) has certainly not applied to the investigative and accountability institutions today. On the contrary, there appears to be a virtuous competition among the different organizations and branches to see who is most effective by aligning their behavior to the dominant sentiment of the majority of the population.

Of course, it is not known whether these forces and reactions are enough to sustain and complete a reaction against the forces that are pushing the country away from its current set of beliefs and institutions. There is no doubt that recent events indicate a potential window of op-portunity that may herald in a new set of beliefs and institutions. Yet, so far, the dominant belief in fiscally sound social inclusion remains. If it does come to happen that the current window of opportunity is realized and the current set of beliefs lose traction, what belief will take its place? We do not venture a prediction, but we pose three possible scenarios: (1) stagnation or "muddling through," (2) populist leadership, and (3) resig-nation/impeachment of the president.

Without a clear mandate from the president or Congress, Brazil faces the possibility of three-plus years of stagnation until the next election. The result would be painful with increasing unemployment and infla-tion along with policy stagnation. But, three years is a long time to wait without signs of dramatic action from some quarter. If stagnation is the short-term outcome, this could usher in a populist leader who promises much but delivers little. In some ways, this could be a return to the 1980s of mounting inflation and economic volatility. Alternatively, Congress could move to impeach Dilma, who might choose to fight it or resign. If impeachment or resignation transpires, a more dramatic move back to fiscally sound social inclusion seems likely. This scenario would be akin to the administration of President Itamar Franco, who assumed the presidency after the impeachment of President Collor. Franco turned economic policy over to Fernando Henrique Cardoso and his economic team, who initiated the *Real Plan*, which tamed inflation. Today's Vice President Michel Temer could turn over policy more directly to an economic team capable of undertaking a painful adjustment back to fiscally sound social inclusion but with the support of markets. Will history repeat itself?

REFERENCES

Abrucio, Fernando. 1998. *Os Barões da Federação*. São Paulo: Hucitec.

Acemoglu, Daron, Simon Johnson, and James A. Robinson. 2005. "Institutions as the Fundamental Cause of Economic Growth." In *Handbook of Economic Growth*, ed. Philippe Aghion and Steve Durlauf, 385–472. New York: North Holland.

Acemoglu, Daron, Simon Johnson, James A. Robinson, and Pierre Yared. 2008. "Income and Democracy." *American Economic Review* 98(3): 808–42.

Acemoglu, Daron, and James A. Robinson. 2000. "Why Did the West Extend the Franchise? Democracy, Inequality, and Growth in Historical Perspective." *Quarterly Journal of Economics* 115(4): 1167–99.

———. 2006. *Economic Origins of Dictatorship and Democracy*. New York: Cambridge University Press.

———. 2012. *Why Nations Fail: The Origins of Power, Prosperity, and Poverty*. New York: Random House.

———. 2013. "Economics versus Politics: Pitfalls of Policy Advice." *Journal of Economic Perspectives* 27(2): 173–92.

Acemoglu, Daron, James Robinson, and Ragnar Torvik. 2011. "Why Do Voters Dismantle Checks and Balances?" NBER Working Paper No. 17293.

Aghion, Phillipe, and Patrick Bolton. 1997. "A Theory of Trickle-Down Growth and Development." *Review of Economic Studies* 64(2): 151–72.

Ahlquist, John, and Margaret Levi. 2011. "Leadership: What It Means, What It Does, and What We Want to Know about It." *Annual Review of Political Science* 14: 1–24.

Alesina, Alberto F., and George-Marios Angeletos. 2005. "Fairness and Redistribution." *American Economic Review* 95(4): 960–80.

Alesina, Alberto F., Guido Cozzi, and Noemi Mantovan. 2012. "The Evolution of Ideology, Fairness and Redistribution." *Economic Journal* 122(565): 1244–61. (Also published as NBER Working Paper No. 15587.)

Alesina, Alberto F., and Paola Giuliano. 2009. "Preferences for Redistribution." NBER Working Paper No. 14825, http://www.nber.org/papers/w14825.

Alesina, Alberto F., and Edward L. Glaeser. 2004. *Fighting Poverty in the US and Europe: A World of Difference*. Oxford: Oxford University Press.

Alesina, Alberto F., Edward L. Glaeser, and Bruce Sacerdote. 2001. "Why Doesn't the United States Have a European-Style Welfare State?" *Brookings Papers on Economic Activity* 2001(2): 187–254.

Alesina, Alberto F., and Eliana La Ferrara. 2005. "Preferences for Redistribution in the Land of Opportunities." *Journal of Public Economics* 89: 897–931.

Almeida, Mansueto. 2011. *Nota Técnica: Restos a Pagar e Artifícios Contábeis*. Brasília: IPEA.

Almeida, Rita, and Pedro Carneiro. 2009. "Enforcement of Labor Regulation and Firm Size." *Journal of Comparative Economics* 37(1): 28–46.

Alston, Lee J., and Andrés A. Gallo. 2010. "Electoral Fraud, the Rise of Peron and Demise of Checks and Balances in Argentina." *Explorations in Economic History* 47(2): 179–97.

Alston, Lee J., Gary Libecap, and Bernardo Mueller. 1999. *Titles, Conflict, and Land Use: The Development of Property Rights and Land Reform on the Brazilian Amazon Frontier*. Ann Arbor: University of Michigan Press.

———. 2010. "Interest Groups, Information Manipulation in the Media, and Public Policy: The Case of the Landless Peasants Movement in Brazil." NBER Working Paper No. W15865, http://www.nber.org/papers/w15865.

Alston, Lee J., Marcus André Melo, Bernardo Mueller, and Carlos Pereira. 2008. "On the Road to Good Governance: Recovering from Economic and Political Shocks in Brazil." In *Policymaking in Latin America: How Politics Shapes Policies*, ed. Ernesto Stein and Mariano Tommasi, 111–54. Cambridge, MA: Harvard University Press.

———. 2010. *The Political Economy of Productivity in Brazil*. IDB Working Paper Series No. 104. Washington, DC: Inter-American Development Bank.

———. 2013. "Changing Social Contracts: Beliefs and Dissipative Inclusion in Brazil." *Journal of Comparative Economics* 41: 48–65. (Also published as NBER Working Paper No. 18588.)

Alston, Lee J., and Bernardo Mueller. 2006. "Pork for Policy: Executive and Legislative Exchange in Brazil." *Journal of Law, Economics, and Organization* 22(1): 87–114.

———. 2011. "Brazilian Development: This Time for Real?" CESifo Forum 1: 37–46, www.cesifo-group.de/DocDL/forum1-11-focus6.pdf.

Alston, Lee J., Bernardo Mueller, and Tomas Nonnenmacher. Forthcoming. *Institutional and Organizational Analysis: Concepts and Applications*. New York: Cambridge University Press.

Ames, Barry. 1995a. "Electoral Rules, Constituency Pressures, and Pork Barrel: Bases of Voting in the Brazilian Congress." *Journal of Politics* 57(2): 324–43.

———. 1995b. "Electoral Strategy under Open-List Proportional Representation." *American Journal of Political Science* 39(2): 406–33.

Amorim Neto, Octavio. 2002. "Presidential Cabinets, Electoral Cycles and Coalition Discipline in Brazil." In *Legislative Politics in Latin America*, ed. Scott Morgenstern and Benito Nacif, 48–78. New York: Cambridge University Press.

Amorim Neto, Octavio, and Fabiano Santos. 2001. "The Executive Connection: Presidentially Defined Factions and Party Discipline in Brazil." *Party Politics* 7(2): 213–34.

Arantes, Rogério B. 1999. "Direito e Política: O Ministério Público e a Defesa dos Direitos Coletivos." *Revista Brasileira de Ciências Sociais*, São Paulo, 14(39): 83–102.

———. 2002. *Ministério Público e Política no Brasil*. São Paulo: Sumaré Press.

———. 2004. "Judiciário: Entre a Justiça e a Política." In *Sistema Político Brasileiro: Uma Introdução*, ed. Lucia Avelar and Antônio Octávio Cintra, 79–108. Rio de Janeiro e São Paulo: Fundação Konrad-Adenauer and Unesp Press.

Arida, Pérsio, ed. 1986. *Inflação Zero: Brasil, Argentina e Israel*. São Paulo: Paz e Terra.

Arinos, Afonso. 1999. "Parecer do Relator Especial da Comissão da Câmara dos Deputados Sobre a Emenda Parlamentarista n. 4, de 29 de Março de 1949." In *Presidencialismo ou Parlamentarismo?*, ed. Afonso Arinos de Melo Franco and Raul Pila, 15–110. Brasília: Senado Federal.

Avritzer, Leonardo. 2009. *Participatory Institutions in Democratic Brazil*. Baltimore: Johns Hopkins University Press.

Baer, Werner, and Paul Beckerman. 1989. "The Decline and Fall of the Brazilian Cruzado." *Latin American Research Review* 24(1): 35–64.

Báez, Javier E., Aude-Sophie Rodella, Ali Sharman, and Martha Viveros. 2015. "Poverty and Shared Prosperity in Brazil: Where to Next?" In *Shared Prosperity and Poverty Eradication in Latin America and the Caribbean*, ed. Louise Cord, Maria Eugenia Genoni, and Carlos Rodriguez-Castelan, 65–95. Washington, DC: World Bank.

Baker, Andy. 2005. "Who Wants to Globalize? Consumer Tastes and Labor Markets in a Theory of Trade Policy Beliefs." *American Journal of Political Science* 49(4): 924–38.

———. 2009. *The Market and the Masses in Latin America: Policy Reform and Consumption in Liberalizing Economies*. New York: Cambridge University Press.

Banerjee, Abhijit V. 2008. "Big Answers for Big Questions: The Presumption of Macroeconomics." Paper presented at the Brookings Global Economy and Development Conference "What Works in Development? Thinking Big and Thinking Small," May 21, http://www.brookings.edu/~/media/Events/2008/5/29%20global%20development/2008_banerjee.PDF.

———. 2009. *Investment Efficiency and the Distribution of Wealth*. World Bank, Commission on Growth and Development Working Paper No. 53, http://economics.mit.edu/files/6966.

Banerjee, Abhijit V., and Esther Duflo. 2008. "What Is Middle Class about the Middle Classes around the World?" *Journal of Economic Perspectives* 22(2): 3–28.

Barro, Robert, and Xavier Sala-i-Martin. 2004. *Economic Growth*. 2nd ed. Cambridge, MA: MIT Press.

Barros, Ricardo Paes de, and Carlos Henrique Corseuil. 2004. "The Impact of Regulations on Brazilian Labor Market Performance." In *Law and Employment: Lessons from Latin America and the Caribbean*, ed. James J. Heckman and Carmen Pagés, 273–350. Chicago: University of Chicago Press.

Barros, Ricardo Paes de, and Rosana Silva Pinto de Mendonça. 1994. "Geração e Reprodução da Desigualdade de Renda no Brasil." In *Perspectivas da Economia Brasileira 1994*, vol. 2, 471–90. Rio de Janeiro: IPEA.

Bates, Robert H., Rui J. P de Figueiredo Jr., and Barry R. Weingast. 1998. "The Politics of Interpretation: Rationality, Culture, and Transition." *Politics and Society* 26: 603–42.

Baumann, Renato. 2002. "Trade Policies, Growth, and Equity in Latin America." In *Models of Capitalism: Lessons from Latin America*, ed. Evelyne Huber, 53–80. University Park: Penn State University Press.

Bénabou, Roland. 2000. "Unequal Societies: Income Distribution and the Social Contract." *American Economic Review* 90(1): 96–129.

Bénabou, Roland. 2002. "Tax and Education Policy in a Heterogeneous-Agent Economy: What Levels of Redistribution Maximize Growth and Efficiency?" *Econometrica* 70(2): 481–517.

———. 2005. "Inequality, Technology and the Social Contract." In *Handbook of Economic Growth*, vol. 1B, ed. Philippe Aghion and Steven Durlauf, 1595–638. Amsterdam, Netherlands: Elsevier.

Bénabou, Roland, and Jean Tirole. 2006. "Belief in a Just World and Redistributive Politics." *Quarterly Journal of Economics* 121(2): 699–746.

Bidner, Chris, and Patrick François. 2013. "The Emergence of Political Accountability." *Quarterly Journal of Economics* 128(3): 1397–448.

Boix, Carles. 2003. *Democracy and Redistribution*. Cambridge: Cambridge University Press.

Bolt, J., and J. L. van Zanden. 2013. "The First Update of the Maddison Project: Re-estimating Growth before 1820." Maddison Project Working Paper No. 4, http://www.ggdc.net/maddison/maddison-project/home.htm.

Brasil, Presidência da República, Casa Civil. 2003. "Análise e Avaliação do Papel das Agências Reguladoras no Atual Arranjo Institucional Brasileiro: Relatório do Grupo Interministerial." Brasília: Dezembro.

Bresser-Pereira, Luiz Carlos. 1984. *Development and Crisis in Brazil, 1930–1983*. Boulder, CO: Westview.

———. 2004. "Proposta de Desenvolvimento para o Brasil." *Revista de Economia Política* 24(4): 625–30.

Brinks, Daniel M., and Varun Gauri. 2012. "The Law's Majestic Equality? The Distributive Impact of Litigating Social and Economic Rights." World Bank, Policy Research Working Paper No. 5999.

Bruns, Barbara, David Evans, and Javier Luque. 2012. *Achieving World-Class Education in Brazil: The Next Agenda*. Washington, DC: World Bank.

Calomiris, Charles W., and Stephen H. Haber. 2014. *Fragile by Design: The Political Origins of Banking Crises and Scarce Credit*. Princeton, NJ: Princeton University Press.

Campelo, Daniela. 2011. "The Politics of Redistribution in Less Developed Democracies: Evidence from Brazil, Ecuador, and Venezuela." In *The Great Gap: Inequality and the Politics of Redistribution in Latin America*, ed. Merike Blofield, 185–216. University Park: Penn State University Press.

Cardoso, Fernando Henrique. 2006. *A Arte da Politica: A Historia que Vivi*. Rio de Janeiro: Civilização Brasileira.

———. 2010. *Relembrando o que Escrevi: Da Reconqusita de Democracia aos Desafios Globais*. São Paulo: Civilização Brasileira.

Cardoso, Renato F. 2013. "Política Econômica, Reformas Institucionais e Crescimento: A Experiência Brasileira (1945–2010)." In *Desenvolvimento Econômico: Uma Perspectiva Brasileira*, ed. Fabio Giambiagi, Fernando Veloso, Pedro Cavalcanti Ferreira, and Samuel Pessoa, 166–210. São Paulo: Campus.

Carvalho, Carlos Eduardo. 2003. "O Fracasso do Plano Collor: Erros de Execução ou de Concepção?" *ECONOMIA Niterói* 4(2) (July–December): 283–331.

Castro, Antonio Barros de. 1994. "Renegade Development: Rise and Demise of State-Led Development in Brazil." In *Democracy, Markets, and Structural*

Reform in Latin America, ed. William Smith, Carlos Acuña, and Eduardo Gamarra, 183–213. Boulder, CO: Lynne Rienner.

Castro, Jorge Abrahão, and José Aparecido Carlos Ribeiro. 2009. *As Políticas Sociais e a Constituição de 1988: Conquistas e Desafios*. Brasília: IPEA.

Ciria, Albert O., and Carlos Alberto Astiz. 1978. *Parties and Power in Modern Argentina, 1930–1946*. Albany: State University of New York Press.

CNI-Ibope. 2013. "Pesquisa CNI-Ibope: Avaliação do Governo." Brasília: Confederação Nacional da Indústria.

Collier, David. 2011. "Understanding Process Tracing." *PS: Political Science and Politics* 44(4): 823–30.

Comissão Pastoral da Terra. 2010. *Conflitos no Campo no Brasil*. Brasília: CPT, http://www.cptnacional.org.br/index.php?option=com_content&view=article &id=734.

Cornia, G. A., ed. 2014. *Falling Inequality in Latin America: Policy Changes and Lessons*. Oxford: Oxford University Press.

Cruz, Sebastião V. 1995. *Empresariado e Estado na Transição Brasileira: Um Estudo Sobre a Economia Política do Autoritarismo (1974–1977)*. Campinas: Unicamp.

DaMatta, Roberto. 1991. *Carnivals, Rogues, and Heroes: An Interpretation of the Brazilian Dilemma*. Notre Dame, IN: University of Notre Dame Press.

Della Paolera, Gerardo, and Alan M. Taylor. 1998. "Finance and Development in an Emerging Market: Argentina in the Interwar Period." In *Latin America and the World Economy since 1800*, ed. John H. Coatsworth and Alan M. Taylor, 139–70. Series on Latin American Studies. Cambridge: David Rockefeller Center for Latin American Studies; distributed by Harvard University Press.

———. 1999. "Economic Recovery from the Argentine Great Depression: Institutions, Expectations, and the Change of Macroeconomic Regime." *Journal of Economic History* 59(3): 567–99.

———. 2001. "Bailing Out: Internal versus External Convertibility." In *Straining at the Anchor: The Argentine Currency Board and the Search for Macroeconomic Stability, 1880–1935*, ed. Gerardo della Paolera and Alan M. Taylor, 165–87. National Bureau of Economic Research Series on Long-Term Factors in Economic Development. Chicago: University of Chicago Press.

Díaz Alejandro, C. F. 1970. *Essays on the Economic History of the Argentine Republic*. New Haven, CT: Yale University Press.

Djankov, S., E. Glaeser, R. La Porta, F. Lopez-de-Silanes, and A. Shleifer. 2003. "The New Comparative Economics." *Journal of Comparative Economics* 31: 595–619.

Easterly, William. 2000. "The Middle Class Consensus and Economic Development." Policy Research Working Paper 2346. Washington, DC: World Bank.

Easterly, William, and Sergio Rebelo. 1993. "Fiscal Policy and Growth." *Journal of Monetary Economics* 32: 417–58.

Economist. 2009. "Getting It Together at Last." November 14. http://www .economist.com/node/14829485.

———. 2011. "The Servant Problem." December 17, http://www.economist.com /node/21541717.

Economist. 2013. "Has Brazil Blown It?" September 28. http://www.economist
.com/news/leaders/21586833-stagnant-economy-bloated-state-and-mass
-protests-mean-dilma-rousseff-must-change-course-has.

Eggertsson, Thráinn. 2005. *Imperfect Institutions: Possibilities and Limits of Reform*. Ann Arbor: University of Michigan Press.

Elkins, Zachary, Tom Ginsburg, and James Melton. 2009. *The Endurance of National Constitutions*. New York: Cambridge University Press.

Engel, Eduardo A., A. Galetovic, and C. E. Raddatz. 1999. "Taxes and Income Redistribution in Chile: Some Unpleasant Redistributive Arithmetic." *Journal of Development Economics* 59: 155–92.

Engerman, Stanley, and Kenneth Sokoloff. 2000. "Institutions, Factor Endowments, and Paths of Development in the New World." *Journal of Economic Perspectives* 14(3): 217–32.

———. 2012. *Economic Development in the Americas since 1500: Endowments and Institutions*. New York: Cambridge University Press.

Ferejohn, John, and Pasquale Pasquino. 2007. "Rule of Democracy and Rule of Law." In *Democracy and the Rule of Law*, ed. José María Maravall and Adam Przeworski, 242–60. New York: Cambridge University Press.

Fernandez, Raquel, and Dani Rodrik. 1991. "Resistance to Reform: Status Quo Bias in the Presence of Individual-Specific Uncertainty." *American Economic Review* 81(5): 1146–55.

Ferreira, Francisco H. G., Phillippe G. Leite, Luiz A. Pereira da Silva, and Paulo Picchetti. 2008. "Can the Distributional Impacts of Macroeconomic Shocks Be Predicted? A Comparison of Top-Down Macro-Micro Models with Historical Data for Brazil." In *The Impact of Macroeconomic Policies on Poverty and Income Distribution*, ed. François Bourguignon, Maurizio Bussolo, and Luiz Pereira da Silva, 119–75. Washington, DC: World Bank.

FIESP. 1997. "Quanto Custa para o País a não Realização das Reformas Tributária, da Previdência e Administrativa." In FIESP/CIESP *Fórum das Reformas—A Nação tem Pressa: O Custo do Atraso*, 6–39. São Paulo: FIESP/CIESP.

Figueiredo, Argelina, and Fernando Limongi. 2006. "Poder de Agenda na Democracia Brasileira: Desempenho do Governo no Presidencialismo Multipartidário." In *Reforma Politica: Lições da Historia Recente*, ed. Glaucio Soares and Lucio Renno. Rio de Janeiro: FGV Press.

Fiorina, Morris, and Kenneth Shepsle. 1989. "Formal Theories of Leadership: Agents, Agenda-Setters, and Entrepreneurs." In *Leadership and Politics*, ed. Bryan D. Jones, 17–40. Lawrence: University Press of Kansas.

Fishlow, Albert. 2011. *Starting Over: Brazil since 1985*. Washington, DC: Brookings Institution Press.

Fogel, Robert W. 1982. "Circumstantial Evidence in 'Scientific' and Traditional History." In *Philosophy of History and Contemporary Historiography*, ed. D. Carr, W. Dray, and T. Geraets, 61–112. Ottawa, Canada: University of Ottawa Press.

Follath, Erich, and Jens Gluesing. 2012. "From Poverty to Power: How Good Governance Made Brazil a Model Nation." *Spiegel Online International*, August 10, http://www.spiegel.de/international/world/good-governance-series-how-brazil
-became-a-model-nation-a-843591.html.

Fong, Christina. 2001. "Social Preferences, Self-Interest, and the Demand for Redistribution." *Journal of Public Economics* 82: 225–46.

Franco, Gustavo. 1995. *O Plano Real e Outros Ensaios*. Rio de Janeiro: Editora Francisco Alves.

———. 1999. "Seis anos de Trabalho: Um Balanço (Discurso de Despedida)." In *O Desafio Brasileiro: Ensaios sobre Desenvolvimento, Globalização e Moeda*, 264–82. São Paulo: Editora 34.

Frieden, Jeffry A. 1987. "The Brazilian Borrowing Experience: From Miracle to Debacle and Back." *Latin American Research Review* 22(1): 95–131.

Frischtak, Claudio, and Katharina Davies. 2014. "O Investimento Privado em Infraestrutura e seu Financiamento." In *Gargalos e Soluções na Infraestrutura de Transportes*, ed. A. C. Pinheiro and C. Frischtak. Rio de Janeiro: FGV Editora IBRE.

Frohlich, N., J. Oppenheimer, and O. C. Young. 1971. *Political Leadership and Collective Goods*. Princeton, NJ: Princeton University Press.

Gallo, Andrés A., and Lee J. Alston. 2008. "Argentina's Abandonment of the Rule of Law and Its Aftermath." *Journal of Law and Policy* 26: 153–82.

Galor, Oded. 2011. "Inequality, Human Capital Formation and the Process of Development." NBER Working Paper No. 17058, http://www.nber.org/papers/w17058.

Galor, Oded, Omer Moav, and Dietrich Vollrath. 2009. "Inequality in Landownership, the Emergence of Human-Capital Promoting Institutions, and the Great Divergence." *Review of Economic Studies* 76(1): 143–79.

Gama Neto, Ricardo Borges. 2011. "Plano Real, Privatização dos Bancos Estaduais e Reeleição." *Revista Brasileira de Ciências Sociais* 26(77): 129–50, http://dx.doi.org/10.1590/S0102-69092011000300012.

Garcia, Marcio. 2010. "Brazil: Creative Accounting and Fiscal Risk." *EconoMonitor*, October 21, http://www.economonitor.com/blog/2010/10/brazil-creative-accounting-and-fiscal-risk/.

Ginsburg, Tom, Zachary Elkins, and Justin Blount. 2009. "Does the Process of Constitution-Making Matter?" *Annual Review of Law and Social Science* 5: 201–23.

Giuliano, Paola, and Antonio Spilimbergo. 2009. "Growing Up in a Recession: Beliefs and the Macroeconomy." NBER Working Paper No. 15321, http://www.nber.org/papers/w15321.

Greif, Avner. 2006. *Institutions and the Path to the Modern Economy: Lessons from Medieval Trade*. New York: Cambridge University Press.

———. 2008. "The Normative Foundations of Institutions and Institutional Change." Unpublished manuscript.

———. 2012. "Institutions and Leadership." Book manuscript in progress.

Greif, Avner, and Jared Ruben. 2014. "The Institutional Basis of Political Legitimacy: The Reformation and the Origin of the Modern Economy in England." Working Paper, Chapman University.

Hadfield, Gillian K., and Barry R. Weingast. 2014a. "Constitutions as Coordinating Devices." In *Institutions, Property Rights, and Economic Growth: The Legacy of Douglass North*, ed. Sebastian Galiani and Itai Sened, 121–50. New York: Cambridge University Press.

Hadfield, Gillian K., and Barry R. Weingast. 2014b. "Microfoundations of the Rule of Law." *Annual Review of Political Science* 17: 21–42.

Haggard, Stephan. 2000. "Interest, Institutions, and Policy Reform." In *Economic Policy Reform*, ed. Anne Krueger. Chicago: University of Chicago Press.

Haggard, Stephan, and Robert Kaufman. 1995. *The Political Economy of Democratic Transitions*. Princeton, NJ: Princeton University Press.

Hall, Peter. 1989. *The Political Power of Economic Ideas: Keynesianism across Nations*. Princeton, NJ: Princeton University Press.

Hambloch, Ernest. 1936. *Her Majesty the President of Brazil*. New York: E. P. Dutton.

Handler, Joel F. 2003. "Social Citizenship and Workfare in the US and Western Europe: From Status to Contract." *Journal of European Social Policy* 13(3): 229–43.

Hanushek, Eric A., Paul E. Peterson, and Ludger Woessmann. 2012. *Achievement Growth: International and U.S. State Trends in Student Performance*. Harvard's Program on Education Policy and Governance, PEPG Report No. 12-03. Cambridge, MA: Harvard University.

Harberger, Arnold C. 1998. "A Vision of the Growth Process." *American Economic Review* 88(1): 1–32.

Heritage Foundation. 2012. "Index of Economic Freedom." http://www.heritage.org/.

Herkenhoff, João Baptista. 1986. *Como Participar da Constituinte*. Rio de Janeiro: Vozes.

Heston, A., R. Summers, and B. Aten. 2009. *Penn World Table*. Version 6.3, Center for International Comparisons of Production, Income and Prices. Philadelphia: University of Pennsylvania.

Higgins, Sean, Nora Lustig, Whitney Ruble, and Timothy Smeeding. 2013. "Comparing the Incidence of Taxes and Social Spending in Brazil and the United States." CEQ Working Paper No. 16, Center for Inter-American Policy and Research and Department of Economics, Tulane University and Inter-American Dialogue.

Higgins, Sean, and Claudiney Pereira. 2013. "The Effects of Brazil's High Taxation and Social Spending on the Distribution of Household Income." CEQ Working Paper No. 7, Center for Inter-American Policy and Research and Department of Economics, Tulane University and Inter-American Dialogue.

Higgs, Robert. 1987. *Crisis and Leviathan: Critical Episodes in the Growth of American Government*. New York: Cambridge University Press.

Holmes, Stephen, and Cass Sunstein. 1995. "The Politics of Constitutional Revision in Eastern Europe." In *Responding to Imperfection: The Theory and Practice of Constitutional Amendment*, ed. Sanford Levinson, 275–306. Princeton, NJ: Princeton University Press.

Howard, A. E. Dick. 1996. "The Indeterminacy of Constitutions." *Wake Forest Law Review* 31(2): 383–410.

Hunter, Wendy. 2010. *The Transformation of the Workers' Party in Brazil, 1989–2009*. New York: Cambridge University Press.

IBP (International Budget Partnership). 2010. *The Open Budget Survey*. Washington, DC: IBP.

IDB (Inter-American Development Bank). 2006. *The Politics of Policies: Economic and Social Progress in Latin America*, http://www.iadb.org/res/ipes/2006/.

ILO (International Labour Organization). 2011. *Understanding the Brazilian Success in Reducing Child Labour: Empirical Evidence and Policy Lessons.* Understanding Children's Work Programme Working Paper Series, June. Rome: ILO Office for Italy and San Marino.

Immervoll, Herwig. 2006. "Fiscal Drag—An Automatic Stabiliser?" *Research in Labor Economics* 25: 141–64.

IPEA. 2009. *Vinte Anos da Constituição Federal.* Vol. 1. Brasília: IPEA.

———. 2011. "Comunicado IPEA No. 108—Gasto Federal: Uma Análise da Execução Orçamentária de 2010." Brasília: IPEA.

Jones, Benjamin F., and Benjamin A. Olken. 2005. "Do Leaders Matter? National Leadership and Growth since World War II." *Quarterly Journal of Economics* 120(3): 835–64.

Jusko, Karen Long. 2011. "The Politics of Redistribution in Diverse Societies." Working Paper, Department of Political Science, Stanford University.

Kaplan, Steve B. 2013. *Globalization and Austerity Politics in Latin America.* New York: Cambridge University Press.

Kerche, Fabio. 2007. "Autonomia e Discricionaridade do Ministério Público no Brasil." *Dados* 50: 259–79.

Kernell, Samuel. 1997. *Going Public: New Strategies of Presidential Leadership.* Washington, DC: CQ Press.

Kindleberger, Charles P., and Robert Z. Aliber. 2011. *Manias, Panics, and Crashes: A History of Financial Crises.* 6th ed. New York: Palgrave Macmillan.

Kingstone, Peter. 1999. *Crafting Coalitions for Reform: Business Preferences, Political Institutions, and Neoliberal Reform in Brazil.* University Park: Penn State University Press.

Knight, Frank H. 1921. *Risk, Uncertainty, and Profit.* Boston: Hart, Schaffner, and Marx; Houghton Mifflin.

Knight, Jack. 2001. "Institutionalizing Constitutional Interpretation." In *Constitutional Culture and Democratic Rule*, ed. John Ferejohn, Jack Rakove, and Jonathan Riley, 361–92. New York: Cambridge University Press.

Kuran, Timur. 1995. *Private Truths, Public Lies: The Social Consequences of Preference Falsification.* Cambridge, MA: Harvard University Press.

Lamounier, Bolivar. 1989. "Authoritarian Brazil Revisited: The Impact of Elections on the Abertura." In *Democratizing Brazil: Problems of Transition and Consolidation*, ed. Alfred Stepan, 43–79. New York: Oxford University Press.

Lemann, Nicholas. 2011. "The Anointed." *New Yorker*, December 5, 50.

Levy, Bryan, and Pablo Spiller, eds. 1996. *Regulations, Institutions, and Commitment: Comparative Studies of Telecommunications.* New York: Cambridge University Press.

Lijphart, Arendt. 1999. *Patterns of Democracy: Government Forms and Performance in Thirty-Six Countries.* New Haven, CT: Yale University Press.

Lindert, Kathy, Emmanuel Skoufias, and Joseph Shapiro. 2006. "Redistributing Income to the Poor and the Rich: Public Transfers in Latin America and the Caribbean." SP Discussion Paper No. 0605. Social Safety Nets Primer Series. Washington, DC: World Bank.

Lindert, Peter H. 2003. "Why the Welfare State Looks Like a Free Lunch." NBER Working Paper No. 9869, http://www.nber.org/papers/w9869.

Longo, Carlos Alberto. 1992. "State and the Liberalization of the Brazilian Economy." *Análise Econômica* 10(18): 3–23.

Longo, Francisco. 2006. "Análisis Comparativo por Indices." In *Informe Sobre la Situación del Servicio Civil en América Latina*, ed. Koldo Echebarría, 573–92. Washington, DC: Inter-American Development Bank.

Lustig, Nora, Luis F. Lopez-Calva, and E. Ortiz-Juarez. 2012. "Declining Inequality in Latin America in the 2000s: The Cases of Argentina, Brazil, and Mexico." Center for Global Development Working Paper 307. Washington, DC: Center for Global Development.

Lustig, Nora, Carola Pessino, and John Scott. 2013. "The Impact of Taxes and Social Spending on Inequality and Poverty in Argentina, Bolivia, Brazil, Mexico, Peru and Uruguay: An Overview." CEQ Working Paper No. 13, Tulane University, New Orleans, LA.

Machiavelli, Nicolló. [1532] 1998. *The Prince*. 2nd ed. Chicago: University of Chicago Press.

Martínez-Lara, Javier. 1996. *Building Democracy in Brazil: The Politics of Constitutional Change, 1985–95*. New York: St. Martin's.

Marx, Karl. [1852] 1963. *The Eighteenth Brumaire of Louis Bonaparte*. New York: International Publishers.

McCloskey, Deirdre. 2006. *The Bourgeois Virtues: Ethics for an Age of Commerce*. Chicago: University of Chicago Press.

———. 2010. *Bourgeois Dignity: Why Economics Can't Explain the Modern World*. Chicago: University of Chicago Press.

Medeiros, Danilo Buscato. 2012. "Organizando Maiorias, Agregando Preferencias: A Assembleia Nacional Constituinte de 1987–1988." MA thesis, University of São Paulo.

Medeiros, Marcelo. 2001. "A Trajetória do Welfare State no Brasil: Papel Redistributivo das Políticas Sociais dos Anos 1930 aos Anos 1990." Brasília: IPEA, Texto para Discussão, No. 852.

Melo, Marcus André. 2002. *Reformas Constitucionais no Brasil*. Rio de Janeiro: Revan.

———. 2004. "Institutional Choice and the Diffusion of Policy Paradigms: Brazil and the Second Wave of Pension Reforms." *International Political Science Review* 25(3): 297–319.

———. 2005. "O Sucesso Inesperado das Reformas de Segunda Geração: Federalismo, Reformas Constitucionais e Politica Social." *Dados* 48(4): 845–90.

———. 2013. "Mudança Constitucional no Brasil: Dos Debates sobre as Regras de Emendamento na Constituinte à Megapolítica." *Novos Estudos Cebrap* 97 (November): 187–207.

Melo, Marcus André, and Carlos Pereira. 2013. *Making Brazil Work: Checking the President in a Multiparty System*. New York: Palgrave Macmillan.

Melo, Marcus André, Carlos Pereira, and Saulo Souza. 2010. *The Political Economy of Fiscal Reform in Brazil: The Rationale for the Suboptimal Equilibrium*. IDB Working Paper Series No. 117. Washington, DC: Inter-American Development Bank.

Meltzer, Allan H., and Scott F. Richard. 1981. "A Rational Theory of the Size of Government." *Journal of Political Economy* 89(5): 914–27.

Mendes, Marcos. 2015. "Restrições Legais à Abertura do Mercado Brasileiro de Projetos e Serviços de Engenharia." Texto para Discussão 171, Núcleo de Estudos e Pesquisas do Senado Federal.

Miller, J. H., and S. E. Page. 2007. *Complex Adaptive Systems: An Introduction to Computational Models of Social Life*. Princeton, NJ: Princeton University Press.

Mokyr, Joel. 2009. *The Enlightened Economy: An Economic History of Britain, 1700–1850*. New Haven, CT: Yale University Press.

Montclaire, Stephane, et al. 1991. *A Constituição Desejada: As 72.719 Sugestões Enviadas Pelos Cidadãos Brasileiros à Assembléia Nacional Constituinte*. Brasília: Senado Federal.

Mueller, Bernardo. 2010. "The Fiscal Imperative and the Role of Public Prosecutors in Brazilian Environmental Policy." *Law and Policy* 32(1): 104–26.

Mueller, Bernardo, and A. R. Oliveira. 2009. "Regulation during the Lula Government." In *Brazil under Lula: Economy, Politics, and Society under the Worker-President*, ed. Joseph L. Love and Werner Baer, 93–114. New York: Palgrave Macmillan.

Mueller, Bernardo, and Carlos Pereira. 2002. "Credibility and the Design of Regulatory Agencies in Brazil." *Brazilian Journal of Political Economy* 22(3) (July–September): 65–88.

Musacchio, Aldo, and Sergio G. Lazzarini. 2014. *Reinventing State Capitalism: Leviathan in Business, Brazil and Beyond*. Cambridge, MA: Harvard University Press.

Neal, Larry. 1993. *The Rise of Financial Capitalism: International Capital Markets in the Age of Reason*. New York: Cambridge University Press.

Neri, Marcelo C. 2012. *De Volta ao País do Futuro: Projeções, Crise Europeia e a Nova Classe Média*. Fundação Getúlio Vargas, Centro de Políticas Sociais.

Neustadt, R. 1990. *Presidential Power and the Modern Presidents: The Politics of Leadership from Roosevelt to Reagan*. New York: Free Press.

North, Douglass C. 1981. *Structure and Change in Economic History*. New York: Norton.

———. 1990. *Institutions, Institutional Change and Economic Performance*. New York: Cambridge University Press.

———. 2005. *Understanding the Process of Economic Change*. Princeton, NJ: Princeton University Press.

North, Douglass C., John Joseph Wallis, Steven B. Webb, and Barry R. Weingast. 2012. *In the Shadow of Violence: Politics, Economics and the Problems of Development*. New York: Cambridge University Press.

North, Douglass C., John Joseph Wallis, and Barry R. Weingast. 2009. *Violence and Social Orders: A Conceptual Framework for Interpreting Recorded Human History*. New York: Cambridge University Press.

OECD. 2010. "Brazil: Encouraging Lessons from a Large Federal System." In *Strong Performers and Successful Reformers in Education: Lessons from PISA for the United States*. OECD, http://dx.doi.org/10.1787/9789264096660-en.

Payne, Leigh. 1994. *Brazilian Industrialists and Democratic Change*. Baltimore: Johns Hopkins University Press.

Peele, Gillian. 2005. "Leadership and Politics: A Case for a Closer Relationship?" *Leadership* 1(2): 187–204.

Pereira, Carlos, and Andrés Mejía Acosta. 2010. "Policymaking in Multiparty Presidential Regimes: A Comparison between Brazil and Ecuador." *Governance* 23(4): 641–66.

Pereira, Carlos, and Gregory Michener. Forthcoming. "A Great Leap Forward for Democracy and Rule of Law? Brazil's Mensalão Trial." *Journal of Latin American Studies.*

Pereira, Carlos, Timothy Power, and Eric Raile. 2011. "Presidentialism, Coalitions, and Accountability." In *Corruption and Democracy in Brazil: The Struggle for Accountability*, ed. Timothy Power and Matthew M. Taylor, 31–55. Notre Dame, IN: University of Notre Dame Press.

Perotti, Roberto. 1995. "Growth, Income Distribution, and Democracy: What the Data Say." Discussion Paper Series No. 757, Columbia University.

Pessanha, Charles. 1997. "Relações entre os Poderes Executivo e Legislativo no Brasil: 1946–1994." PhD diss., Universidade de São Paulo.

Phelps, E. S. 2008. "Dynamism and Inclusion: What? Why? How?" CCS Working Paper No. 25, May, http://capitalism.columbia.edu/files/ccs/workingpage/2015/ccswp25_phelps.pdf.

Pilatti, Adriano. 2008. *A Constituinte de 1987–1988: Progressistas, Conservadores, Ordem Econômica, e Regras do Jogo.* Rio de Janeiro: Lumen Juris.

Pinheiro, A. C., and C. Frischtak. 2014. *Gargalos e Soluções na Infraestrutura de Transportes.* Rio de Janeiro: FGV Editora IBRE.

Pires, Roberto R. C., ed. 2011. *Efetividade das Instituições Participativas no Brasil: Estratégias de Avaliação.* Diálogos para o Desenvolvimento 7. Brasília: IPEA.

Pocock, J.G.A. 1975. *The Machiavellian Moment: Florentine Political Thought and the Atlantic Republican Tradition.* Princeton, NJ: Princeton University Press.

Powell, G. Bingham. 2000. *Elections as Instruments of Democracy: Majoritarian and Proportional Visions.* New Haven, CT: Yale University Press.

Praça, Sérgio, and Lincoln Noronha. 2012. "Políticas Públicas e a Descentralização da Assembléia Constituinte Brasileira, 1987–1988." *Revista Brasileira de Ciências Sociais* 27(78): 131–47.

Prado, Maria Clara R. M. 2005. *A Real Historia do Real: Uma Radiografia da Moeda que Mudou o Brasil.* São Paulo: Record.

Przeworski, Adam. 1991. *Democracy and the Market.* Cambridge: Cambridge University Press.

Rakove, Jack, Andrew R. Rutten, and Barry R. Weingast. 2004. "Ideas, Interests, and Credible Commitments in the American Revolution." Working Paper, Hoover Institution, Stanford University, August.

Ramos, Lauro, and José Guilherme A. Reis. 1995. "Salário Mínimo, Distribuição de Renda e Pobreza no Brasil." *Pesquisa e Planejamento Econômico* 25(1): 99–114.

Reich, Gary M. 1998. "The 1988 Constitution a Decade Later: Ugly Compromises Reconsidered." *Journal of Interamerican Studies and World Affairs* 40(4): 5–24.

Riker, William H. 1983. "Political Theory and the Art of Heresthetics." In *Political Science: The State of the Discipline*, ed. Ada W. Finifter. Washington, DC: American Political Science Association.

———. 1984. "The Heresthetics of Constitution-Making: The Presidency in 1787, with Comments on Determinism and Rational Choice." *American Political Science Review* 78(1): 1–16.

———. 1986. *The Art of Political Manipulation.* New Haven, CT: Yale University Press.

———. 1996. *The Strategy of Rhetoric: Campaigning for the American Constitution.* New Haven, CT: Yale University Press.

Ríos-Figueroa, Julio, and Jeffrey Staton. 2008. "Unpacking the Rule of Law: A Review of Judicial Independence Measures." Committee on Concepts and Methods (C&M) Working Paper Series 21, International Political Science Association (IPSA).

Rodrik, D., A. Subramanian, and F. Trebbi. 2004. "Institutions Rule: The Primacy of Institutions over Geography and Integration in Economic Development." *Journal of Economic Growth* 9: 131–65.

Roett, Riordan. 2010. *The New Brazil.* Washington, DC: Brookings Institution Press.

Rosenn, Keith. 1990. "Brazil's New Constitution: An Exercise in Transient Constitutionalism for a Transitional Society." *American Journal of Comparative Law* 38(4): 773–802.

Saboia, João. 2007. "A Redistribuição de Renda não Pode Parar." *Valor Econômico,* February 13.

Saint Paul, Gilles, and Thierry Verdier. 1996. "Inequality, Redistribution and Growth: A Challenge to the Conventional Political Economy Approach." *European Economic Review* 40: 719–28.

Sala-i-Martin, Xavier. 1997. "Transfers, Social Safety Nets, and Economic Growth." *Staff Papers—International Monetary Fund* 44(1): 81–102.

Samuels, David. 2000. "The Gubernatorial Coattails Effect: Federalism and Congressional Elections in Brazil." *Journal of Politics* 62(1): 240–53.

Sarotte, Mary Elise. 2014. *The Collapse: The Accidental Opening of the Berlin Wall.* New York: Basic Books.

Sartori, Giovanni. 1994. *Comparative Constitutional Engineering.* New York: New York University Press.

Schneider, Ben Ross. 1992. "Privatization in the Collor Government: Triumph of Liberalism or Collapse of the Development State?" In *The Right and Democracy in Latin America,* ed. Douglas A. Chalmers, Maria do Carmo Campello de Souza, and Atilio A. Boron, 225–38. New York: Praeger.

———. 1997–1998. "Organized Business Politics in Democratic Brazil." *Journal of Interamerican Studies and World Affairs* 39(4): 95–127.

———. 1998. "Business Politics in Democratic Brazil." *Journal of International Studies and World Affairs* 39(4): 95–127.

———. 2004. "Organizing Interests and Coalitions in the Politics of Market Reform in Latin America." *World Politics* 56(3): 456–79.

———. 2013. *Hierarchical Capitalism in Latin America: Business, Labor, and the Challenges of Equitable Development.* New York: Cambridge University Press.

Schofield, Norman. 2006. *Architects of Political Change: Constitutional Quandries and Social Choice Theory.* New York: Cambridge University Press.

Sharma, Ruchir. 2012. *Breakout Nations: In Pursuit of the Next Economic Miracles*. New York: Norton.

Silva, José Afonso da. 2002. *Poder Constituinte e Poder Popular: Estudos sobre a Constituição*. São Paulo: Malheiros.

Simonsen, Mario Henrique. 1991. "*Aspectos Técnicos do Plano Collor*." Special issue, *Revista Brasileira de Economia* 45 (January): 113–28.

Skidmore, Thomas. 1988. *From Castelo to Tancredo: 1964–1985*. Rio de Janeiro: Paz e Terra Press.

Souza, Amaury de, and Bolivar Lamounier. 1989. "A Feitura da Nova Constituição: Um Reexame da Cultura Política Brasileira." *Pesquisa e Planejamento Econômico* 2 (December): 17–37.

Spiller, Pablo T., and Mariano Tommasi. 2009. *The Institutional Foundations of Public Policy in Argentina: A Transaction Cost Approach*. New York: Cambridge University Press.

Staton, Jeffrey K. 2010. *Judicial Power and Strategic Communication in Mexico*. New York: Cambridge University Press.

Stein, E., M. Tommasi, C. Scartascini, and P. Spiller. 2008. *Policymaking in Latin America: How Politics Shapes Policies*. Cambridge, MA: Harvard University Press.

Taleb, Nicolas Nassim. 2010. *The Black Swan: The Impact of the Highly Improbable*. New York: Random House.

Ter-minassian, Tereza. 2013. "Improving Social Spending for a Better Life for All in Brazil." Vox LACEA, http://www.vox.lacea.org/?q=brazil_social_spending.

Tetlock, Philip E. 2006. *Expert Political Judgment? How Good Is It? How Can We Know?* Princeton, NJ: Princeton University Press.

Torres, Ernani T. Filho, Luiz Macahyba, and Rodrigo Zeidan. 2014. *Restructuring Brazil's National Financial System*. International Research Initiative on Brazil and Africa (IRIBA) Working Paper No. 06, University of Manchester.

US Department of Agriculture. 1936. *Agricultural Statistics 1936*. Washington, DC: US Department of Agriculture.

Vanberg, Georg. 2005. *The Politics of Constitutional Review in Germany*. Cambridge: Cambridge University Press.

———. 2008. "Establishing and Maintaining Judicial Independence." In *The Oxford Handbook of Law and Politics*, ed. Keith E. Whittington and Daniel Kelemen, 99–118. New York: Oxford University Press.

Villela, Anibal. 1997. *The Collor Plan and the Industrial and Foreign Trade Policy*. Rio de Janeiro: Institute of Applied Economic Research.

Wagner, R. 1966. "Pressure Groups and Political Entrepreneurs." *Public Choice* 1(1): 161–70.

Wallis, John Joseph. 2011. "Institutions, Organizations, Impersonality, and Interests: The Dynamics of Institutions." *Journal of Economic Behavior and Organization* 79(1–2): 48–64.

———. 2014. "Leviathan Denied: Rules, Governments, and Social Dynamics." Book manuscript in progress.

Weingast, Barry. 1995. "The Economic Role of Political Institutions: Market-Preserving Federalism and Economic Development." *Journal of Law, Economics, and Organization* 20(1): 1–31.

Weyland, Kurt. 2002. *The Politics of Market Reform in Fragile Democracies: Argentina, Brazil, Peru, and Venezuela*. Princeton, NJ: Princeton University Press.

Whitehead, Laurence, and Javier Santiso. 2012. "Ulysses and the Sirens: Political and Technical Rationality in Latin America." In *The Oxford Handbook of Latin American Political Economy*, ed. Javier Santiso and Jeff Dayton-Johnson, 550–609. New York: Oxford University Press.

Williamson, John, ed. 1985. *Inflation and Indexation: Argentina, Brazil, and Israel*. Cambridge, MA: MIT Press.

World Bank. 2011. "Social Expenditure and Fiscal Federalism in Russia." Report No. 54392–RU. Human Development Sector Unit, Europe and Central Asia Unit. Washington, DC: World Bank.

INDEX

Page numbers in italics refer to figures and tables.

THE PRINCETON ECONOMIC HISTORY OF THE WESTERN WORLD

Joel Mokyr, Series Editor